Institutions by Artists
Volume Two

Institutions by Artists
Volume Two

Edited by
Jeff Khonsary
Antonia Pinter

Folio Series: E

Fillip, Vancouver

Contents

Contents

Preface

Some ten years after the release of *Institutions by Artists: Volume One*, we turn our attention again to the complex, often contested, cultural landscape that is institutions initiated, led, and transformed by artists. These two publications—and the eponymous 2012 convention they were released in conjunction with—crib their name from a significant anthology series published by Art Metropole through the 1970s, '80s, and '90s (later relaunched in 2011). Published in 1983 and edited by AA Bronson and Peggy Gale, *Museums by Artists* (the third anthology in that series) explored the relationship of the artist to the institutional space of museums: their roles, responsibilities, functions, and physicality. As the introduction to the first volume of *Institutions by Artists* explained, our project utilized a foundation laid by Bronson and Gale—among others—in an attempt *to open up the institutions of art by creating a space for institutions by artists in order to correct, or at least complicate, the record on the relationship between artists and institutions, which has been determined by delimitation rather than expansion.*

Continuing this theoretical framework, we present here a second anthology that carries on the work of unpacking artists' relationships to—and creation of—a larger set of structures that increasingly regulate, demarcate, and codify contemporary artistic practice: centres of economic and cultural capital; state and private apparatuses; and sites of display, storage, and production. The trajectory of these relationships is hardly unified, nor are the institutional practices of artists autonomous from the structures they sometimes operate in opposition to. As Tania Willard and Dana Claxton summarize in a coda that appears in the present volume: *The claim that artist-run spaces can exist free from hegemonic influence seems slippery, and the nature of the dissemination of art knowledge within fixed frameworks of thought and hierarchies makes artist-run culture complicit in how the circulation of art power continues in ways that are not always identified and perhaps reside within the realm of denial, refusal, and enclosure.* They continue: *The possibility of transformation requires the collapse of hierarchies and rules to allow the nuanced, the unspoken, the spirit to be heard.*

With the set of complicated relationships to internal and external forces very much in mind, this volume's contributing authors present a series of historical and contemporary case studies, investigating artists' connections to various manifestations of institutionalized practice. These case studies describe practices that developed in places as disparate as Vancouver, London (Ontario), East Los Angeles, Scotland, and Trinidad and Tobago—building on examples published in the first volume documenting artistic practices in Toyko, Mexico City, Santiago, Amman, Barcelona, Brisbane, Dubai, and Zurich, to name just a few. Rather than providing a fully comprehensive overview to the worldwide phenomenon of institutional practices by artists, this volume—like its predecessor—offers intriguing points of reference that aim to expand, rather than summarize, the discursive environment with which it engages.

The approach and content of this book are very much informed by the intense discussions that emerged from the week-long world congress of artists, curators, critics, and academics produced in parallel to the first *Institutions by Artists* Folio. Organized by Fillip in collaboration with the Pacific Association of Artist Run Centres and the Artist-Run Centres and Collectives Conference, and with the support of Simon Fraser University, the *Institutions by Artists* Convention hosted more than fifty presenters and provided the context for a city-wide constellation of related exhibitions, projects, and public programming. To the reader, the link between the present volume and the 2012 convention will be most clearly evident in the transcripts of two Oxford-style debates appearing near the end of this second volume. Addressing the fundamental questions of artists' relationships to the market and the state and various positions vis-à-vis professionalization respectively, these two debates form a conceptual backbone to the discussions fleshed out around them, just as they set the tone for the convention as a whole. Even more crucially, the *Institutions by Artists* Convention established a sort of networked, highly divergent international brain trust that coalesced momentarily, only to leave a lasting mark both on the practitioners in attendance in Vancouver and those who witnessed the conversations from elsewhere.

It is thus vital to thank a number of people who curated, organized, and produced the 2012 convention. The truly inspired substance of the event—some of which appears here, including commissioned contributions by Tania Bruguera, Julia Bryan-Wilson, Sean Dockray, and others—was coordinated through a Program Committee consisting of Kristina Lee Podesva (Chair), Lorna Brown, Jeff Khonsary, and Jonathan Middleton operating in collaboration with Anton Vidokle and Pelin Tan, who served as outside advisors. The event itself would not have been possible without the hard work and dedication of *Institutions by Artists* Project Manager Lorna Brown, Event Manager Allison Collins, and Research and Communications Assistants Jesi Khadivi and Mariane Bourcheix-Laporte. A note of thanks should also be given to the convention's documentation team—Ian Barbour, Darren Heroux, Josh Olson, and Ron Tran—whose hard work provided some of the raw materials which you see reproduced in a transcribed, edited form in the pages that follow. We would also like to thank the collective efforts of the Pacific Association of Artist Run Centres—the copublisher of both volumes of *Institutions by Artists*—for their steadfast commitment to both the convention and these resultant publications.

Because this project spans so many years, there are innumerable additional people who played a role in seeing this material manifest in the final form you hold in your hands. Special thanks should be given to Fillip Editorial Supervisor Kate Woolf, whose sheer will and dedication played a large part in getting this present volume completed despite numerous roadblocks and setbacks. The timing of the release of this title, on the cusp of Fillip's fifteen-year anniversary, seems completely appropriate. Many of the texts in this volume emerged from a larger editorial series on the topic explored in *Fillip* magazine over many years. As with several other series in *Fillip* (Kate Steinmann's *Apparatus, Capture, Trace* and Antonia Hirsch's *Intangible Economies*), the larger *Institutions by Artists* project formed a significant through-line within Fillip's broader editorial perspective from the very initial years of our work in 2005. It's important, then, to also recognize the significant work of past Fillip Editorial Board members Paloma Campbell, Kristina Lee Podesva, Jonathan Middleton, Sadira Rodrigues, Jordan Strom, Kate Steinmann, and Amy Zion, whose combined work was critical to the commissioning, editing, and support of the texts in this volume. We are also very very grateful to our current fellow Editorial Board members Jaclyn Arndt, Jaleh Mansoor, Sohrab Mohebbi, Jenifer Papararo, and Eric Golo Stone for their unwavering support of Fillip's work more broadly.

It seems a perfect happy accident that this book is being released together with *Services Working Group* (Folio F), a significant volume in the Folio series edited by curator and writer Eric Golo Stone. *Services Working Group* presents complete transcripts from the ground-breaking working group on labour relations and institutional governance in the arts conducted as part of the 1994 exhibition *Services: The Conditions and Relations of Service Provision in Contemporary Project Oriented Artistic Practice*, organized by Helmut Draxler and Andrea Fraser at the Kunstraum Leuphana University of Lüneburg (formerly the Kunstraum of the University of Lüneburg). It perhaps goes without saying that Andrea Fraser's work on Institutional Critique formed much of the intellectual bedrock for the larger *Institutions by Artists* project, and the complex relationships described within the Working Group conversations provide historical background to a conversation that continues to evolve.

In many ways, the 2012 publication of *Institutions by Artists: Volume One* came together in direct conversation with Occupy Wall Street and within the context of a city facing the ongoing impact of the 2010 Vancouver Winter Olympics. The publication of this second volume now—very much in the wake of the human and economic impact of a worldwide pandemic and the rise of right-wing populism in the Americas and abroad—exaggerates both the distance and the overlaps between moments documented in this book and in our constantly evolving present. It's our hope that this gap provides additional perspectives, allowing the discussions that follow to resonate in new and perhaps unpredictable ways.

—Jeff Khonsary and Antonia Pinter
Fillip

Tania Bruguera

Manifesto on Artists' Rights

Art is not a luxury. Art is a basic social need to which everyone has a right.

Art is a way to build thinking, of being aware of oneself and of others at the same time. It is a methodology for the search of a here and now in constant transformation.

Art is an invitation to question; it is the social place of doubt, of wanting to understand and of wanting to change reality.

Art is not only a statement of the present, it is also a call for a better future. Therefore, it is a right not only to enjoy art, but to be able to create it.

Art is a common good that does not have to be understood in its totality.

Art is a space of vulnerability from which what is social is deconstructed to construct what is human.

Artists not only have the right to disagree, but the duty to do so.

Artists have the right to disagree not only with affective, moral, philosophical, or cultural aspects, but also with economic and political ones.

Artists have the right to disagree with power, with the status quo.

Artists have the right to be respected and protected when they dissent.

The governments of nations in which artists work have the obligation to protect the right of artists to dissent because that is artists' social function: to question and address what otherwise is too sensitive to confront.

Artists also have the right to be understood in the complexity of their disagreement. Artists should not be judged but discussed. And certainly artists should not be put in jail for proposing an "other" reality, for sharing their ideas, for wanting to strike up a conversation on the way the present unfolds. If the artist proposal is not understood, it should be discussed by all, not censored by a few.

Governments, corporations, and religious institutions too easily declare, if one publicly expresses and manifests differently from those in power, that one is irresponsible—using guilt and inciting the masses to violent reactions as their best defense strategy instead of processing criticism and making a call for public debate. There is nothing that justifies the use of violence against an idea or the person that proposes it.

Governments have the duty to provide a space for self-criticism in which they are accountable for their actions, a space where the people can question them. No government is infallible; no human being—even if elected—has the right to talk for all citizens. No social solution is permanent and artists have the opportunity and the duty to propose the imaginary of other social alternatives, of using their communication tools from a space of *sensitive responsibility*.

Governments must stop fearing ideas.

Governments, corporations (contemporary alternative governments), and religious institutions are not the only ones with a right to build a future; this is the right of citizens, and artists are active citizens. That is why artists have the right and the responsibility not only to think up a different and better world, but to try to build it.

Artists have the right to be *artivists* (part artists/part activists), because they are an active part of civil society, because art is a safe space in which people can debate, interpret, construct, and educate. And this space must be defended because it benefits all; art is a social tool.

Governments should not control art and artists. They should protect them.

Artists have the right to create the work they want to create, with no limits; they have the duty to be responsible without self-censure.

Society has the right for public spaces to be spaces for creativity and artistic expression, since they also are collective spaces for knowledge and debate. Public space belongs to civic society, not to governments, corporations, or religious institutions.

Freedom of artistic expression does not emerge spontaneously; it is something one learns to reach by leaving behind pressure, emotional blackmail, censorship, and self-censorship. This is a difficult process that should be respected and appreciated.

Artistic censorship not only affects artists but also the communities they inhabit. It creates fear and self-censorship. It paralyzes the possibility to exercise critical thinking.

Art is a complex product without one single and final interpretation. Artists have the right to not have their oeuvre reduced or simplified as a schematic that can be manipulated by those in power to consequently result in public offenses they can direct to the artists so as to invalidate their proposals.

The right to decide the value of an artistic statement is not a right of those in power. It is not the right of governments, or corporations, or religious institutions to define what art is. It is the right of the artists to define what art is for them.

In order to create a space for dialogue and the protection of works of art that question established ideas and realities, governments should provide educational platforms from which artistic practice may be better understood.

In moments of high sensitivity (wars, legislative changes, political transitions), it is the duty of the government to protect and guarantee dissident, questioning voices because these are moments in which one cannot do away with rationality and critical thought, and it is sometimes only through art that some ideas can emerge and make a public appearance. Without dissent there is no chance for progress.

Socially and politically committed artists talk about difficult moments, deal with sensitive topics, but, unlike journalists, they have no legal protection when doing their work. Unlike corporations, they have no significant economic backing. Unlike governments, they have no political power. Art is a social work based on a practice that makes artists vulnerable and—as is the case with journalists, corporations, and governmental or religious institutions—artists have the right to be protected because they are doing a public service.

We must be cautious of the increasing criminalization of socially committed artistic creation and the rationale of national security used to censure artists who dissent.

Many types of strategies are used for political censorship: direct political pressure on the artist; not accessing economic support; bureaucratic censorship that postpones production processes and marginalizes visibility by drawing artists away from circuits of legitimization and distribution; control of the right to travel. Sometimes "popular sensibility" is used as censorship, but all are a centralized decision for power not to be challenged.

On the other hand, there are artists who are internationally acknowledged and admired for being artivists in their countries of origin and who, at a given time, for one reason or another, migrate and establish themselves temporarily in other countries where they find a new type of censorship, a censorship that relegates, pigeonholes, and sets them inside a limited mental geography where they are only allowed to talk critically of the country they come from and not the country to which they have arrived. This is a situation of censorship where artists are relegated to being unidimensionally political: as political objects of use.

The process of discovering a different society, the inner negotiation one requires to understand the place to which one has arrived and the place one has left, is inherent in the contemporary condition, which is increasingly a migrant condition. This is a condition that artists embody and that they have the right to express. A national culture is the hybridization of the image those who do not live in the country have of it, as well as the one built by all of those present, day by day, in the place, no matter where they have come from before.

We cannot ask artists, whose work is to question society, to keep silent and resort to self-censure once they cross a territorial border.

Artists have the right not to be fragmented as human beings or as social beings.

Artistic expression is a space to challenge meanings, to defy what is imaginable. This is what, as time goes by, is recognized as culture.

A society with freedom of artistic expression is a healthier society. It is a society where citizens are allowed to dream of a better world where they have a place. It is a society that better expresses itself, because it expresses itself in its entire complexity.

There is no other type of practice in the public sphere providing the qualities of the space created by art; that is why this space must be protected.

Governments have the duty to protect all their citizens, including those who may be considered uncomfortable because they question government and what is socially established.

Critical thinking is a civic right that becomes evident in artistic practices. Therefore, when this is threatened we should not talk of censorship, but of the violation of artists' rights.

Ken Becker

Not Just Some Canadian Hippie Bullshit

The Western Front as Artists' Practice

It may help to think of [The Eternal Network] as being part of the wider network where artistic activity just becomes one of the elements.

—Robert Filliou[1]

In the above quote, the French Fluxus artist Robert Filliou describes the conception of an Eternal Network made up of artists and their production, among other pursuits. Filliou sees in this system exchanges between different points on a map creating an art world that draws its energy from artists and their actions and that exists as a connective tissue in a nexus of ideas and operations, rather than a single, centralized location.[2]

At the time that the artist made this statement in the late 1970s, correspondence art, video exchanges, performance, radio, and sound art were helping to form new systems of authorship and distribution. Artists had already begun to develop and use nonhierarchical group formations and public systems of transmission, such as the postal service and broadcast media. Such strategies for production and distribution existed globally, but for artists across Canada they contributed to the foundation of new, burgeoning arts communities. In fact, in the 1970s, Filliou's presence, with a Fluxus influence, contributed to the development of the Western Front (alternately identified as WF or the Front), an artist-run centre (ARC) based in Vancouver, Canada.[3] Filliou's first of many visits to the Western Front took place in 1973,[4] which was the year the society formed and acquired the former Knights of Pythias Hall at 303 East 8th Avenue. Five artists—Kate Craig, Glenn Lewis, Eric Metcalfe, Michael Morris, and Vincent Trasov—as well as architect Mo Van Nostrand, composer Martin Bartlett, and writer Henry Greenhow, purchased the building together.

All eight were members of the Vancouver arts community and interested in having "stable living/working spaces."[5] By purchasing this specific space, the founding members also acquired the capacity to present public exhibitions, performances, and expanded collaborative productions. Their extended network of friends, in Vancouver and abroad, became both audience members and collaborators.[6] With little previous existing infrastructure around them, members of the Western Front assumed a multitude of roles in order to fulfill an immediate set of administrative needs. Artist Hank Bull, who moved into the Western Front six months after it opened, illustrates this point when he states: *Imagine a scenario that is architecturally determined. There is this building in which people live and produce; visiting artists live in the building. Managers, curators, and artists producing are all the same group of people.... We made work together, showed it to each other, and created not only the work, but the distribution system and the audience.*[7]

Although it is impossible to claim that all ARCs in Canada are direct descendants of Fluxus practice, it is worth tracing the influence of Filliou on the Western Front's artists,[8] for there are noteworthy affinities and relationships to explore here. For instance, attempts by the Front artists to create a functioning live/work space mirrors the pursuit of an art/life connection that also propelled artists associated with Fluxus production, such as George Maciunas, Dick Higgins, Geoffrey Hendricks, and Nam June Paik. In an essay entitled "Between Water and Stone,"[9] Kristine Stiles describes Fluxus as having "originated in the context of performance and the nature of its being—the ontology of Fluxus—is performative." She continues by writing: *Fluxus performance stresses interaction between the material and the mental worlds, and its actions negotiate degrees of human freedom in relations between the private and the social worlds—directions that recall philosophical descriptions of the phenomenological character of the body as an instrument acting in the world.*[10]

Thus, the Fluxus performer is not a mere character or role, but an individual or group of individuals consciously interacting with their physical and social surroundings. By viewing themselves as a sort of social sculpture,[11] artists at the Western Front actively merged the performative with daily life activities.

It is my goal in this text to examine the Western Front as a mode and a space vis-à-vis artistic production: the site of daily performance, rather than as simply an artist-run gallery or site of artistic presentation. Consequently, by extrapolation, ARCs might be viewed more fully as an extension of artists' practice rather than solely as an attempt to emulate or create organizational and administrative structures as platforms for their work. In this case, I will therefore consider the Western Front as a manifestation of *how* artists operate, instead of as a place *where* artists showcase the collective results of their activities

Historical Context

The Western Front is part of a larger story of artist-generated culture in Vancouver and Canada.[12] In 1957, seventeen years before the Front opened, the Canadian government began a program to support artists, via the newly formed Canada Council for the Arts. Created through an Act of Parliament, the Canada Council was founded "to foster and promote the study and enjoyment of and the production of works in the arts, the humanities and social sciences,"[13] and such support was vital to growing the cultural life in Canada. In the case of Vancouver, for instance, prior to the 1960s there was only one commercial gallery in the city, the New Design Gallery, and by the mid-1960s, the list had expanded to include only four more.[14]

The first noncommercial spaces in Vancouver formed less than a decade after state funding became available through various programs. The Sound Gallery formed in 1965, and the artists' collective Intermedia emerged in 1967.[15] Front members Michael Morris and Vincent Trasov started Image Bank[16] in 1969 with ties to *FILE* magazine,[17] published by the members of the Toronto-based collective General Idea. In 1967, Intermedia received the staggering sum of $40,000[18] from the Canada Council, validating the collective's existence and jumpstarting its public programming. By making their video equipment publicly available, Intermedia became one of the energizing factors for Vancouver's growing art scene, and its dissolution in 1972 catalyzed the formation of a number of new artist-run spaces in the city, including the Western Front.

From 1973 to 1981, during what Bull describes as the "freewheeling experimental stage of the Front,"[19] the building operated, in theory, similarly to a communal version of Andy Warhol's Studio[20] or a countercultural Shaker community, rather than a museum or gallery space. The Front's expansive architecture functioned as communal living quarters, a performance venue, a residency for visiting artists, and a production studio. The building accommodated time-based events: dance, film, music, poetry,[21] and other forms of social and artistic practice (although these sorts of distinctions were not made by the participants at the time), which mainly took place in two large halls.[22]

The room that would eventually become the designated art gallery originally served as the group's dining area, where elaborate nightly communal meals took place. It is worth noting that unlike some prior spaces in Vancouver, such as the one occupied by members of Intermedia, the Western Front did not provide public access to equipment and facilities.[23] Instead, what eventually developed was a video artist residency program, through which artists were invited to stay at the building, utilize the equipment, and produce new work. This set-up restricted public access to the new video technology but allowed for a sustained system of facilitation and oversight, which Intermedia had lacked. Works made during such residencies are today stored in the Western Front's archive and constitute the primary research for this text.

An example of how the Western Front's founders combined art and life was in their adoption of pseudonyms or stage personas, further complicating the identifications of each individual within their collective, performative platform.[24] Morris has described the motivation for these personas in the following way: *We felt we had to create a context to live and make art that was independent from the museum and the marketplace but nonetheless would address issues and the public in totally new ways.... I think the personas and mythologies were a necessary step in making such a radical break with existing roles and traditions: they created for us a world where the serious ground we were breaking could be taken as "business as usual."*[25]

One could argue that the process of creating identities facilitates both a certain creative distance from one's actions but also allows the individual to expand outside of his or her own perceived limitations. One criticism of what was taking place at the Front was that these roles and personas were theatrical, light, or camp, undermining the merits of the artists involved. Robert Ballantyne sums up this critique of the Western Front artists by describing a parallel criticism levelled against *FILE* magazine in the following: *The article…condemning* File *was written as part of a rising backlash against increasingly idiosyncratic and playful impulses towards the evacuation of the category of the self. The years following the international events of 1968 were increasingly dominated by conflictual demands from both the left and the right for a serious art, which we can read as a high art, capable of redeeming lost virility.*[26]

When mentioning the desire for a "serious art," it might be revealing to return to Fluxus practice as a counterpoint. Humour, the obvious inverse to seriousness, was one of the favoured tools of George Maciunas, who said: *We never intended to be high art. We came out to be like a bunch of jokers. In fact, I gave an answer to one banker [who] asked me when we applied for a mortgage. They asked Bob Watts what was his profession, he said, well he was a professor for twenty-five years. Then they asked what do I make and what do I do, and I said, I make jokes!*[27]

This apparent split (between the serious and the humorous/theatrical) would indicate at least two very different impulses in the art production of 1970s Vancouver—i.e., Jeff Wall, Ian Wallace, and artists who became known as members of what would eventually be called the "Vancouver School" and the practices that arose out of the Western Front. More than an active *conflict*, however, these two systems would seem to demonstrate basic differences in approach, two very different sets of goals and governing principles. In some ways the divide seems to be an example of two distinct movements occurring in the same moment within a shared geography. In reference to the same article Ballantyne mentioned regarding *FILE* magazine, curator Scott Watson draws parameters for the variances between the two positions: *The difference between [the artists involved in the Western Front] and the circle of Jeff Wall is about precisely this. It came out into the open in the early seventies. There was a review of one of the first issues of* FILE *magazine.... The article was written by Dennis Wheeler...a protégé of Robert Smithson and a friend of Jeff Wall's. It really attacks...this kind of un-rigorous, devil-may-care attitude as being fundamentally unserious. I would say that for years there was a felt split between these two camps of artists. I don't think that is true anymore. It's all in the past.... While Wall and his companions pursued an art that was conceptual, cinematic, and theoretical toward a progressive revolutionary politic, the Western Front were more eager to investigate process, revisions of the everyday, provisionality, in an apolitical, anarchist, sort of Buddhist subversion.*[28]

To further reinforce this notion of revising the everyday in terms of their attitude toward the established structures surrounding the Western Front, Bull states succinctly: "As an artist you don't have to fit into an institutional or an economic system. You can make your own up."[29]

That process of self-definition and openness to broader forms, definitions, and practices seems to have fuelled artist-run spaces. The concept of rigour in Watson's statement suggests a connection to academic diligence, which prioritizes that distinctive process, but rigour and energy might be equally valid components of nonacademic pursuits. Inclusion, or the inclusive strategy of opting to obliterate any differentiation between one's art and one's daily life, connects back to Filliou, Fluxus, and creating spaces for pursuits that run in contradiction to supposedly serious art.

In the early '70s, Filliou found in Canadian artists an actual manifestation of the "Eternal Network" he had imagined.[30] Bull describes Filliou's early connection with the developing scene: *[He] had coined the idea of the Eternal*

Network and then came here [Vancouver] and discovered FILE *magazine. Here were these artists who already had a network.... [Filliou] said, "Oh here are the artists that are doing the exact same thing I have been talking about!"*[31]

Filliou is a convenient stand-in for a larger realm of Fluxus influence. The broader context of Fluxus included a system for engagement that, as Craig Saper, associate professor at Philadelphia's University of the Arts, explains, "offered a research methodology for what I call 'networked ideas' and demonstrated the value of those ideas in various experiments."[32] If we continue to try and separate out what artists do from the end result of their endeavours, Saper's essay "Fluxus as Laboratory" provides some insight. The goal of Fluxus, and one might argue the Western Front as well, was to provide an environment where this sort of learning might take place. Instead of making works, visiting artists at the Western Front, if viewed as conducting experiments, understand that importance of the generative process as the locality under which real change, growth, and learning takes place.[33] Rather than making an artwork or individual pieces, the entirety of the production of the space can be seen as the result of laboratory production. Saper continues: *Fluxus often parodied the kind of art that posits a masterpiece appreciated by a spectator. By contrast, Fluxus works highlighted socio-poetic interaction and encouraged epistemological experimentation among participant-users.*[34]

One reading of what artists do might be the creation of circumstances in which one can investigate how we interact, relate to the world, learn, change, and evolve. The ideological shift away from art as an elite consumer good and toward a manifestation of that interaction and its social impact connects to Filliou's piece *Telepathic Music no. Now* made in 1980 during his last residency at the Western Front.

Telepathic Music no. Now

During his first three visits to the Front, Filliou made work that was the continuation of projects conceived in other mediums. So, for instance, his *Teaching and Learning as Performing Arts, Part II,* made in 1979 at the Front, is the continuation of ideas formed in his book *Teaching and Learning as Performing Arts I* (1970).[35] Most of these early works can be seen via the Front's online archive.[36] The focus here will be on *Telepathic Music no. Now,* an unfinished work, buried in the archive, and an interesting document in terms of its content, time frame, and direct connection to the discussion at hand.[37]

Lasting twelve minutes, *Telepathic Music* begins with Filliou sitting at a table, so only the upper half of his body can be seen. Next to him is a full-sized, brown-paper grocery bag. The table is a saturated red and the backdrop a baby blue. The artist wears a white sack over his head with the eyes, nose, and mouth cut out. His glasses perch awkwardly over the hood. The overall visual effect, which might be a little disturbing, is offset, somewhat, by Filliou's voice and delivery. His halting, repetitious, circular speech addresses great-great-great-great-great-great-great-grand-children five million years into the future. He attempts to explain what he, the artist, is doing and why.

Filliou continues to speak as he empties two apples out of the paper bag (the apples remain in front of him on the table untouched), then places the bag briefly over his head (and over the hood), and at the halfway point of the piece, removes the hood, continually addressing the camera, and replaces the hood again, this time with his glasses on underneath the hood. The grocery bag is placed out of sight at this point and remains off-screen for the duration of the piece.

With this work Filliou communicates a dissertation on artistic energy as the new driving force for a new approach to society's failings. He collapses time so that his address of the distant future is in fact aimed simultaneously at the present. The position conveyed is one of the artist as a communicator, or poet, with the imperative to simply convey information across space and time. Filliou passes information, concepts, and instructions from artist to audience. The entirety of the argument, inherent in the work, lies in the conceit that words (i.e., ideas) are as powerful as actions (i.e., art) and are conduits that facilitate change.

If the connection between art and life is something that the artist actively pursues, his or her actions (i.e., process) constitute a form of self-reflexive meditation. This awareness process, the act of living with both art and life and attempting to do so without judgment between these two facets, requires actively ignoring any difference between both functions. This, in itself, is the performative act. And through this performance, the artist facilitates an alternate relationship with his or her own actions and self-realization. The performative component also allows for a distancing of one's activities from the self,[38] creating a space to explore new facets in a manner similar to an actor playing a role. Treating the ongoing performance as a communicative task, similar to an active meditation, or sustained concentration toward the act of being, is an idea that potentially extends well beyond artistic endeavours. Within Filliou's title, *Telepathic Music no. Now*, exists the notion of mentally transmitting information from one person to another (what could be more direct than telepathy?) through an artistic gesture.[39] The title also conveys a certain degree of concentration and effort on the part of the individual engaged in the act of communicating.

On an overly simple level the piece is a transmission of the state of what it means to be in the world and the capacity for art and communication to operate as energy for social change. Saper writes: *The social project of the Fluxus laboratory involves disseminating knowledge. This is the social situation of learning.... Fluxus work has no intrinsic value. The value of the work resides in the ideas it implies to the reader, the spectator and to other participants.*[40]

The role of the viewer, my role, becomes activated while watching the piece thirty-five years later and is the continuation of a thinking-through of ideas related to learning, not as Filliou necessarily meant them, but as they are understood in the present. The artist's oration focuses on art's function and dynamic potential outside an art context. The videotape on which he appears is not a precious object, but a reproducible form that lends itself to dispersal throughout the network outlined at the beginning of this discussion. That network is not hemmed in by the limitations of time and space, but rather continues as long as the ideas are active in their engagement with an audience. The Eternal Network, as the name implies, is perpetually operational.

Argument

Absurdity heightens rigour.

—Glenn Lewis[41]

Through an examination of ARCs, one can extrapolate the motivations for artistic attempts at achieving greater levels of self-determination.[42] Striving for control of the space of production, control of one's living situation, and melding the two into a social-artistic mixture were strategies exemplified by the founders/participants in the Western Front. The questions that form the basis of this essay concern the strengths, weaknesses, and opportunities inherent in such systems. As part of this analysis, it would seem necessary to separate an artist's works from his or her practice (i.e., separating the *product*, the art itself, from the productive function of being an artist). The first is a result (i.e., the effects of a practice) and the second is the process or system (i.e., the means of doing). The *product* exists ordinarily as the preserve of the market, disassociated from the location of its own production, existing instead among abstract systems of art commerce. Here, however, I am more concerned with an artist's practice as a viable daily exercise that proceeds from self-discovery and contributes to individual growth. As such, my argument attends more to artistic labour (or, practice) instead of its product (or, art).

An artist-run centre can actively facilitate an artist's development by providing an entry point, a supportive environment in which to work and expand. Ideas, in general, need testing grounds, receptive audiences, and a laboratory setting in which to fully develop. Do ARCs allow for artistic experimentation but fail to provide a larger critical audience to test one's ideas against? Exhibiting work, truly exhibiting work, it could be argued, is an act that requires a certain criticality, the public, outside one's own peer, friend, and social groups. This broader audience can theoretically access new works from a perspective unimpeded by a personal relationship with the artists and their work. By combining artistic and social contexts, the Western Front provided a space to experiment and test out ideas in the early stages of development among members of a like-minded peer group without the pressure to display work, which could be a perceived strength, but read equally as insular and limiting.

In a 1983 interview, founding member Kate Craig makes the following statement about her own approach to art making within the context of the organization:

Certainly there is the issue of the amount of time required for organizing events, and working for others: it obviously gets in the way of your own work. But you also have to understand my attitude.... It wouldn't make sense to me to work on my own. I don't relate to the world that way. I consider working on videotapes with other people very much part of my work. It's the ideas that are exciting, the production. I have no intention to be famous; it doesn't interest me.... How one organizes one's life is political.... I know with my own work...it's not so much a critique as it is an alternative, a way of dealing with one's life 24 hours a day, how one relates to the outside world or to one's own community.[43]

The specific set of priorities stated here stresses a co-authored approach to art making in which the support role functions not as an inferior position but as a valid form of contributing to the process. The artist prioritizes the benefits gained through developing systems of organization that promote interaction between individuals toward a set of common goals.

Craig's perspective also highlights an unapologetic stance toward the value systems associated with a larger art market. Her administrative role within the Western Front was as much a part of her own creative process as her individual art practice. In other words, Craig integrated the work she performed as a facilitator into her work as an artist. In fact, by imagining all of her activities—collaborating, making, thinking, reading, conversing, arguing, filing paperwork—as part of a singular practice,[44] Craig articulates her own realization of the Western Front's aims. This epitomizes the combining of, to return to Stiles's definition of Fluxus, *the material and the mental worlds, and its actions negotiate degrees of human freedom in relations between the private and the social worlds—directions that recall philosophical descriptions of the phenomenological*

character of the body as an instrument acting in the world.[45]
It also might mean that the Western Front, as an entity,
was the external structure in which the enactment of such
ideals took place. The space is the location where artists,
whose practices extend into all of their daily actions, perform that role.

Residency Program (1976)

*It was a sanctuary. It was a school. It was a place where I
developed technical skills, a place where I could make friends
and community, where I could share laterally. Where I could
have the freedom to explore without the pressure of creating
a product. It was like the ideal free school in a kind of way.
I never went to art school, I never went to university, and so
this was a really important continuing part of my training.
I still needed to learn all sorts of things, plus I was attracted to
this new technology.*

—Margaret Dragu[46]

In 1976, Kate Craig took over from Glenn Lewis as
director of the Western Front's artists-in-residence program.
She inherited what had been a video program designed primarily to document events at the Front and turned it into a
video production residency[47] and outlined the goals of that
project clearly: *When I took over the video program I decided
that given the facility, what we should really be doing is producing special production tapes. So, I started a program where
we would invite artists to come to the Western Front specifically to make new video works. The artists that were invited
were not necessarily video artists. They were people who were
very interested in exploring the medium.*[48]

Craig brought in artists who often had little to no video

experience and gave them access to the technology and the space's collective expertise. When she refers to special production tapes she means those that were distinct from recorded performances of live events, or the making of documentaries. There were no requirements placed on visiting artists. They were simply provided with the resources to make video works that were stand-alone pieces. A circumstance that was rare then, unheard of now, and which allowed them to work and produce as they wished, and even to burn the end result if they saw fit.[49] Craig followed the basic model she and Filliou had developed during his first few visits, whereby artists would pitch ideas to her and a discussion would take place regarding the viability and parameters of a proposed project.

In 1978, she and visiting artist Margaret Dragu generated *Backup*, a relatively cinematic production for the Western Front at the time. *Backup* was a film that combined dual, fractured narratives through three clearly defined chapters consisting of multiple vignettes, and its script focuses loosely on the lives of two women played by Craig and Dragu, as themselves, and a set of female graduates at a finishing school.[50]

Backup (37:36 minutes) begins with Craig and Dragu standing on the roof of the Western Front with Vancouver's skyline behind them.[51] Craig can be heard through a voiceover, discussing the possibility of a city that prioritizes urban gardening. The second set of scenes depicts a group playing billiards. During this part, the narrative gets murky and the trajectory of action becomes unclear. Dragu and Craig share a hot dog. They have a conversation with another woman. A pool player makes a series of difficult shots. The video then cuts to a new scene where a group of young women, led by a matron of sorts, jogs out of the Western Front building and around the block.

The same women are now seated in a French class, a tutorial follows on the proper way to make mayonnaise, and then a physics lesson, a life-drawing class, and a quick, confusing jilted-lover-and-murder scene where one woman drowns another in a bathtub for being in love with the same man.

Later in the video the alleged murderer and her lover-professor leave the building on bikes. The camera continues rolling as the teacher loses the contents of his bag on the street and has to improvise a clumsy recovery. He exclaims as they flee, "Let's leave this madhouse!"

The next scene features a formal graduation banquet and some after-dinner flirting between the female students and a group of older men in suits (played by local lawyers) at a long dinner table. Food is served, conversation takes place, and in a later scene leg touching is apparent as the table is removed and the two groups continue to mingle.

Toward the end of the film there is a long shot of Dragu and Craig cleaning and ironing (to the song "Work to Do" by the Isley Brothers)[52] in a small room. During this sequence, they work, take breaks, and share a cigarette. Each disrobes to iron the outfits they have on, and there is a pleasant meditative tedium to these tasks. This is followed by a set of carefully shot vacuuming scenes framed to mirror angles used in dance performances. The gender politics at play seem purposely oblique. In the final shot of the movie the two artists walk casually down the alley behind the Western Front as if enjoying the day together.

Despite the informal feel to these scenes, *Backup* was in fact a semi-professional production, demonstrated by the fact that it was filmed in colour and that its camerawork is steadier than much of the earlier videos in the Front archive. Although the shots are lengthy, the cuts are clean, and the progression of scenes appears to be reasonably logical.

Backup also occupies an odd position between a movie or TV program (with a narrative or script) and a performative work, or art. Rather than integrating itself into the standard parameters of production, editing, etc., it purposefully contradicts these practices, facilitating an increased awareness of the conceits of normal, as evinced by mass media, mediation and leaves an audience constantly trying to position themselves within the (non-)structure of the piece. Its overlapping narratives and unfinished story arcs leave one searching to create connections that are not present in the film. Dragu and Craig's refusal to satisfy our expectations in the constructed relationship between media and viewer might cause one to reconsider the expectation itself.

After filming the bathtub scene, Dragu and Craig[53] (who was incidentally deeply uncomfortable with the depiction of a murder) agreed to completely abandon their storylines. Dragu credits the process with venerating her impulse to be suspicious of narrative and allowing herself to actively deconstruct the form.[54] The film's authors were too smart to impose a rigid moral structure on the proceedings, and that ambiguity feels exploratory and oddly rigorous. The downside of *Backup* is that scenes do drag on, the sound is often difficult to decipher, and the extended meditations on single scenes may lose the viewer's attention after a time. Dragu and Craig's collaboration communicates information about their characters, with a choppy narrative, sexual innuendo, and a complete abandonment of the multiple story arcs. It also, on some level, manages to combine elements of daily life at the Western Front along with a fictitious plot, blurring the lines, again, between art and life, leading to a film that is nuanced and enigmatic.

Conclusion

What excites me about DIY culture is that it is about craft and community and it is generally less about art, or at least it tends not to inspire toward that art market. It typically happens on a local level or in an affinity group. And it often seeks to intervene in the same space that it is born. And it raises a question to me that is key, just because we have the capability and the tools to make mass media, or make high-art, should that be our highest goals. The rewards from working within particular communities often outweigh the actual benefits of mass distribution.

—Rick Prelinger[55]

Rick Prelinger's above quote about DIY culture applies equally to this discussion of artist-run spaces. It focuses on perceptions concerning the relative value of artistic production within a broader context. The argument of this essay takes the position that high art has more than its fair share of promoters. A consideration of other value sets is not meant to supplant the dominant systems of thinking, but rather to provide skeptics with a possible tool kit with which to move forward.

In Vancouver in the 1970s, work shown in state-funded artist-run centres was disengaged from the art market. The benefits of exhibiting in ARCs during that period were instead connected to attention economies. The often repeated refrain about the city is that it has never had much of an economic infrastructure in the form of commercial galleries and private collectors.[56] Both market and attention economies cater to positions concerning degrees of accomplishment. One gauges achievement based on the exchange of money and the other on degrees of perceived recognition of an artist's production. The long-standing impact of the Canada Council's funding of artists and art spaces provides a certain state-funded alternative by which support is allocated based on a remarkable awareness of the actual need of artist-controlled spaces.[57] On some level, the majority of the Western Front's modes of production, such as correspondence art, video exchanges, magazine publishing, and radio, have that element of projecting outward. These modes acted as forms of promotion engineered through that extended network of friends and collaborators, as a means of increasing visibility, self-promotion, and networking. The act of creating one's own buzz also links back to the quote from Hank Bull concerning the creation of one's own systems, be they economic or institutional. Although the dissemination of artwork through these new artistic and communicative arrangements was generated by artists and ARCs, with their reliance on external funding sources such as the Canada Council, or even the postal service, public radio frequencies, public television stations, etc., to some degree this model could be perceived as being less about the creation of innovative strategies and more about integrating, or piggybacking, oneself into and onto pre-existing schemes that suit one's economic, communicative, or self-promotional needs.[58] Even the concept of the residency program is on some level a method to bring people into your space with the notion that when they leave they will talk about, and promote, their experience. To some degree, then, the choice to support others functions as a way to promote and support oneself.

It would be too complex to chart the benefit of the Western Front's model of production to an individual in this paper, except perhaps anecdotally. All of the standard gauges for success are dependent on monetary and/or institutional values: the price of work, the number of exhibitions, the scale of future production, and so on. If the individual bases his or her practice, in part, on the rejection of these criteria for judgment because of ideological differences, what other factors might one consider? Mel Ramsden in his 1975 article "On Practice" speaks to the challenge of reprioritizing what constitutes value in regard to the outcome of artistic processes. He writes: *In an integrated society, workers, as skilled craftspeople, control their activities and hence the attributes of their products. Hence the worker's attachment to his or her product results not only from pride in the object of their labor but also and I think, crucially, in their personal regard for the community it serves…under reigning Capitalism, the worker's hopes, community goals…cultural life…need not be, and are usually not, compatible with the products of their labor.*[59]

The overarching goal of production in a space such as the Western Front was to provide individual and communal benefits derived from specific modes of and environments for making. The Canada Council, partially comprising artists, must have understood the value of structures that attempted to reach past art making and embed themselves in the way individuals relate to one another and as a group, forming the basic tenets of a society. Without that connection, Ramsden continues, "we reach a state where our work becomes totally alienated from our psyche, and finally our community—and to such an extent that we may be eventually incapable of helping ourselves."[60] Practice—the daily act, the negotiation, the relationship, the work of being not only an artist but an ever-evolving individual—moves beyond art, becoming "just one of the elements,"[61] to return to Filliou. The greater ramifications for society of this line of thinking play out in the manner in which the individual performs those daily acts. Again, Scott Watson defines some of the basic notions embodied by the Western Front in its opposition to prevalent lines of thinking from that period: *Vancouver is a periphery, and is self-consciously that.*

That is part of the raison-d'etre of the Front is to be a node in a wider network. The Front has always been about process, networking, and collaboration. It has never been about product. I would say for a long, long time, they would have been ideologically opposed to any criteria of quality as coming from a foreign, outmoded, and oppressive ideological aesthetics system; the one that Clement Greenberg stood for, for example. That offhandedness that you see, which eventually bores, is a position. It is not just the result of a lack of talent or no ideas. It also reflects the abiding commitment to not being very careful with the distinction between art and life, that avant-garde position. Trying to embody it and trying to live it.... We see that in Glenn Lewis's work, for which there is an abiding respect, around here.[62]

Vancouver is a city with a strong history of poetry and literature converging with a newly emerging visual art scene created through the development of a counterculture and the rise of feminism, racial politics, and academic institutions. Within that mixture exists a more recognized history, albeit an uneven and inconsistent one: that of the Vancouver School, comprising artists Jeff Wall, Ken Lum, Rodney Graham, Ian Wallace, Stan Douglas, Roy Arden, et al., which situated itself within larger, mainstream international art discourses and broadcast itself externally (but in an internationalism distinct from the Front's connection to the Eternal Network). This model favours engagement and discourse with an art *world*. In this case the work and the support of the work, exhibitions, texts, and philosophical substructure push outward and attempt to tie into, contrast with, and compare to broader, more international networks and discussions. Criticism and context, publication and exhibition, extend beyond the known entities. The artists engaged with broader audiences, abstracted communities, and commercial spaces, museums, galleries, and Art History, with a capital "A" and "H."

In the Western Front's archive[63] one can access the other history of Vancouver, one charting the rise of state-funded artist-run centres—a self-supporting artist community that acts for and of itself (even though organizations within this mode competed and continue to compete for the same funds), and that allows for all modes of expression, discourse, and experimentation. A community composed of like-minded individuals with a shared goal of noncommercial, self-reinforced production, focusing on a wide-open model of acceptance with links to Fluxus, the emerging counterculture, and feminism. The networks and their casts of characters perform and share ideas that are co-authored, and commingled, with the production of the space.

The strengths of the artist-run-centre model can be seen specifically in terms of access and opportunity. This access manifests not only in the form of otherwise unavailable equipment, workspace, time, and skill sets of the members of the Front, but also as an ideological platform for making work. That platform is connected with an alternative vision of what artists do and links to a continued, ongoing investigation, teaching, and learning, and its impact on the individual and the community.

In contrast, one might argue that actors within academia and the commercial gallery system have a distinct set of goals, a different set of ambitions. In the 1970s, those systems were, and maybe still are, set up partially to determine quality and value based on a set of parameters connected with the market and dominant art-historical discourses, determined primarily by those with a certain knowledge base, a certain position, and an investment in the continuation and supremacy of those ideals. The creation of spaces that actively respond to the prevailing systems by calling for increased openness and accessibility to people on all the various levels of engagement and production provides a counterbalance and rightfully challenges the authority of such systems. If those same alternative spaces initiate and maintain active archives, the ongoing record created allows access to alternate histories. Rather than repeatedly having to reinvent the wheel, future initiators of projects driven by forces other than the market can access the accumulated knowledge of the histories of artist-run projects. This also means confronting the basic principles of fitting into pre-existing, or creating new, substitute economies. The two relevant examples here may be the Fluxus artists' implementation of retail shops selling multiples and the Western Front's eventual maturation into a professional, state-funded arts organization.

From 1965 to 1968, Filliou and George Brecht ran La Cédille Qui Sourit, a shop, for lack of a better word, in Villefranche-sur-Mer. In her article on their venture, Natilee Harren uses an excellent phrase to explain what they were attempting: "Fluxus practices in terms of a *deregulation* of the art object"—and then goes on to extrapolate—"deregulation not only of the art object but also of its movement through certain art networks, motivated by artists' frustration and disgust at networks' paradoxical tendency to consolidate power."[64] The notion of deregulating the art object, opening up new paths and modes of transmission for them to exist and move, fits perfectly into the notion of new networks and the dispersal of power throughout. It also coincides with an attempt to take the structure of the market, represented by the store, as a place to sell goods at a profit, and subvert the accepted configuration to meet the needs of the participants. Filliou and Brecht's shop was by all accounts a prop shop.[65] It was a shop mimicking the idea of a shop without having to adhere to the basic principles of the thing itself, taking on the form and forgetting the function.

Postscript

A number of people who have read this essay prior to its published state provided feedback directed toward the concern that the Western Front receiving long-term funding from the state prevented other potential artist-run spaces from developing. The other consistent argument was that over time, because of any number of factors, the Western Front "institutionalized." Framed as a negative feature, this discourse equates institutionalization with what can be reduced to simply selling out. It was proposed that artist-run projects have a specific shelf life and perhaps they should be built to fold after they have run their initial course. Those are all fine points. In regard to the politics of the distribution of state aid, the lifespan of ARCs, and the formalization of the administrative function of the space, these are probably points for a discussion better suited to the members of the community they belong to. As an outside voice, with little stake in the proceedings, it would likely be a misstep for me to interject into local politics.

The Western Front met the needs of the producers as a place of production and presentation as well as a hub of transmission for all the activities within. It wasn't a space to see work that had been previously vetted by art professionals and it wasn't a place that monetized the art experience. As was discussed, the artists at the Western Front were attempting to put into action a theory about how and what being an artist meant. Their definition was broad, inclusive, and experimental. They also established their own platform for defining a set of priorities and operating strategies within the community under which to operate.

Returning to Mel Ramsden's musing in his essay "On Practice" may provide an expanded context for how and why we institute structural priorities amongst ourselves: *In this article [I am] trying to suggest…regarding "art" not as a definition outside of conversation but as a "social" matter embedded in (our) conversation, may be both an effective opposition to the bulldozer of Official Culture as well as a way of affirming our own sociality outside of "mere" contractual role relations.*[66] He goes on to say that the community must engage in that conversation, and participate in the determination of its own "methodological base." Rather than being an external imposition, the rules and the imposition of how art operates in the world become activated and exist only through the social enactment of the conversation and a running definition of what the members of that particular community deem of importance.

How that ties into the vast art-world trajectory is a matter for debate. In Ramsden's case he is talking about New York City in the '70s and it seems baffling to imagine a less singular community. It would appear important to recognize that within the notion of a local conversation, a monolithic solution, an answer, or a general consensus is unachievable. What may emerge are pockets of well-considered arguments and artists making work that reflects the intentions of that conversation and debate. The economics of urban spaces are increasingly enveloped within larger networks of international complexity. Discourse in the ramifications of these intricacies is one possible way groups who share geography remain connected to one another. The art community in Vancouver has a commitment to a long-running dialogue about all facets of artistic production within the city and how they both absorb from external sources and conversely project outward. As a subject, the city exists as a collective archive to outlining an argument about, in this case, ARCs. That archive, and this argument, exists because of the sustained existence of an ongoing conversation within the community and the veracity with which that intercourse takes place.

In all likelihood, when it comes to artist-run anything, projects are bound to peter out, or professionalize, as needs, circumstance, and economics shift over time. This essay is focused on zoning in on that area of being an artist that isn't obsessed with the final result, but rather inhabits that murky, shifting notion of individuals processing information, together, within an artist mode. What that is, or what people need to operate in that capacity, may stay in the realm of constant conjecture. What seems to be important, and what the Western Front represents here, is the notion that artists in the moment may inherently possess insight, or at least the proximity to the source, allowing them to empower new work and meet each other's immediate needs. Artist-run centres should be embedded forever in the evolving present, thus providing for artists what other facilities lack.

For instance, the response toward the development of commercial spaces and museums that have adopted mannerisms previously exhibited by ARCs (producing original work, providing space for experimentation, etc.) as a sign that artist-generated culture is no longer needed assumes that this appropriated form is still what artist-run spaces should look like. ARCs' existence and expansion in the future may take on other forms entirely, adapting to the developing needs.

Debating provincial politics or the decreased vitality of ARCs over time can, again, be left to someone else. Instead, this essay recommends looking around and making spaces that meet the needs of your cohort. Have a stake in the production of others and embrace the necessary administrative function as a component of your own practice. To be accepting and immersed in art while it is being made, before others lay judgment on the end result, requires faith and excitement in the process, in the performance, and in the performer, rather than the requisite documentation, the essay, criticism, or review. And the effective artist-run space, for its active lifespan, inherently understands what is happening in the present tense.

It is also easier to connect the time spent working, the artists' daily acts, to the place where those acts take place. This is opposed to the final product, which, as a commodity, can easily be dissociated, travelling from the place of its making. If one realizes that the importance of one's actions are inherent in the actions themselves; that the location of said actions connects the maker to his or her immediate environment; and that the immediate environment is paramount, as are the actions of the local network with which one interacts, then one's connection to that locale is strengthened, and maybe to "real" production too.

The counterpoint to all the perceived leisure-class-driven art-world drivel/malarkey is not as simple as establishing collectives, or co-authoring work, or abiding by a nonmaterial mode of (non-)production. What the Western Front was attempting to examine in its early years was the space in-between making, the moments of living, the running conversation that comprise an active participation in life and work. It's not a notion exclusive to artists. It is being present in one's own life and community. It is valuing the process and the interaction beyond the end result. It is an attempt at nonjudgment when it comes to one's own and others' processes. If an attempt was to be made to disentangle art and commerce, the place to start might exist here.

1. Robert Filliou, "Robert Filliou Defines the Eternal Network," clip from *Porta Filliou* (1977), YouTube video, 3:07, posted by Clive Robertson, January 17, 2013, http://fillip. ca/7ogl.
2. *Perhaps one of the most important byproducts of the "artworks" generated by the [Network] methodology is that the work is defined by the artists themselves and does not necessarily depend on more traditional forms of validation from museums, the conventional art market or art history. The network activity began as an experiment in communications on a creative level, correspondence by mail proving to be the most convenient, accessible and inexpensive means available. It led inevitably, to a wider understanding of the use of media.* Luis Jacob, "Golden Streams: Artists' Collaboration and Exchange in the 1970s" (exhibition essay), CCCA Canadian Art Database, 2002, http://ccca. ca. Also found in the Western Front Archive at the University of British Columbia, Vancouver, Box 16, File 1.
3. *When Robert Filliou developed his concept of the "Eternal Network," he was thinking of the human condition rather than of art. Filliou held that the purpose of art was to make life more important than art. That was the central idea of the Eternal Network. In the years since Filliou coined the term, it has taken on a life of its own. The Eternal Network has come to signify a global community of people who stand for many of the ideas that Filliou cherished. This community is fluid, comprised of people who may never meet one another in person.... From the early 1960s, using the postal system, the Eternal Network foreshadowed other networks that would become possible later through the use of such technologies as computer, telefax and electronic mail.* Ken Friedman, quoted in Jacob,

"Golden Streams." Originally published in *Eternal Network: A Mail Art Anthology* (1995).
4. *A member of the Fluxus movement, Filliou's visit affirmed and acquainted the Western Front with some social principles. Filliou had dedicated his Principles of Poetic Economy to Charles Fourier, a 19th-century thinker and utopian who, before Marx wrote and before Freud was born, succeeded in reconciling both. Fourier was the precursor of many liberation movements. He thought he had discovered the secret to social harmony—work as play.* Keith Wallace, *Whispered Art History: Twenty Years at the Western Front* (Vancouver: Arsenal Pulp, 1993), 13.
5. In the introduction to *Whispered Art History*, Wallace writes: *Eight potential shareholders—Bartlett and Von Nostrand as well as Kate Craig, Henry Greenhow, Glenn Lewis, Eric Metcalfe, Michael Morris and Vincent Trasov— were secured. All were friends involved in some aspect of the arts that included painting, photography, video, performance, literature and music. All of them were also looking for stable living/working spaces* (1).
6. *1973 was one of those periodic booms in Vancouver. Many artists found themselves on the street, turfed out of old studios to make way for new building. Martin Bartlett, electronic composer, artists Michael Morris, Vincent Trasov, Glenn Lewis, Kate Craig, and Eric Metcalfe, architect Mo Van Nostrand, and writer Henry Greenhow found themselves homeless. By pooling their resources and obtaining two mortgages, they managed to buy the old Knights of Pythias Lodge Hall, a three-story wooden building, constructed in 1922. As Western Front, the society received its first grant for new music programming and performance from the Explorations Section of Canada Council in 1974.... [The] Western*

Front set out to be a centre for all the arts, complete with artists in residence. Subsequently many other artists became involved in the Western Front, including Hank Bull, Jane Ellison, Daina Augaitis, Elizabeth Van der Zaag, Karen Henry, Annette Hurtig, Susan Milne, Corry Wyngaarden, Elizabeth Chitty, David Kelln, Patrick Ready, Babs Shapiro, Mark Corwin, Donna Zapt, Owen Underhill, Charles Watts, Bob Richardson, Kye Goodwin, Doug Brown, Paul Wong, Mary Beth Knechtel, Gerry Gilbert, Bill Little, Alex Varty, and Judy Radul. AA Bronson, *From Sea to Shining Sea: Artist-Initiated Activity in Canada* (Toronto: Power Plant, 1987), 64.

7. Hank Bull, in discussion with the author, October 2013.

8. *Through the correspondence art network, from 1969 on, Image Bank had been in touch with Filliou and other Fluxus artists. Filliou characterized the correspondence and collaboration between artists as the "Eternal Network." His attitude of ephemerality, life as art, and philosophy of equivalence had a powerful impact on the direction of the Western Front. Other Fluxus artists Dick Higgins, Emmett Williams, and Geoff Hendricks, who were subsequent artists-in-residence, reinforced this view of art. They all did performance and made video tapes during their residencies.* Bronson, *From Sea to Shining Sea*, 66.

9. Incidentally, Stiles dedicates this essay to Robert Filliou, whom she cites as one of her most valued teachers.

10. Kristine Stiles, "Between Water and Stone: Fluxus Performance, A Metaphysics of Acts," in *In the Spirit of Fluxus*, ed. Elizabeth Armstrong and Joan Rothfuss (Minneapolis: Walker Art Center, 1993), 62–99.

11. *It's very much art and life superimposed.... Your practice is this social sculpture, in Beuysian terms. Life is a performance, it's collaboration, there are all sorts of ways in for all sorts of people and it is something that is being done together, there is no one in charge and it's a collective experience.* Bull, in discussion with author, January 2014.

12. *There was no art scene no art collectors nor art dealers no art media no museums. As artists we found ourselves isolated both geographically and culturally. The tremendous distances between us prevented us from seeing ourselves as an art scene. Culturally we had none of the supporting institutions most art scenes take for granted...as artists we had to construct not only our art but the fabric of an art scene. We had to start our own institutions, start our own galleries, publish our own magazines and develop our own networks. Since there was no market we had to develop our own raison d'etre. The result of this activity was not only the accumulated activity itself, but also an institutional network of artist-run centres from sea to sea. In fact the entire face of contemporary Canadian art has been, no, not altered, but created as a result of this activity.* Bronson, *From Sea to Shining Sea*, 10.

13. From *Twenty Plus Five*, an unauthored "discussion paper on the role of the Canada Council in the arts, after the first twenty years (1957–1977) and over the next five." Found in the WF Archive at the University of British Columbia, Vancouver, Box 1, File 26.

14. *Such as the Odyssey Gallery, or short-lived artist-initiated commercial ventures such as the Tempus Gallery, the Focus Gallery and later the Magan Ghetto.* Keith Wallace, "A Particular History: Artist-Run Centres in Vancouver," in *Vancouver Anthology*, ed. Stan Douglas (Vancouver: Talonbooks and Or Gallery, 2011), 30.

15. WF member Glenn Lewis served

on the Intermedia Board of Trustees from 1970–72.

16. *Image Bank, the creation of Michael Morris and Vincent Trasov…came into being as a response to Ray Johnson's New York Correspondence School and the subsequent correspondence art involvement with many artists in North America and abroad…. Image Bank was primarily a structure for setting up, extending and reinforcing correspondence, creating a network using the postal system as a means of communication. An International Image Request Directory was instigated as the form of "exchange." Requests were published quarterly in General Idea's* FILE *Megazine and annually as a complete directory.* Bronson, *From Sea to Shining Sea*, 41.

17. *Vol. 1, No. 1 of FILE Magazine, was published by General Idea, originated with the help of a federal LIP (Local Initiatives Project) grant. Its original purpose was to create a cross-Canada link-up between artists, and it featured Image Bank's "Image Request Lists" from Vancouver and across-Canada gossip as means of doing this. The first issue featured Vincent Trasov of Vancouver in his Mr. Peanut costume, against the Toronto skyline. As the artists became more involved in the magazine format, it became General Idea's first major step into appropriating and reinhabiting formats of mass culture.* Ibid., 60.

18. Ibid. The Canada Council spent $639,300 in the first year of its existence.

19. Bull, in discussion with the author, October 2013.

20. *We wanted an art scene, a real art scene, and we knew we had to start with what we had before us: a theatre scene, a literary scene, a music scene, and so on. We also knew that we wanted to be connected cross-Canada and to the world at large…and so we were very aware of* connecting with other communities and artists and creating an infrastructure that would hold together over time. This was a lesson we learned from Warhol: so much of his work was contextualized by the Factory community, which he built around him. He was very much a scene builder and we knew we had to be too…but on a larger scale. AA Bronson, quoted in Jacob, "Golden Streams."

21. A major influence on Vancouver's visual artists was the strong literary presence existing in the city since the '50s. Poets and writers informed a sophisticated political, artistic, and literary discourse. From the Western Front's inception, poetry readings have taken place every Monday night. *The cross-fertilization of poetry and visual art is the most distinctive aspect of the west coast avant-garde, the germ of which was the San Francisco Renaissance of the 1950s. Black Mountain poets Robert Duncan and Robert* Creeley *moved to San Francisco, bringing their poetics with them."* (Lara Halina Tomaszewska, "Borderlines of Poetry and Art: Vancouver, American Modernism, and the Formation of the West Coast Avant-Garde, 1961–69" [PhD dissertation, University of British Columbia, 2007], 17.) *In 1963, the University of British Columbia hosted the Vancouver Poetry Conference, the culmination of a three-year frenzy of poetic activity on the west coast. The San Francisco Renaissance had traveled and taken hold in Vancouver. This was only the beginning: Creeley, Duncan, Ginsberg, Spicer, Persky, and Blaser all taught in Vancouver during the 1960s. In 1961, the first Festival of the Contemporary Arts took place on the university campus. It was to be an annual event for the next decade—a multi-disciplinary festival that featured experimental film, visual art, dance, and music produced on*

the west coast (ibid., 19).

22. From the 1978 Financial Statement in the WF Archive: the Western
Front "is specifically designed for
presentation, research, production and
distribution to define and understand
the art of the seventies." The upstairs
hall is known as the Grand Luxe Hall
and the downstairs space was/is the
dance studio.

23. *However, by keeping a tight lid on
access to facilities and equipment, even
to the point of installing a buzz-in entry
system, the Western Front assumed its
own particular form of institutionalization. As only invited artists could exhibit,
perform, produce a video, or stay as part
of the artist-in-residence program, this
policy created a perceived exclusivity
during the 1970s, one that alienated a
considerable segment of the local art community and basically ignored the public*
(Wallace, "A Particular History," 36).
It's difficult to determine whether having a lock on the front door of your
home counts as imposing institutionalization or exclusivity. The odd set
of parameters that factor into having
public functions in a semi-private residence undercut what must have been
an ongoing negotiation for members
of the space. Whether the public was
"ignored" by not being granted open
access to video equipment is also up
for debate. The Western Front con-
tinuously displayed an ability to professionalize in order to facilitate the
sustained existence of the society. To
a certain degree, the continued function of the institution forty years later
in the same building, etc., rather than
as a historical footnote, would seem to
imply at least a semblance of forward-
thinking pragmatism.

24. See Wallace's introduction to
Whispered Art History, where he
lists the various personae of the WF
members: *Eric Metcalfe (Dr. Brute),
Kate Craig (Lady Brute), Henry
Greenhow (S.S. Tell of Borderline
Studios), Glenn Lewis (Flakey Rosehip
of the New York Corres Sponge Dance
School of Vancouver), Michael Morris
and Vincent Trasov (Marcel Idea and
Mr. Peanut of Image Bank)*. Wallace,
Whispered Art History, 3.

25. Michael Morris, quoted in Jacob,
"Golden Streams."

26. Robert Ballantyne, "Glamour
Pageantry and Knives: Gay Identity
in File Megazine" (PhD dissertation,
University of British Columbia, 1994).

27. George Maciunas, quoted in Larry
Miller, "Transcript of the Videotaped
Interview with George Maciunas," in
The Fluxus Reader, ed. Ken Friedman
(Hoboken, NJ: John Wiley & Sons,
1998), 197.

28. Scott Watson, head of the Department of Art History, Visual Art and
Theory and director/curator of the
Morris and Helen Belkin Art Gallery
at the University of British Columbia, in discussion with the author,
January 2014.

29. Bull, in discussion with the author,
January 2014.

30. *The Decca Dance and the celebra-
tion of the "1,000,011th" anniversary of
art, organized by Image Bank, Lowell
Darling, Willoughby Sharp, Ant Farm,
General Idea and the Western Front. The
fall of 1973 was spent in preparation for
this momentous occasion, a celebration
of the Eternal Network that took place in
the splendid ballroom of the former Elk's
Lodge on MacArthur Park in Hollywood.
Susan Subtle, Les Petits Bonbons, John
Jack Baylin, John Dowd, Irene Dogmatic,
Anna Banana, Victor Coleman, Andy
Graffiti, and a host of correspondence
artists from across North America
appeared for the ritual celebration of
"Art's 1,000,011th Birthday" and Mail*

Art Awards Ceremony. The stage show, a parody of the Academy Awards, featured a male chorus resplendent in tuxedos and Shark Fin Bathing Caps moving in stately symmetry to the inimitable crooning of androgyne Pascal. It could be said to mark the peak of the Mail art movement, and for many, signalled the end of it. Copiously documented on film, video and in print. "Hollywood Decca Dance and Art's Birthday," CCCA Canadian Art Database, accessed October 3, 2013, http://fillip.ca/sxbr.

31. Bull, in discussion with the author, January 2014.

32. Craig Saper, "Fluxus as a Laboratory," in *The Fluxus Reader*, 136.

33. If one is compelled by economics or other internal and external forces to prioritize the end product (which this essay does not disparage), the process of composing may exist as a hurdle to overcome en route to a finished idea.

34. Saper, "Fluxus as a Laboratory," 136.

35. Robert Filliou and John Cage, *Teaching and Learning as Performing Arts* (New York: Koenig, 1970).

36. Western Front's private online archive is accessible via Vimeo. See http://fillip.ca/0upo.

37. There are documents in Filliou's artist file at the WF implying that the tape was to be added to by other artists, a plan which never came to fruition.

38. Again tied to the Western Front's founding members' development of performative personas.

39. With effective performers there is the feeling that they are communicating to each member of an audience individually. This experience is the closest I can imagine to group telepathy.

40. Saper, "Fluxus as a Laboratory," 137.

41. "Artists: Glenn Lewis," Trench Gallery (website), accessed March 29, 2014, http://trenchgallery.com.

42. Which are often more difficult to realize in commercially driven systems.

43. Kate Craig, "Personal Perspectives," in *Vancouver: Art and Artists, 1931–1983*, ed. Luke Rombout (Vancouver: Vancouver Art Gallery, 1983), http://fillip.ca/w84s.

44. Ambition, which Watson links in terms of Jeff Wall to individual, grand results and personal success, could be seen here in Craig's case as a desire to see others, or the Western Front itself, succeed.

45. Stiles, "Between Water and Stone," 62–99.

46. Margaret Dragu, in discussion with the author, February 2014.

47. Glenn Lewis, email message to author, February 16, 2014.

48. Kate Craig, from a short essay on the making of *Backup* and her administrative role in the space. Dated July 27, 1980. Written on Craig and Bull's personal letterhead, found in Dragu's artist's file in the Western Front Archive.

49. The Western Front had video equipment that was unavailable elsewhere in Canada at the time: the first JVC editing decks, new colour video cameras, etc.

50. Margaret Dragu and Kate Craig met in Toronto in 1975. Members of the Western Front performed in a show called *Spots Before Your Eyes* at A Space. Dragu was hired on to tighten up the group's sloppy choreography. With a background in dance, at Judson Church, Dragu was well suited to the task. Craig invited her to be an artist-in-residence. Dragu would visit on a regular, yearly basis thereafter, to work on projects and participate in the life of the Front. The tape they put

together turned out to be the largest production made at the WF up to that point, with the collaborators having actual production meetings, renting props, and dyeing costumes. Dragu had acted in theatre and television and brought some of that industry professional experience to the endeavour. Her original concept was to make a murder mystery about a private all-girls' school. Dragu, in discussion with the author, February 2014.

51. Each chapter in the film has a title, or mode. The scene on the roof is titled "Mode 31: Get It On." The pool hall scene is titled "Mode 4: Get Down." The classroom scenes are titled "Mode 13: Get Up." The banquet scenes are titled "Mode 112: Get Around." The cleaning scenes are titled "Mode 202: Get Behind."

52. From the group's 1972 album, *Brother, Brother, Brother*.

53. Craig's own works such as *Delicate Issue* (1979) and *Still Life cont.* (1976) are explorations of the artist's body and living space from exceedingly close up. Craig narrates over the footage discussing the roles of the viewer and the person being viewed and what information can be ascertained the closer the gaze gets to the object, in this case her body. Shots blur and abstract as the camera loses the ability to focus that close to the artist's body. Often it is difficult to tell what is on the screen until a nipple, an armpit, or shoulder blades appear. This piece is reminiscent somewhat of Joan Jonas's *Mirror Piece* (1969), in which the artist attempts to view the entirety of her body with a small handheld mirror in front of an audience. Craig's piece reads more as an exploration of landscape, and through the voiceover implicates the person on display within the exchange as well. The mediation of the video camera, the intimacy of the camerawork, performed by her husband, Hank Bull, adds to the voyeuristic nature of the experience. Late in the piece when the camera suddenly pulls into focus on the artist's asshole it's difficult not to still have a visceral reaction to the scene.

54. Dragu, in discussion with the author, February 2014.

55. Rick Prelinger, "Appropriation: Is it Finished? (A Manifesto)," lecture at the Wattis Institute, San Francisco, March 14, 2014.

56. I have no idea if this is true or not. It certainly was mentioned like a mantra by nearly everyone I spoke with concerning Vancouver's art scene. Wallace comments on the status of ARCs and the market in the 1970s: "Twenty years ago, few Vancouver collectors ventured into the world of ARCs to explore, and perhaps support, what was considered new or experimental art." Keith Wallace, "Artist-Run Centres: A Reflection on Three Texts," in *Institutions by Artists*, ed. Jeff Khonsary and Kristina Lee Podesva (Vancouver: Fillip, 2012), 262.

57. For instance, in the 1977 publication from the Canada Council outlining their funding rules and regulation, there is a funding category titled "Aid to Parallel Galleries." It reads: "This program is for cooperative galleries, founded, and operated by professional artists for at least one year. Grants may cover operating expenses and costs of experimental exhibitions and other artistic productions." For me, the phrase "experimental exhibitions and other artistic productions" seems remarkable. Canada Council, "Aid to Artists," 1977, found in the Western Front Archive, University of British Columbia, Vancouver, Box 1, File 26.

58. So on a certain level this runs in

direct contrast to Bull's prior quote: "As an artist you don't have to fit into an institutional or an economic system. You can make your own up." The Western Front found a way to integrate itself into both an economic system (via Canada Council grants) and institutionalized in order to continue to qualify for said funding. Even the residency program was not a new system but rather one that operated based on a set of principles venerated here.
59. Mel Ramsden, "On Practice," *The FOX*, no. 1 (1975), 182.
60. Ibid.
61. "It may help to think of it as being part of the wider network where artistic activity just becomes one of the elements." Filliou, "Robert Filliou Defines the Eternal Network."
62. Watson, in discussion with the author, January 2014.
63. Those tapes are breaking down and are in need of digitization, which may or may not occur based on budgets and time and luck to some degree. The tapes that are considered of most historical value and slated for digitization are actually connected with the Vancouver/West Coast literary scene of the '60s and '70s. Viewing any part of the archive from the first twenty-five years of the Front means there is a chance you could be the last to see that particular tape.
64. Natilee Harren, "La cédille qui ne finit pas: Robert Filliou, George Brecht, and Fluxus in Villefranche (deregulation version)," *Art & Education*, 2011, http://fillip.ca/fr3u.
65. A shop that is more or less a prop, rather than a shop selling props.
66. Ramsden, "On Practice," 187.

Philip Monk
Battle Stances

*General Idea, CEAC, and the Struggle for
Ideological Dominance in Toronto, 1976–78*

Everyone knows the story of CEAC, of how it crashed and burned. It's been told thoroughly before, significantly by Dot Tuer in her monumental, archival research article, "The CEAC Was Banned in Canada," published in *C Magazine* in 1986. It's the story of how an ambitious, tightly controlled, and guarded artist-run centre amassed its own building, declared a radical political program, and advocated kneecapping, Red Brigade style, before it lost its council funding and closed down in 1978. Not only during its brief history was the Centre for Experimental Art and Communication (CEAC) a rival of A Space, the latter billing itself as Canada's oldest and most important artist-run space, "it was cast in opposition to A Space," Tuer suggests.[1]

In telling the story, or, rather, in setting it up, Tuer casts another opposition—that between CEAC and General Idea—by opening her article with two contrasting epigraphs drawn from two rival publications, the house organs of General Idea and CEAC: *FILE* and *Strike*, respectively. The first she presents is General Idea's famous Glamour manifesto of 1975, in which they wrote: *We wanted to be famous, glamourous and rich. That is to say we wanted to be artists and we knew that if we were famous and glamourous we could say we were artists and we would be. We never felt we had to produce great art to be great artists. We knew great art did not bring glamour and fame. We knew we had to keep a foot in the door of art and we were conscious of the importance of berets and paint brushes.*

And the second is Amerigo Marras's not-so-well-known 1978 article "On Organization": *What perpetuates the reactionary mystification of the role of the artist is the "world of scarcity" and the "incapacity to survive" in a capitalist society. The artist defends the privilege and the entrenchment he/she holds in a capitalist society. Also symptomatic, even and not less so among the vanguard, alternative and co-op artist's groups, is the sense of hopelessness for social change, as these same groups mimic those repressive methods of economical capitalization adopted by the art world.*[2]

One might argue that perhaps this set-up was too easy, judging General Idea against CEAC, given that General Idea already ironically set itself up in its reactionary mystification of the role of the artist. However, I am not here to advocate for General Idea (having a few years earlier delivered a lecture and published an article arguing for the capitalist basis of General Idea's mystifying system of Glamour).[3] Nevertheless, in Tuer's article General Idea's empty shell of history becomes the empty rhetorical figure against which the fullness of CEAC's forgotten revolutionary materialist practice was contrasted.

"Miss General Idea hangs around the left stage area for much of the action," Tuer wrote of CEAC's cast of characters,[4] as if General Idea's muse sought inspiration there for the artists' plagiarist, intellectual parasitism. But what if General Idea and CEAC were in secret communication, especially through their respective publications? And what if this communication naturally was one of rivalry? Let's extend Tuer's epigraphic opposition between the two to see whether we can productively trace their communication through this period when both *FILE* and *Art Communication Edition (ACE)*, later to become *Strike*, were publishing. Doing so would enable us to read certain editorials and articles as critiques of the other's practice. It would cast CEAC and General Idea's competitive relationship in a whole new light. Moreover, it would, to a degree, reveal a struggle for the assertion of a particular practice. Let's, for the moment, call this practice political—in effect, theirs was a struggle for the ideological domination of the Toronto art community.

It was more than just a battle of words. We can trace parallels through much of their activities. Both originating in commune-like situations, each instituted major multifaceted artist-run organizations. The Kensington Arts Association began in 1973 and became CEAC when it moved to Toronto's warehouse district, soon to become the centre of the art scene, in 1976; Art Metropole started on Yonge Street in 1974 and moved a couple blocks away from CEAC in 1978. Both conducted campaigns in Europe and New York to publicize themselves. And, significantly, both published magazines.

But in the end it was the words that mattered. This record is found in the magazines that each group individually published. Eventually self-serving, both publications originally fulfilled other functions. For instance, modelled on *LIFE* magazine, *FILE* (1972–89) was the house organ of the short-lived correspondence movement before it became a vehicle mainly for General Idea's own mythological production and promotion of international fellow travellers (e.g., the *mondo arte*). *Art Communication Edition* published for about a year (from late 1976) when it changed its name to *Strike* and produced three issues in 1978 before expiring. Publishing nearly monthly, it began really as a newsletter for CEAC activities but soon became a broadsheet in which the war of words, with General Idea sometimes as target, eventually escalated. While a target, General Idea was never named specifically; nonetheless, a close reader of both magazines would recognize the code words indicating a critique of the collective's practice.

Mimic Magazines

The opening communication between CEAC and General Idea took place just before *ACE* started publishing, through the auspices of a third artist-produced newspaper, *Only Paper Today (OPT)*, which A Space published as a journal of experimental art and literary writing that served the Toronto art community.[5] *OPT* published an interview with Amerigo Marras by Robert Handforth, the ostensible purpose of which was to inform readers about the opening of CEAC's new space and, indeed, remarkably, the ownership of a whole building, which CEAC purchased in September 1976, in addition to articulating the artistic program and direction of this elusive organization.[6] Handforth was then one of the directors of A Space, soon to resign in September 1977. As he was already an Art Metropole employee, perhaps he was seen to be fully in General Idea's camp, so in conveying information about CEAC to *OPT*'s readers, Marras thus obliquely spoke, through his interlocutor, to General Idea. When asked whether CEAC was just another name for the Kensington Arts Association, Marras replied: "Well you see, the K.A.A. is still alive and well. But the K.A.A. is now behind the props—the frame of reference." This was a noteworthy description because, with its props and frames of reference, it exactly repeated the language of General Idea's fictitious *The 1984 Miss General Idea Pavillion*, which included props and plans that had been unveiled by General Idea in its Carmen Lamanna Gallery exhibition *Going thru the Notions* in fall 1975, still fresh in memory. Handforth continued, "So now it's K.A.A. operating as CEAC," and Marras replied, "Yeah. CEAC is the public front. We wanted it to be descriptive." As in the case of General Idea's *Pavillion*, Marras projected CEAC as the rhetorical—you could say, performative—front for a collective activity, but one not so visibly focused on an artwork as in the case of General Idea. If this front was "descriptive," did Marras then mean—here adopting the language of General Idea—that he considered it to be mythological too? For "description" was the classifying term used by General Idea for the mythological universe of correspondence art: *I am not concerned with breaking myths, nor with making myths, but with the structural implications implicit in mythology's view of the universe. In myth it is clear that every-*thing *must be accounted for. Unlike science, myth starts with a vision and fills in the blanks. It structures a cosmology through description, not analysis.*[7]

Myth was a disjunctive, even destructive, model allied to the cut-and-paste of collage that led to a synthesis—to new myths of alternate lifestyles: *In this article seeing art as a system of signs in motion as an archive and indicator and stabilizer of culture as a means of creating fetish objects as residence for the field of imagery defining a culture, seeing all this and more in many ways we have become aware of the necessity of developing methods of generating realizing stabilizing alternate myths alternate lifestyles.*[8]

From 1973 to 1976, when these two statements were written, there was already a different world, so Marras's "accounting for" could now be considered not to be based on Claude Lévi-Strauss's structural anthropology (as in the case of General Idea), but as proceeding from another, all-inclusive, "mythic" model: Marxism. (With the beginning of publication of *The FOX* in New York in 1975, Marxism became the art world's au courant discourse.) Not for him any synthesis; Marras simply preferred disjunction. Refusing to answer Handforth's question about "artistic policies," he said instead: "Usually what we try to do is build up contradictions—without ambiguity."[9] With this turn of phrase, Marras turned CEAC in opposition to General Idea, for General Idea was for ambiguity without contradiction, evident in the title of one of its 1975 *Pavillion* blueprints, *Luxon Louvre (Ambiguity without Contradiction)*. Marras's clever, chiasmatic inversion contradicted General Idea's enterprise at its core by attacking its fundamental principle of ambiguity. He would always fundamentally oppose contradiction to ambiguity.

What would the antithesis of ambiguity and contradiction be? It would pose a system of meaning to a system of conflict, of fluctuating interpretation to an explicit provocation that was nonstop.[10] It was not that General Idea saw itself beyond conflict. General Idea considered Glamour a "battleground," but the artists also thought of it as beyond Marxism. With the insouciance of a fashion-magazine caption, General Idea wrote: "Glamour replaces Marxism as the single revolutionary statement of the twentieth century."[11] Marras himself would rather forestall that replacement. He would prefer Marxism tout court, a Marxism unadorned, or at least adorned with nothing but rhetoric.

Yet he was not ready to quit his dialogue with General Idea and set the journals in strict opposition on divergent paths. It appears that Marras saw *ACE* as a means of a continuing critique of General Idea. For instance, the second issue of *ACE*, from early 1977, carried the article "Four Leading Questions as Principles of Revolutionary Practice." Simply stated, it was a radicalized answer to *General Idea's Framing Devices*, the artists' five-point agenda or master plan first promulgated in 1975, but it assumed the same format. To the question "What is Art & Communication?," the answer responded: *It is interface impact conducive within social forms as frames, structures, behaviour. Art as materialist practice and communication as dialectics in juxtaposition along contextual layerings produce revolutionary effects. Art & Communication is basically this: dialectical materialism practiced as ideology.*[12] Compare this to General

Idea: *THE FRAME OF REFERENCE is basically this: a framing device within which we inhabit the role of the general public, the audience, the media. Mirrors mirroring mirrors expanding and contracting to the focal point of view and including the lines of perspective bisecting the successive frames to the vanishing point. The general public, the audience, the media playing the part of the sounding board, the comprehensive framework outlining whatever meets their eye.*[13]

Despite their obscurity, the manifesto-like character of both pronouncements implied, theoretically at least, an incitement to action. The measure of success for both was not just an "effect" determined by vocabulary but also the practice's (pretended) effectiveness in the public realm. Yet, we have to consider whether the closed frameworks of "mirrors mirroring mirrors" or "juxtaposition along contextual layerings" were not just self-serving rhetorical devices that had no practical effect outside their art context. However, these statements were themselves performative: they were means of their own enacting. They were their own effect, so to speak. They were an analysis of their own intentions as much as they were an analysis in extension, outside themselves. In the end it would be a matter of how CEAC and General Idea negotiated their specialized rhetoric in relation to a purported public realm. Effectiveness would be a matter of survival.

In its July 1977 editorial, CEAC strategically chose its enemy and thereby specified a role for *ACE*: "Art Communication Edition proposes for itself the role of being the 'antithesis to dominant ideologies,' rather than the role of being alternative to the hegemony of commercially motivated journals."[14] An interesting distinction: Why discriminate between dominant ideologies and a specific form of transmission, even if it was the type one operated through? One wonders whether the "antithetical" versus the "alternative" was the new formula of the previous antithesis of "contradiction" and "ambiguity." For, once again, the article was a veiled attack on General Idea, who was not mentioned by name but obviously was the representative—though a common art and political term—of the "alternative" (see above). Only halfway through the article, at the mention of *People* magazine, one of those commercially motivated journals, do we realize that it was not only the Time Life publication being analyzed but also General Idea's newly formatted *FILE*. Or at least we were made to understand that *FILE* basically operated in the same manner as *People*: "How does 'people' magazine communicate to us? It teaches a 'popular' language" that reflects its audience as stereotypes of its own repression.[15] Marras's critique was topical. In the recent spring 1977 issue of *FILE*, General Idea revealed the Time Life lawsuit against the artists for *FILE*'s simulation of *LIFE*. General Idea had eventually complied by changing the look of the cover but surreptitiously got the last laugh by making that issue into a "SPECIAL PEOPLE ISSUE": "FILE was entering the no-no-nostalgia age in preparation for 1984 and in keeping abreast of the TIMEs was becoming increasingly concerned with PEOPLE."[16]

Marras thought the joke rather was on General Idea, still playing its game of mimicry by inhabiting various popular-culture formats: that is, merely playing a "role of being alternative to the hegemony of commercially motivated journals." *FILE*, of course, was a vehicle for simulation of mainstream *LIFE* magazine. *We maneuver hungrily, conquering the uncontested territory of culture's forgotten shells— beauty pageants, pavillions, picture magazines, and other contemporary corpses. Like parasites we animate these dead bodies and speak in alien tongues*, General Idea wrote in its 1975 Glamour manifesto.[17] Two years later, in an *ACE* 6 article articulating the accompanying editorial, Marras responded: *We know that mimicry is only the immature and most immediate response. We respond with safe patterns that are recognizable as the parody of the dominant "culture". The mimicry is only falling into the same view of history (of heroes). The correct pattern is, instead, being antithetical to the dominant culture; to completely break away from the main direction is to deny classifying oneself as alternative. We reject the process of absorption. We reject the process of parodying.*[18]

That is, Marras rejected General Idea, rejecting its artistic practice of simulation (parody) and inhabitation of roles (absorption). To be antithetical was *not* to be alternative. One was either for contradiction or for alternative. There was no other choice. Marras concludes: *This argument brings in an important issue in the so-called alternative circles. We do not stand as alternative but as antithetical to dominant ideologies. To be antithetical is to reject any "coming back" syndromes so pedantically proposed in reaction to revolutionary activisms.* Presumably "'coming back' syndromes" referred to General Idea's retro camp sensibility. Retro was the wrong camp. To be revolutionary meant first being factional. CEAC's factional enemy in the Toronto art community obviously was General Idea.

The Punk Effect

Yet, a new antithetical faction surfaced in the Toronto art community that briefly united the two groups—*for*, however, rather than against. For the one thing General Idea and CEAC temporarily could agree on, when it broke in Toronto in summer 1977, was punk. Significantly, CEAC helped spawn it by playing host to the Crash 'n' Burn punk club in the basement of their Duncan Street building. General Idea, too, had a role to play promoting it by devoting a whole issue of *FILE* that fall to "Punk 'til You Puke!"—creating an international roster of punk bands with Canadian groups following in the rear. Yet, by all accounts Toronto was one of the main centres, along with London and New York, and it was kicked off in that basement by a couple of groups that respectively became CEAC's and General Idea's house bands: the Diodes and the Dishes.

General Idea knew a good incendiary performance when it saw one, so under the influence of punk, it "burnt down" its *Pavillion* soon after. The fuse was lit in the "Punk 'til You Puke!" issue, where the editorial concluded: "The sentimentalism of late sixties early seventies essentially surrealistic aesthetic has been replaced by a certain prag- matic anarchy which is now the theme of this issue."[19] In an article from that same issue, "Pogo Dancing in the British Aisles," the ever-astute AA Bronson aligned his paean to punk to Gilles Deleuze and Félix Guatarri's description of desiring machines from their recently translated *Anti- Oedipus: Capitalism and Schizophrenia*. Bronson saw the desiring punk machine as anti-capitalist and "an anarchist motion by definition"[20]—but he equally recognized punk for its subversive fashion sense.

Already in July, CEAC had sent a letter from the front- line trenches, ambivalently titled "Spanking Punk": "The latest rebellious form for Toronto's youth scene is the rave of *crash 'n burn* punk rock groups."[21] Yet *the punk rock scene in Toronto is considerably different from that in Britain, where the youth are the victims of working class conditions. The Canadians, instead, exist on the edge of a capitalist sur- plus, having grown up in homogeneous suburban settings*, the anonymous author observes with a dismissive sneer. None- theless, revolutionary potential, the author concluded, existed beyond the "frustrated consumerism" of "broken beer glasses and make-up applied with razor blades."

CEAC would use the hard edge of punk to deliver its own hard-line message. *ACE* 8 (October 1977)—the complementary issue to *FILE*'s "Punk 'til You Puke!"—actually was a 45 rpm record, with CEAC slogans ("you people are the police") interspersed between the Diodes' raucous short-burst instrumentals. As always, the two magazine issues were assembled within spitting distance of each other, but they soon began to deviate from one another on the subject of punk, antithetically so. The editorial to *ACE* 9 (November 1977) reads: *In the western capitalist countries the Fall has cooled the steam produced by the 1977 summer of rock. Punks, mannerists, opportunists, nouveaux riche, promoters, fashion burnt, and all the other idiots fallen into the image of anarchy as dictated by the vogue punk, rush towards the cliché of fashion like flies to a mound of shit. The fashion, the image, the shit has been widely explored and exploited by the mass media. Even the usual "avant garde" magazines [read:* FILE *magazine] have covered the news while putting themselves into the picture.*[22]

As if answering in advance to the pragmatic anarchy of General Idea's showcard "Fascism and anarchy join forces to make a work of art," exhibited at the Carmen Lamanna Gallery that December, or anticipating *FILE*'s "$UCCE$$ Issue" of March 1981, the editorial goes on: *Capitalization has taken place as the time to cash in arrived. At last, the idea of anarchy makes money and the economical statement that punk rock might have made in the beginnings is forgotten.*[23]

The editorial coyly, yet strangely, concludes: "And we are ready to place the right device in the right place. Does any one understand what we mean?"

For those who did not understand, perhaps not exactly comprehending the turn from punk anarchy to revolutionary politics, CEAC placed that device and exploded a bomb in the second issue of the newly renamed *Strike* (May 1978): *We are opposed to the dominant tendency of playing idiots, as in the case of "punks" or the sustainers of the commodity system.... In the manner of the [Red] Brigades, we support leg shooting/knee capping to accelerate the demise of the old system.*[24] In a turn to world-historical revolutionary politics, *Strike*'s editorial board could not resist one last localizing dig here at General Idea. Who were these players, either punks or (art) supporters of the commodity system, but those who self-identified with "the creampuff innocence of idiots"? General Idea, that is.[25]

What Is Effective Art?

By the evidence of print, the rivalry between CEAC and General Idea seems one-sided. We do not find the same linguistic obsession with a rival in the language used in *FILE*. Was this then a case of mimetic rivalry on CEAC's part? That is, was it more mimesis than antithesis? Or was *ACE* actually a serious critique of General Idea, unnamed though the artists were? This is part of a larger question: Was antithesis merely a rhetorical device on CEAC's part or was it actually effective? That is, how seriously do we take a statement of theirs such as this: "We want to simply eliminate the dominant culture 'tout court'"?[26]

In the process, did CEAC want as well to eliminate General Idea tout court? In an *ACE* 7 (August 1977) article by Marras titled "VENOM," under the heading "Introduction of poison into the system of the victim," we read: *The relationship (distance) between individuals/groups determines the conflict/agreement between them. Each set of individuals tends to include/exclude the other as a process of elimination-dissent. Others call it generation gap, cold war, class struggle, or simply asphyxiation.*[27] In this internecine counterplotting we recall that poisoning was also a primary counterstrategy of Glamourous General Idea in its viral inhabitation of media. Indeed, mimesis itself was a subtle, invasive form of venom (what Marras had earlier rejected as "absorption").[28] It is more than a little revealing that the next heading to Marras's article is "malignant virulence." Had General Idea all along infected CEAC, especially virulent Marras in his "conflict/ agreement" with this rival group? The theory of mimetic rivalry is that one kills what one copies.

Yet, CEAC believed being antithetical was effective, especially in the move from the art system, where it considered consumerist General Idea to malinger, to the social realm of politics per se, where CEAC itself wanted to operate. So the editorial board explained in the inaugural issue of *Strike*: *Are we supposed to explain the switch from Art Communication Edition to STRIKE? We want to come out closer to the de-training programme, opposed to service systems. We want to effectively move on and merge with the social stance that we foster. We know that within consumerist tactics, the antithetical position, as explained in issue 6 of Art Communication Edition, is an* effective *strategy.*[29]

"Effective" was *the* word, as when later in that issue the collective continued to explain: *During the last couple months the discussions have been centered around the meaning of counter-information, counter-productivity, terrorism, the possible actions that create* effective *change, to a practice of scrutinizing texts and pinning down its obscurantist ideological incorrectness.*[30] In these discussions, CEAC may have passed beyond General Idea and its "obscurantist ideological incorrectness," but General Idea, at the same moment, was talking about "effectiveness," too—as in "What do you mean by 'effective' art?"

Such was the lead question to General Idea's "Punk 'til You Puke!" editorial—of all places. The answer was a little less effective…or was it? "Obviously art that has effect. Obviously art that affects an audience. Being effective requires an audience. Obviously art that has an effect is art that has an audience."[31] This exercise in circular reasoning did not really answer the questions: But what of the effect? What was the effect? More than asking the question, General Idea was making art about it as well. Not that it was necessarily making *effective* art, because who, for instance, was its intended audience; but it was *posing* the answer—performing it. So it is the artwork *Press Conference* from March 1977—with its faux media set-up—rather than the "Punk" editorial that we must look to for an answer to this pertinent question.

The faux *Press Conference* (conducted at Western Front, Vancouver, in front of an art audience with the purpose of making this tape) was called to address "effective art." It seemingly cynically concluded with the statement: "It isn't art unless it sells." But "selling" meant being "culturally operational," a situation where the artwork sold itself and its context, and where the objective was to "get the public to act on the basis of your work." Art was "not merely a medium for personal expression but potentially also a powerful cultural tool" and an "effective generator of cultural information that warrants consumer acceptance." As to the method of effectiveness, "the best way is to test an idea first in a controlled situation like the art scene, look at your feedback, and then continue from then on." "Content must be allowed to maneuver its way into the people's cultural needs or context."[32]

A press conference is a vehicle of dissemination, but General Idea framed it as a *format* within which to enact its so-called analysis of effectiveness. (The performance assumed not just the format of a press conference but also the language of a marketing sales pitch, as if culture was business and art its product.) Nonetheless, format and audience were contained within the artificiality of the set-up: performing to camera with a participating audience. For all the language of audience of its "Punk" editorial, the artists chose to remain within the cultural framework of the art system, using it as a "control group" to test their "product," the effectiveness of which did not exceed the art frame. The artists never intended to. General Idea's statements were a framework for discussion; they were not meant to be taken literally as some, in light of their own idea of political effectiveness, proceeded to do.[33]

But what of CEAC and its *Strike* editorial statement "We want to effectively move on and merge with the social stance that we foster"? How effectively did they manage their crossover from art world to public domain? In his article in that issue, "On Organization," Marras admitted right away: "I am approaching the toleration limit to any further internalization of the notion of 'art' and/or of 'art as something else.'"[34] Presumably, effectiveness was to be found outside the art system, not, as in the case of General Idea, internal to it. "On Organization" had a solid Marxist title, in the lineage, for instance, of Mao Zedong's "On Practice" or "On Contradiction," but it said nothing on the organization of workers or the masses, let alone the art community, whose attempts at collectivity, through the artist-run system of parallel galleries or artists union (Canadian Artists' Representation), Marras (intolerantly) dismissed. Instead, artists in Canada and New York were accused of being careerist petite-bourgeois supporters of the class system. Art essentially was a "cover-up" for maintaining the class system; even its discourse was suspect: "When we discuss 'art', we are actually using the discourse as a pretext for established relationships in a class structure."[35]

CEAC, however, never could abstain from a discussion of art, although exempting itself presumably from the stigma of maintaining class relations for doing so. Immediately, in the controversial second issue of *Strike* (May 1978), it inserted a four-page broadsheet, "Dissidence in the 1978 Venice Biennale," that complained of the National Gallery of Canada's selection of artists for the national pavilion in Venice and provided an analysis of the "socio-political function of art and art institutions" and of how "the legitimating [and ameliorating] function of art serves the interests of power" as an "ideological tool" of capitalism.[36]

In this "Joint Statement by the Central Strike Committee," analysis began to diverge somewhat from that found, for instance, in Marras's "On Organization." Past practices, too, came in for self-criticism: "such as the idealist conceptions of Alternative Perceptions, Deviant Behaviour, Punks, etc." But in any intended crossover, merging with the social stance it wanted to foster, the Central Strike Committee wavered on the line. "Dissidence in the 1978 Venice Biennale" was long on art analysis, short on class analysis. In their defense, the authors admit: "so long as we remain even vaguely connected to an art context, a thorough critique of art practice is necessary." Yet, they are clear that art is part of the problem and not the solution: *We do not rule out the possibility of a truly radical function for art, but in the present socio-political contexts it seems that a radical function for art can only exist as a negative one. Only criticism is possible and not a positive practice, or at least criticism must be an integral part of any model of practice.*

The committee states: *Our general purpose is to communicate not posture; avant-garde mystification must be countered by de-mystification. Therefore we wish to be as clear as possible so that response is to our ideas and not to their appearance; not as recent modernists who now use politics as yet another gambit.* (Here the committee implicates but does not name both mystifying artists such as General Idea as well as those in on the "political" gambit, such as the artists around *The FOX* magazine in New York and Carole Condé and Karl Beveridge particularly in the Toronto context.[37]) In that "art must question its own sociology, its place in the relation of production," these relations were best seen not as strictly determined by an economic base (as the relations of production), as you might expect, but rather recognized to be ideological: being the pervasive forms or representations through which men live their imaginary relationship to reality.[38] Here, Louis Althusser's particular inflection of the notion of ideology was essential to its discussion since art—CEAC following Althusser—is conceded to be "superstructural and not materially based."[39] (CEAC's analysis of the relation of art to the Canadian state contradictorily belies this superstructural independence, however.) Recourse to theory was necessary, but theory alone was not enough: "Our oppositions must be made clear against concrete examples and lead towards active transformation."

Yet in a statement of over ten thousand words, few concrete examples of active transformation are offered, other than the brief mention of "proper preoccupations" for art such as an "oppressed native population or the structure of wage labour" or the belief "in the need to broaden the scope of the battle from the shop floor to everyday life." *Art* remained the framework of discussion. The committee admits that *the complete rejection of art is not the point and transition to activism is not automatic. Both strategies are effected by the need to account for pervasive ideology. When this is done we see that art may serve as one of its battle grounds and that it reveals the ideological function of all art and the class embeddedness of all artists which must be dealt with. Our only valid purpose can be the transformation to real democracy and conscious participation of all which entails the overthrow of capitalism.*

They conclude: *Towards this goal de-myst-ification is an important action for art—the dispersal of imaginary relations which have intervened and disarmed the material struggle.*

In their desire "to communicate not posture," the committee was "as clear as possible" that, while art still had a role to play in the dispersal of imaginary, ideological relations (the dispelling of which was the critical function of *Strike*), the ultimate aim was to *re*-arm the material struggle in the overthrow of capitalism. Everything about *Strike* began to point to the journal as that vehicle. Take the May 1978 *Strike*: from its cover image of Aldo Moro's bullet-ridden bodyguards' corpses; to the Brigate Rosse red star predominant on its back cover, indeed underscoring many of its pages as a red stamp of approval; to its translation of the theatre-of-the-absurd court transcripts "Red Brigades on Trial"; to the printing of the Red Brigade slogans "carry out the strike against the imperialist state of the transnational" and "build the unity of the revolutionary movement"; to the publishing of Mao's "Combat Liberalism" directly beneath the issue's editorial.[40] By the image projected both graphically and verbally, it would seem that the *Strike* editorial committee wanted to "move on and merge" with the Brigate Rosse. (Remember, they said, "We want to effectively move on and merge with the social stance that we foster.") Unless all this was *posturing*, it was the armed framework within which to read the short and to the point, indeed striking, editorial that was to be so explosive:

We are opposed to the dominant tendency of playing idiots, as in the case of "punks" or the sustainers of the commodity system. The questioning through polemics of the cultural, economical and political hegemony should be fought on all fronts.

To still maintain tolerance towards the servants of the State is to preserve the status quo of Liberalism. In the manner of the Brigades, we support leg shooting/knee capping to accelerate the demise of the old system. Despite what the "new philosophers" tell us about the end of ideology, the war is before and beneath us. Waged and unwaged sector of the population is increasing its demands for "less work." On the way to surpass Liberalism we should prepare the barricades.[41]

The editorial was not so much an argument as strung together slogans, with the odd political demand thrown in—for "less work."[42] But what an effect it had! The reaction was swift. Even before the issue had been delivered from the printer, it was leaked to the tabloid the *Toronto Sun*, to predictable result: "Our taxes aid 'blood-thirsty' radical paper," the headline read. Then followed the predictable outcome to this funding scandal: questions on the floors of the provincial and federal legislatures and quick revocation of every level of arts council funding. Without ongoing funding, CEAC lost its building and suspended operations, but not without publishing one final issue of *Strike* a few months later.[43]

This final issue of *Strike* was dedicated to human rights but it served as a vindication of CEAC's position under the hands of a repressive regime: the Canadian government and its puppet arts councils. "Foremost, what we wish to make clear is that what happened to *Strike* and CEAC is a definite case of censorship, in fact, political repression."[44]

The aim of the earlier offending *Strike* issue, which supposedly became the cause of the clampdown on CEAC's activities, was to show that "liberal democracies are essentially repressive regimes." The authors of "Snuff," the article that made this claim in the final issue, thought that *Strike's radical analysis coupled with provocation proved to be very successful as a means of creating debate on the issues of our analysis within a wider audience, and as a social experiment to prod liberal democracies to reveal their true nature as concluded in our analysis.* This analysis "was coupled with a provocative visual and verbal imagery." The problem, the writers claimed, was that the government concentrated only on the imagery, not its analysis, which was the greater part of their work and, besides, the imagery was no more violent than other examples found in art and entertainment. Why the censorship and repression? *Why? Partly because our imagery was drawn from reality, but primarily because it was coupled with a radical analysis of liberal democracies, and it was that analysis that the media and the government, the pillars of liberal democracies, feared.*

Was it a case of censorship? No. The second issue of *Strike* was freely circulated, as was the final October issue. Was CEAC suppressed...or banned, as it later claimed when it advertised, "As the futurists were in fascist Italy, as the Bauhaus was in Nazi Germany, as the constructivists were in the Soviet Union, the CEAC was banned in Canada"?[45] No. It could continue its activities—both artistic and political—only without government funding. As Marras had earlier written in "On Organization": "When I refer to Canada, I refer to it as a concrete reality: the economical base that allows my work to happen but not my revolt (since I should be able to revolt without its economical support)."[46] Was this still the case? Indeed, was it ever the case that CEAC's revolt was not paid for by its funding?

CEAC allowed that it was surprised by the scandal: "We did not anticipate the extremity of their reaction," it said of the governments' and councils' responses.[47] In reaction, did CEAC reveal its true nature, its "true face"? ("If only words and images caused the reaction that they did, then little is needed as a lever of provocation to force liberal democracies to show their true face.") CEAC's "true face" was revealed in its face-to-face with the "true face" of the government. Indeed, nothing seemed to exist outside this relationship between the two. When push came to shove, it seems that CEAC's *effectiveness* only existed in relationship to the government. Initially, CEAC stated, "Our intention, working from the insular art context, was to provoke debate and elicit reaction from outside the art world." In the end, it acknowledged, "We have actually achieved illiciting [*sic*] a response from outside of art and from the most powerful sectors of society." You have to admit that CEAC was successful. It was effective. Its success was its failure, however.

Through its success and failure, CEAC defined itself solely in relation to the state: "As far as the government was concerned, it was very easy for them to put an end to our activities, for they had only to cut off our funding." As a result, "now pushed as [they were] to this brink at which all [their] alternatives ha[d] been deliberately cut off," the writers came to the conclusion: "Now not only is it clear that there are no legitimate means to effective change, but *Strike* has been denied any means of legitimate change if such a possibility has ever existed."[48] To a degree they were right when they said that they were being punished for their political views.[49] Yes, its funding was stopped, but it was naive of CEAC to expect that it wouldn't be and disingenuous to argue that suspension of funding was censorship and repression and, moreover, that there were no alternatives available to it once this funding was cut off. Isn't it a bit strange to realize that, for all its radicalism, CEAC eventually defined itself *solely* in terms of its government funding? Moreover, that it reconciled itself to this dependent condition. Only in Canada could this happen, you might say!

It did not take the government's provocation, though, to change CEAC's relation to the state. It already preexisted. Just as "Snuff" was to disavow the ideological leeway most contemporary Marxist philosophers then gave to the work of art, so too CEAC misconstrued its analysis of the state. Seeing it akin to a crude economic determinism, CEAC made the state determinant in the last instance, at least in terms of Canada's art funding. The irony is that the writers of "Dissidence in the Venice Biennale" rejected economic determinism in the last instance for the superstructural play of art but maintained it for the state, all in the same article! CEAC overemphasized the power of the state and its determinant role: *In Canada, the state supports art almost exclusively, e.g. by grants, and arbitrates its quality, e.g. by selection for festivals such as V[enice] B[iennale]. By this method the state reflects its own position and reinforces art's position as a universal abstraction above the material, special interests, the ideological. Art then functions as the ideological tool of the dominant class through the state in the same way that the state itself is an ideological tool of the dominant class.*[50]

The authors flattered themselves that it was their radical analysis that brought down the establishment's wrath and not simply their provocative advocacy of kneecapping. "Ten little words," an artist lamented in a letter to the Ontario Arts Council: "Can we now say that these ten words which caused so much controversy are enough grounds to stop the funding of such a crucial centre?"[51] The effect seemed disproportionate to the cause. Ten little words. But what an effect they had. What was CEAC's justification of its advocacy of kneecapping? The authors were insistent that what CEAC published were *only* words and images. "The suppression of what were only pictures and words was quick and severe."[52] But it wasn't words and imagery, it was the specific phrase: "In the manner of the Brigades, we support leg shooting/knee capping to accelerate the demise of the old system."[53] The authors disavowed responsibility for this statement. In fact, the authors of "Snuff" obfuscated the phrase, never repeating it or addressing it specifically—"though we made some strong statements," they admitted in the article. Instead, they subsumed it under the general category of "imagery," as if its words had no semantic meaning.[54] Its meaning instead was drawn from reality, an objective condition over which the authors had no responsibility, having merely reported it: "a powerful imagery whose impact depended on the urgency of the reality it was derived from."[55]

When asked by a reporter whether he supported kneecapping, Marras replied: "Well, we are saying that it should be taken as a metaphorical point to realize that the problem is in recognizing real issues."[56] Well, if kneecapping was metaphor and the rest of *Strike* was only words and images, what do we make of the "radical analysis" they were coupled to? Was it only words and images too? Metaphors and not incitement to action? An imaginary world with no effectiveness? In the end it seems that *Strike*'s rhetoric was the means by which CEAC lived its *imaginary* relationship to revolutionary politics.

CEAC's demise left the field to General Idea. Was General Idea effective? It survived. Survival is effective. Survival of the species, of the genus, of the general idea. *FILE*'s spring 1981 "$UCCE$$ Issue" was "proof" of General Idea's success. To survive, though, meant being adaptable, but also elusive or evasive as they had stated earlier in 1975:

The triple strategy of Glamour is simple but evasive:
1. Concealment, i.e., separation, postured innocence.
2. Hardening of the Target, i.e., closure of the object, a seeming immobility, a brilliance.
3. Mobility of the Target, i.e., the superficial image hides an APPARENT emptiness (changing one's mind, shifting stance, "feminine" logic).[57]

There would be no "effective immobilization" of General Idea's activities by the government, even if "like customs agents on the borders of acceptance, we smuggle transgression back into the picture, mixing doubles out of the ingredients of prohibition."[58] General Idea had always made itself into a moving target. CEAC made itself into a static target: of the media, of politicians. Could it get mobile again, by learning anew, perhaps? Could it take lessons from an old foe? Its final word on the role of art suggested so: *The only valid purposes for art in a pre-revolutionary situation are: as a front which, by its potential for ambiguity, is an easy means of obtaining government and corporate funds to put toward the revolutionary cause; or as a* direct *tool for* explicit *communication and provocation in the class struggle.*[59]

There would be no more "contradictions without ambiguity," it seemed, for CEAC. Rather, the proposed aim was a contradictory "ambiguity" and "explicitness." The issue, perhaps a contradiction given CEAC's immediate circumstance, was keeping the knowledge of one from the other, the funding from the provocation. From whom did CEAC learn to dissemble? From General Idea, perhaps? Or was it dissembling all along?[60]

1. Dot Tuer, "The CEAC Was Banned in Canada," *C Magazine*, no. 11 (1986), 28. In his 1978 article, AA Bronson called A Space "Canada's oldest, largest and most influential" artist-run gallery. "Imagine A Space as Karen Ann Quinlan….," *Centerfold*, September 1978, 104.

2. General Idea, "Glamour," in the "Glamour Issue," *FILE* 3, no. 1 (Autumn 1975), 21; Amerigo Marras, "On Organization," *Strike* 2, no. 1 (January 1978), 5.

3. "Sentences on Art" was presented at the Rivoli, Toronto, November 22, 1982, and published as "Editorials: General Idea and the Myth of Appropriation," *Parachute*, Winter 1983, 12–23. Reprinted in Philip Monk, *Struggles with the Image: Essays in Art Criticism* (Toronto: YYZ Books, 1988), 131–82.

4. Tuer, "The CEAC Was Banned in Canada," 25.

5. *Only Paper Today* was published by A Space under the editorship of poet Victor Coleman from 1973 until fall 1978, when a schism, caused by a "takeover" of A Space, led Coleman to publish it under the auspices of the Eternal Network. It continued publishing until 1980.

6. Amerigo Marras, interview by Robert Handforth, "Amerigo Marras Talks about CEAC," *Only Paper Today* 4, no. 2 (November/December 1976), 2.

7. AA Bronson, "Pablum for the Pablum Eaters," in *Video by Artists*, ed. Peggy Gale (Toronto: Art Metropole, 1976), 197. This is a revised reprint of the anonymous *FILE* article of the same name from 1973.

8. General Idea, "Pablum for the Pablum Eaters," *FILE* 2, nos. 1 and 2 (May 1973), 20. Note the title of the article "The Lumpen and the Lumpen-Eaters," published in *Art Communication Edition*, no. 3 (February 1977).

9. Marras, "Amerigo Marras Talks about CEAC," 2.

10. "A resonance which is ambiguity flips the image in and out of context. Layers of accumulated meaning snap in and out of focus." "Glamour: Image Lobotomy," in the "Glamour Issue," *FILE* 3, no. 1 (Autumn 1975). For Glamour as a system of meaning in General Idea's work, see Philip Monk, *Glamour Is Theft: A User's Guide to General Idea* (Toronto: Art Gallery of York University, 2013).

11. General Idea, "Battleground," in the "Glamour Issue," *FILE* 3, no. 1 (Autumn 1975), 31.

12. "Four Leading Questions as Principles of Revolutionary Practice." Dated 1976, it was published in *Art Communication Edition*, no. 2 (January 1977), 5.

13. "General Idea's Framing Devices" was published in *FILE* 4, no. 1 (Summer 1978), 12–13, but was part of the 1975 performance and video *Going thru the Motions*. Also consider the quotation by Marras: "The quantitative approach I proposed indicated the possibility of going from one system to another by using contextual outlines or structures that formed multiple reference systems or empty frames" (Amerigo Marras, "Notes and Statements of Activity. Toronto, 1977," *La Mamelle*, 1977, 31). And cf.: "Itself being a context out of content back into context, that is ideological praxis back into social praxis or vice versa" ("Four Leading Questions as Principles of Revolutionary Practice," *Art Communication Edition*, no. 2 [January 1975], 5). For General Idea, ambiguity was the flipping of one context into another or of context into content and

vice versa. It was the principle of their parasitic inhabitation.

14. "Editorial," *Art Communication Edition*, no. 6 (July 1977), 2.

15. Amerigo Marras, "on being antithetical," *Art Communication Edition*, no. 6 (July 1997), 3–4.

16. General Idea, "Editorial," in the "Special People Issue," *FILE* 3, no. 3 (Spring 1977), 17.

17. General Idea, "Artificiality," in the "Glamour Issue," *FILE* 3, no. 1 (Autumn 1975), 32.

18. Marras, "on being antithetical," 4.

19. General Idea, "Editorial," *FILE* 3, no. 4 (Fall 1977), 11. See Monk, *Glamour Is Theft*, 111–13 and 224; and "Crises (and Coping) in the Work of General Idea," *Fillip*, no. 16 (Spring 2012), 106–12. Available online at http://fillip.ca/xmco.

20. "Desire is anti-capitalist." AA Bronson, "Pogo Dancing in the British Aisles," *FILE* 3, no. 4 (Fall 1977), 20. Another Deleuze-Guattari source might have been "Balance Sheet-Program for Desiring-Machines," in the "Anti-Oedipus" issue, *Semiotext(e)* 2, no. 3 (1977), 117–35. At least Hermann Neutics suggested so in "Is This a Photo Book," *Only Paper Today* 5, no. 4 (May 1978), 13: "A.A. Bronson drew largely on that article in his great intro to the 'new wave rock' issue of File."

21. "Spanking Punk," *Art Communication Edition*, no. 6 (July 1977), 24. Actually, bands started playing earlier that year in CEAC's basement. Also see Amerigo Marras, "report from Canada, part 1: the punk scene" (unpublished manuscript), CEAC Fonds, York University.

22. "If Anarchy Succeeds Everyone Will Follow, *Art Communication Edition*, no. 9 (November 1977), 3.

23. The text to the "Fascism and anarchy join forces to make a work of art" *Showcard* 1-084 reads: *Voice over: "The 1984 Miss General Idea Pavillion was the first concrete manifestation of that uneasy union we now take for granted, the first project where fascism and anarchy could join forces to create a work of art—and they did."* The text also was published in *General Idea's Reconstructing Futures* (1977).

24. "Playing Idiots, Plain Hideous," *Strike* 2, no. 2 (May 1978), 3.

25. "We moved in on history and occupied images, emptying them of meaning, reducing them to shells. We filled these shells with Glamour, the creampuff innocence of idiots, the naughty silence of sharkfins slicing oily waters" ("Stolen Lingo," in "Glamour"). In the slippages that accompany the identifications of mimicry, the editorial stated, "We continue to speak in an alien tongue," unconsciously adapting General Idea's terminology: "Like parasites we animate these dead bodies ['culture's forgotten shells'] and speak in alien tongues." ("Artificiality," in "Glamour").

26. Marras, "on being antithetical," 4.

27. Amerigo Marras, "VENOM," *Art Communication Edition*, no. 7 (July 1978), 4.

28. See the 1975 *FILE* "Glamour Issue": Miss General Idea *is more akin to poison, that other natural enemy to culture. Like poison Miss General Idea, objet d'art, posed on stiletto heels and bound in the latest fantasy, represents a violent intrusion into the heart of culture: the Canada Council, for example, or beauty pageants (essentially one and the same).* Or: *With this gesture [a manipulation of the self] we husk Nature, voiding the shell that Culture, that great Amazon, single-breasted but divided, might shoot the poisoned arrow of meaning into its empty shell* ("Glamour," in

the "Glamour Issue," *FILE* 3, no. 1 [Autumn 1975]). Marras's methodology could be called cannibalistic. He would "absorb" a colleague's more fully articulated program of thought then proceed to kill off this individual in print with a stab in the back in *ACE*. Marras's treatment of Hervé Fischer of the Paris Collectif d'Art Sociologique is a case in point.

29. *Strike* 2, no. 1 (January 1978), 2. Italics mine.

30. "Polemics," *Strike* 2, no. 1 (January 1978), 29. Italics mine.

31. General Idea, "Editorial," *FILE* 3, no. 4 (Fall 1979), 11.

32. General Idea, *Press Conference*, performance video, Western Front, Vancouver, 1977.

33. In his review of General Idea's 1979 exhibition *Consenting Adults*, Clive Robertson decided to apply *Press Conference*'s criteria of effective art to the work of that exhibition. See Clive Robertson, "Consenting Adults: General Idea at Carmen Lamanna Gallery," *Centerfold*, April/May 1979, 195. In a letter to the editor, General Idea responded that it considered "*Press Conference*, our videotape of 1977,…more concerned with the language of power than with 'effective art'" ("Letters," *Centerfold*, June/July 1979, 219). As General Idea reveals in this letter, the language of *Press Conference* was based on an advertisement in the American business magazine *Fortune* placed by an advertising company to tout the benefits of advertising to industry.

That the term "effective" continued to lead debates is indicated by the following selection of texts from *Centrefold*: *Politics and therefore culture, to be effective have to do more than simply (and simplistically) nominate their context. In its social practice, as well as in its production, it has to align itself with the social forces that seek its overthrow* (Karl Beveridge, "The Last Conceptual Artist," *Centerfold*, February/March 1979, 127).

The political effectiveness of artworks is not a new problem, rather it's one that has been, over the years, over-discussed…. In a larger sense you can't make art effective without the right context, and the context depends on history (Tim Guest, "Politics Performances Provide…," *Centerfold*, February/March 1979, 105).

If you are an artist, how ineffectual is your art? Honestly, does your art produce the intended or expected result? (Tom Sherman, "Editorial," *Centerfold*, April/May 1979, 148).

34. Marras, "On Organization," 5. Also in "Notes and Statements of Activity. Toronto, 1977," 34.

35. Marras, "On Organization," 5.

36. "Dissidence in the 1978 Venice Biennale," *Strike* 2, no. 2 (May 1978), was issued as a "Joint Statement" by the Central Strike Committee, which consisted of Amerigo Marras, Roy Pelletier, Bob Reid, Bruce Eves, Lily Chiro, and Paul McLellan. You might ask yourself what this small clique was *central* to, having mimicked the language of a centralized party apparatus, but without any cadres or supporters, be they workers or artists.

37. Debates about the political function or politicizing of art in New York centered around *The FOX*, a publication issued by Art & Language in three issues between 1975 and 1976 when a schism ended it. For a period summary, see Nancy Marmer, "Art & Politics '77," *Art in America*, July/August 1977, 64–66. Reviews of the subsequent schism publications, *Red Herring* and *Art Language*, October 1976, otherwise known as *FOX* 4,

were published in *Art Communication Edition*, no. 5 (May 1977). Condé and Beveridge's controversial exhibition *It's Still Privileged Art* took place at the Art Gallery of Ontario January 24–February 29, 1976. For a review, see Walter Klepac, "Carol Condé and Karl Beveridge:…It's Still Privileged Art," *artscanada*, April/May 1976, 67. CEAC participated in these debates with a contextual art conference in Toronto in November 1976. See the report "Contextual Art," *Art Communication Edition*, no. 2 (January 1975), 4. This was followed by seminars in Paris (Ecole Sociologique Interrogative) and Warsaw and Kazimierz (Contextual Seminars) as part of CEAC's European tour in May 1977. See documents in *Art Communication Edition*, no. 6 (July 1977), 9–14.

38. *A developed theory of ideology is important for our discussion of art because art is superstructural and not materially based, therefore art exists within the domain of ideology and an understanding of ideology becomes central to our critique of art* ("Dissidence in the 1978 Venice Biennale").

39. Louis Althusser, "Ideology and Ideological State Apparatus," in *Lenin and Philosophy*, trans. Ben Brewster (London: NLB, 1971), 121–73. An NLB edition of Althusser's *For Marx*, with its essay "Contradiction and Overdetermination," had just been released in 1977; his *Reading Capital* was already available.

40. One cannot but be struck by the discordant juxtaposition of the large image of the Red Brigade red star emblem on the back cover of the second issue of *Strike* and a full-page advertisement for the Bologna Art Fair (Arte Fiera: International Fair of Contemporary Art) on its reverse side. Such advertisements commonly are given in exchange for display tables at these commercial fairs. It demonstrates CEAC's desire to participate in a limited way within the art system at its most capitalistic.

41. "Playing Idiots, Plain Hideous," 3.

42. "Waged and unwaged sector of the population is increasing its demands for 'less work.'" This is one of the rare mentions of what would align CEAC to Italian autonomia and other leftist movements advocating the abolition of work or its refusal. It was always thrown in as one more item in a list but was never really addressed substantially. For instance: "The directing group is allied to the revolutionary cause that intends to create cultural polemics, debates, confrontations and the pursuit of collective education for a new community eliminating labour" (*Strike* 2, no. 2 [May 1978], 5). However, in a note to "Snuff," the authors explained what they meant by "eliminating labour" through a short series of quotations from Marx. The series is quoted from the publication *Zerowork*, a short-lived American journal that published two issues in 1975 and 1977.

43. CEAC managed a European tour during the controversy, with a visit to the Bologna Art Fair. Other activities subsequent to the loss of funding were the publication of the third issue of *Strike* and the creation of a one-hour broadcast for Close Radio, Los Angeles.

44. "Snuff," *Strike* 2, no. 2 (May 1978), 13–14. Who was the writer of this text? Was it the same Strike Central Committee that had penned "Dissidence in the 1978 Venice Biennale"? I don't believe all the members of that committee wrote the first text, because it maintains somewhat of a stylistic whole. Presumably Amerigo Marras,

having been listed first, was one of the authors. But the quality of the writing there, and in "Snuff," changed considerably toward a more fluid reading that suggests one or two others besides Marras contributed significantly, writers for whom English was their first language. (Marras's first language was Italian.) The addition of new members to the CEAC collective perhaps accounts for the "correction" of Marras's position in "On Organization" by statements in "Dissidence in the 1978 Venice Biennale."

45. Advertisement placed in Ontario Association of Art Galleries, *Magazine*, Winter 1978/79, 10.

46. Marras, "On Organization," 6.

47. Quotations in this paragraph and next: "Snuff," 13–15.

48. CEAC defined its activities and effectiveness only in relation to its funding: if funding was cut, there would be no activities, no possibility of effectiveness. It was a strange logic to say, "*Strike* has been denied any means of legitimate change" if denied funding. We can only conclude, as the writers here conclude, that CEAC's politics could only be institutionally supported through government funding.

49. *Through Strike's social experiment of radical analysis and provocation, the powers of liberal democracies were forced to contradict their own principles, revealing them to be the illusions of a false ideology. Through direct censorship our liberal democracy contradicted itself when it acted against individuals for their political beliefs through an economic sanction that intended their effective immobilization. It contradicted itself when a cultural body suppressed individuals for their political beliefs, while the political establishment suppressed their cultural expression. It contradicted itself when a cultural body which is supposed to be autonomous from political interests, is dictated to by the political establishment. It contradicted itself when it based such repressive actions on distortion, or used such distortion as a form of indirect censorship* ("Snuff," 15).

50. "Dissidence in the 1978 Venice Biennale."

51. Gerard Pas, undated letter to Arthur Gelber, vice-chairman of the Ontario Arts Council, CEAC Fonds, York University, as referred to in Tuer, "The CEAC Was Banned in Canada," 37.

52. "Snuff," 15.

53. In its "Statement to the Press," the Strike Collective (Amerigo Marras, Suber Corley, Bruce Eves, Paul McLellan, Roy Pelletier, Bob Reid) stated: *What position do we take in relation to the BR [Red Brigades]? We present their accusations of the ruling order in an extract of their court proceedings published in our paper. We share their anger and we agree that it is the power sector that must be on trial. We do not believe that terrorism makes any sense in the context here and we question the theoretical basis of any vanguard group that intends to lead or speak for the people, as little better than the farce of representation that exists in the present power structures of the state. We have published this material on the BR to rectify the repressed and distorted coverage they have received by all media* (quoted in Tuer, "The CEAC Was Banned in Canada," 35–36).

54. *Our tools were not guns but: radical analysis at the level of general theory; criticism at the level of specific polemics; and the use of a strong visual and verbal imagery drawn from reality, as a means of bringing about a confrontation with a factuality many ignore, and as an aide in provoking debate* ("Snuff," 13).

55. Ibid.

56. A broadcast by CEAC, June 1978, Close Radio, Los Angeles. Available online at http:// fillip.ca/vr35.

57. "Glamour," in the "Glamour Issue," *FILE* 3, no. 1 (Autumn 1975), 31. Having been left the field with CEAC's demise did not mean that General Idea had won the battle. It was confronted on another front by the battle for A Space that was raging at the same time, which it won. But by the early 1980s, General Idea felt that the tide in Toronto had turned against it in terms of opposition within the art community.

58. General Idea, "Editorial," *FILE* 4, no. 2 (Fall 1979), 17.

59. "Snuff," 15.

60. In "Outline of a Proposal," a 1978 letter in support of an application to the "Artists with Their Work" program administered by the Art Gallery of Ontario, Marras wrote: *In the context of the new Canadian generation of artists and cultural operators, I am participating to* [sic] *the process of cultural dissembling. Such a process of dissembling is carried out around pressing contemporary issues* (Amerigo Marras, "Outline of a Proposal," 1978, CEAC Fonds, York University).

Julia Bryan-Wilson

Implicated

Feminist Art Histories and Affective Pasts

No scholars are truly detached from their objects of inquiry; we become invested in the details of our research no matter how distant our subjects might be from us temporally or geographically. For contemporary art historians like myself, dialogues with living artists enrich our writing and sometimes lead to lasting friendships. Even though such relationships can be viewed with some suspicion in an academic climate that values ostensible neutrality, they are vitally significant to the field of contemporary art history— not least feminist and queer art histories. Yet such intimacies are often veiled, ignored, dismissed, or glossed over rather than addressed forthrightly. I am not advocating for the constant production of simple statements of disclosure; rather, we should endeavour to theorize the affective bonds that feed our work, to account for them in their complexity, and to reflect on them critically. What consequences might this more personally implicated version of art history have for how we grapple with artistic productions and practices that open into the realm of political affiliation building?

In a departure from my usual scholarship, in which I normally investigate the artistic practices of others, this article discusses an aspect of my own past with feminist and queer alternative media production, namely my involvement with Joanie 4 Jackie, formerly called Big Miss Moviola, which was founded by the filmmaker, novelist, and artist Miranda July in 1995. This kind of narration of a personal relationship with an art project demands an affective model of methodology that takes into account emotional histories and networks of allegiances that include friendship and queer kin circles as they relate to the promises of alternative cultural production as well as its compromises and disjunctures.

In 1995, almost ten years before the invention of YouTube, Miranda July was a dropout from the University of California, Santa Cruz, who had moved to Portland, Oregon, to take part in a loose community of punk bands, start-up music labels, fanzines, and do-it-yourself feminist culture that was known informally, and with some self-irony, as riot grrrl. Miranda had thought that she would major in film at Santa Cruz, but found its culture of mostly male students alienating, and she had a vague impulse to harness the DIY energy found in the Pacific Northwest music scene toward a new kind of scrappy, totally self-funded feminist moviemaking. She had no money, had no space, did not own a video camera, and had no access to an editing suite; even more crucially, she had no colleagues and no audience, no way to connect with other women who might be having the same video-making cravings, no way to share work, to brainstorm, to critique, to collaborate, no structure or system to connect with those who might also be borrowing video cameras at local public cable-access stations or bartering for equipment.

So she started a project, entitled Big Miss Moviola, which began as a Xeroxed pamphlet that she'd hand out at rock shows and give to friends to give to their friends. This pamphlet had a deceptively simple idea: "You send me a movie that you made plus $5.00 and a personal statement and I send you a videotape with all movies on it that women like you sent me (including your movie) plus the *Big Miss Moviola* fanzine which has all the filmmaker's personal statement and addresses on it."[1] The basic additive concept here was similar to a chain letter, by which you contribute something and get even more in return (the small fee of five dollars was to cover the cost of dubbing tapes, postage, and Xeroxing). Each tape sent back to a maker had ten videos on it—her own, plus nine others'. Miranda's primary motives were not just to hail a community of other women making videos, but also to actively create an audience of other artists and makers. Hence, this was her promise: at least nine other women will see what you did, and you'll get to see the work of nine other women also, adjacent to and in implicit conversation with your own work.

In this first *Big Miss Moviola* pamphlet, Miranda wrote a lengthy manifesto about the potential of video for political self-representation: *I am starting this network for women filmmakers because I am a woman and I make movies and I know that there isn't really anything to do with them after I make them. If I was writing I could make my own fanzine and pass it out or if it was a song I could start a band and be recorded by my friends and tour around but since it's my heart on a video cassette what do I do with it? Secret, personal art is cool and all but the movies that me and you are making could educate other women filmmakers and everyone else too. The kind of movies/women I'm talking about do not necessarily resemble me in any way except that they make movies and for reasons such as classism, sexism, racism, and ableism are unable to or DON'T WANT TO participate in the institution that teaches prejudice so well in the film industry.*

Articulated in this early document is an explicit acknowledgment of the class, race, gender, and ableist issues that exclude so many from this medium. In addition, Miranda outlines her deliberate refusal to participate in the larger institution of the film industry at that moment; though she has since made movies that have larger audiences, Miranda meant for Big Miss Moviola to be a different type of intervention.

It bears emphasizing that, in its original incarnation, Big Miss Moviola was fuelled totally by snail mail, with letters and VHS cassette tapes sent via the post office, not by the internet, as in the mid-1990s web-based technologies had yet to reach saturation point. Looking back now, some twenty years later, these documents kindle for me a bit of nostalgia for analogue modes, but their entirely amateur aesthetic of handwriting, misaligned Xeroxing, doodling in the margins, and so on was emphatically embraced as a necessity. TV monitors figured prominently in many of these early documents, with a variety of cut-and-pasted female figures inserted in the screens along with statements like "I can do that."

The project initially had a slow start: Miranda handed out her flyer at punk shows and to friends for almost a year before she received the ten women-made short videos she needed for the first chain-letter tape. After that, momentum started to build as Big Miss Moviola began receiving press from local and national venues. Miranda compiled the chain-letter tapes in her apartment by dubbing them using two VCRs onto used VHS tapes bought in bulk, cheaply, at thrift stores. (This kind of reproduction severely degrades the quality of the tapes, but, again, Miranda was operating with no budget at all.) As film and media scholar Lucas Hilderbrand notes in his book *Inherent Vice*, which has a chapter about the video chain letters, *The tapes demonstrate bootleg aesthetics by exhibiting their own assemblage and reproduction. As they appear on the chain letters, low-fi glitches self-reflexively add to the tapes' intimacy as unique person-to-person dubs.*[2]

Importantly, Big Miss Moviola was an entirely non-juried, uncurated project—any video sent in by any self-identified woman was accepted. As Miranda wrote, *There is no one kind of movie that I am asking for." In a later pamphlet, she lists genres that include sci-fi, soap, autobiographical, porno, western, stop-action, confessional, and so on as an indication of how expansive her thinking was about what might be out there, and to generate a sense of wide-open possibility in terms of what would be accepted (anything) within the contours of the project. This was also a forceful statement about the classist presumptions of taste-making, as Miranda was quite defiant in her feminist politics about refusing to make judgments about quality. Instead, she wanted to catalyze "the unseen-underwater movie revolution."*

One of the places Miranda came to drum up more submissions was a video exhibition that I curated in June 1996 with my friends Jon Raymond and Cynthia Star at the storefront for Candy Ass Records, a Portland-based queer-core label. I use the word "curate" in its loosest sense, for the show basically consisted of tapes by people who we personally knew playing on a few borrowed monitors. Miranda and I met at the opening, and I started working with her on Big Miss Moviola, turning a strictly one-woman project into an operation consisting of one woman plus one friend helping out. I was officially involved for roughly two years, from 1996 to about 1998, and in later years I would sometimes act in an advisory role. The email address listed on Big Miss Moviola letters, brochures, and pamphlets from 1996 and 1997 is my email, because Miranda didn't have a computer and I had a day job where I had access to the internet. It was during this time that Big Miss Moviola started to gain traction and attract some visibility, with screenings around Portland, at colleges, and in New York at places like CB's Gallery.

In 1996, Miranda and I were both twenty-two years old, queer identified, and had shared interests in feminist media making. I was not coming from a riot grrrl background but had more academic investments in punk DIY that were both extremely passionate and fairly naive. I had recently graduated from college and had moved to Portland with some friends because of the city's famously cheap rents. I temped at an advertising agency, worked in food service for a catering company holding platters of shrimp at weddings, and had other office jobs as I tried to claw my way out of the gaping hole of my undergraduate debt. I had studied feminist film theory and queer theories of visual culture, and I was interested in figuring out how to develop a praxis that not only thought hard about the structure and form of countercinema but more importantly put into place an alternative method of distribution. That is, I wanted both to experiment with the look of video but also to re-examine the economics of its circulation. In college I had been active in HIV/AIDS awareness and prevention, and my model at that moment for both politics and aesthetics were the HIV/AIDS video collectives that Alexandra Juhasz has written about as a participant as well as a media theorist in her book *AIDS TV: Identity, Community, and Alternative Video.*[3]

In fact, Juhasz taught the very first class I took in college, a freshman-level English course. I mention this to try to map a field of connections that is implicated in proximity, pedagogy, and intimacy. (Juhasz later became an influential supporter of Big Miss Moviola.) It is through such intimacies that you can trace a faint line between the seemingly unlike practices of AIDS video in New York in the late 1980s and DIY punk feminist video in the mid-1990s in Portland. It is not necessarily a direct connection of influence and intention, but rather a series of blurry retracings, echoes, recalls. For instance, when artist and activist Gregg Bordowitz wrote, regarding AIDS alternative video, in 1993, "The production of activist video is primarily concerned with audience and distribution,"[4] this statement resonated with the political aims of Big Miss Moviola.

Looking back through the enormous amount of ephemera I have from this time, several things stand out. One is that the flyers and letters track some of the radical technological changes that have occurred since 1995, especially as the project increasingly migrated online. Another is that Big Miss Moviola was totally uninterested in then still pertinent debates on the medium specificity of video. There has been much ink shed about the discrete histories, aesthetics, and ideological attributions of broadcast TV versus film versus video, but within the rhetoric of Big Miss Moviola, television, film, and video were all collapsed into one shorthand: "movies." Movies encompassed a much bigger rubric than just the literal supporting media; the word signified screens and images, yes, but, more importantly, when we said that we were "making movies," it was a feminist way to describe telling stories about self-scrutiny, self-care, and taking control of gendered visual regimes. The camera was both ever present and irrelevant, a frame for seeing but also an internalized mechanism that could be at once activated and dismantled. In these early Xeroxed booklets, a consistent slippage occurs between media like TV, cinema, and video, for they were not considered distinct sets of equipment but rather all blended together as part of a larger political strategy.

A page from a *Big Miss Moviola* pamphlet from 1997 spells out our attempts to theorize the import of women making independent movies within a system of multiple gazes, self-surveillance, and patriarchy. It states: "Every woman is an expert on the eye. An expert on acting, and an expert on controlling situations while being watched. This is movie making. And making movies also means that you are a watcher." In other words, we moved beyond notions of the male gaze to think about complex circuits of women watching other women, the pleasures of queer women-on-women cruising, the terrors of scrutiny, the unequal ways that power exerts itself, and the absorption of multiple vectors of gazes within our own thoughts. (A similarly complex relay of watcher-watched would later form a large part of Miranda's own experimental short video work, including her brilliant *The Amateurist*, a short she made in 1998.)

The videos on the chain letters were diverse in form: confessional first-person, fictional, camp, outrageous, narrative, abstract, violent, hilarious, tedious. In her article "The Politics of Abstraction," lesbian filmmaker Barbara Hammer argues against narration, writing, "Plot points are male points.... We cannot reproduce radicality using conventional forms."[5] This was decisively not the viewpoint of Big Miss Moviola, which had no interest in gatekeeping but hoped to encourage circulation and promote anything being made by anyone who identified as a woman. Yet despite Big Miss Moviola's best efforts to be inclusive of every axis of difference, the vast majority of movies received were by educated young white women in their early twenties, not only because they had easier access to cameras through college campuses but also because a word-of-mouth strategy only goes so far in terms of outreach. Relying on friends of friends often keeps you in very limited circles, as friendship so often depends upon interclass affinities and tightly bounded milieus.

Increasingly, the project tried to address itself to these exclusions and limitations. In 1996, after seeing the first batch of submissions by mostly white college-age women, Miranda initiated what she called "The Missing Movie Report." Briefly, Miranda walked around Portland with a tape recorder and asked women she encountered on the street, "If you could make a movie, what would it be about?" She recorded their answers on a large poster, including women who had scenarios in their heads at the ready to discuss and those who refused to answer, saying things like "I'm too old for that kind of thing." "The Missing Movie Report" was a way to acknowledge a blind spot within the project itself by chronicling the videos that were *not* being made, not only because many women did not own the means of production but also because of questions of cultural privilege, time, energy, resources, and education. As the poster declares, "The most incredible movies of 1996 will never be made, but that's not a reason to forget about them." Again, Big Miss Moviola considered movies to be not only recordings on videotape but any self-created set of visuals, as we tried to redefine the possibilities of movies to include stories or images that might exist wholly in the imagination.

In response to the growing awareness that there was a whole universe of unmade movies because of these questions of privilege and access, Big Miss Moviola wanted to enable hands-on workshops and facilitate equipment sharing. We envisioned an offshoot project through which we would help high-school students and teenage girls make movies, because, as I state in a brochure from 1997, "dismissing teenagers is part of a conspiracy that wants to keep women silent." To test the waters, Miranda and I held a screening in 1997 at Columbia River High School, near Portland (we served cereal as an after-school snack), but the truth was that, at that point, Big Miss Moviola was not equipped for the production assistance we fantasized about—neither of us yet owned a video camera. The project always existed in this gap between what was actually happening and what might, potentially, some day, be possible: a fertile space where the dreams of the someday help enable the next steps. Those visions helped the project grow, but sometimes we were faced with the realization that our cash-strapped reality was badly mismatched to our ambitious desires, and we had to acknowledge our limits without getting depressed and giving up.

Throughout the late 1990s, the chain letters did become a genuine, if modest, alternative distribution network for women video makers, and eventually the project grew big enough that Miranda began taking on interns to help her keep up with submissions. She also invited guest curators to make special "costar" tapes selected from the vast archive. In 2003, she gave the project over to Bard College, in Annandale-on-Hudson, New York.[6] Big Miss Moviola outgrew Miranda July, and Miranda July also outgrew Big Miss Moviola. In addition, the advent of YouTube made the act of sharing video work feel less urgent and in some ways less political.

Art history, the field that I sometimes uncomfortably occupy, does not always account for the multiple and slippery roles that contemporary art historians can inhabit, including supporter, critic, co-conspirator, and active collaborator. But I here recount my intimate engagement with an artist's project because the residue of what Miranda called "the challenge and the promise" of Big Miss Moviola has stayed with me in my academic scholarship, as I have continued to think about how cultural production can create new publics, can try to open up different spaces for discourse, and, importantly, can stumble as it confronts its own material and ideological limits.

This sort of queer feminist approach requires a more robust accounting of interpersonal relations—what we might term *implications*—that sediment themselves, over time, into histories. These histories are vital to keep alive, because this type of art project often runs not on money but on faith, willpower, and the support of allies; to chronicle those networks of affiliation is to also narrate how such practices actually function and survive. That is, the story of how an artist project was built on friendship or fell to ruin because of duelling lovers should not be a shadow history running parallel to its institutional timeline of getting grants and building infrastructure, or to the meaty matter of analyzing the work produced—these are all coexisting, intertwining tales. Paying greater attention to relational ties between friends and collaborators (including my complex bonds with the subjects I write about, even those whom I have never met) is one way to lay bare my own investments and compromised involvements in the institution of art history.

1. Miranda July, *The Big Miss Moviola Project*, pamphlet 1, 1995. All documents related to Big Miss Moviola are from my personal archive.

2. Lucas Hilderbrand, *Inherent Vice: Bootleg Histories of Videotape and Copyright* (Durham, NC: Duke University Press, 2009), 167.

3. Alexandra Juhasz, *AIDS TV: Identity, Community, and Alternative Video* (Durham, NC: Duke University Press, 1995).

4. Gregg Bordowitz, "The AIDS Crisis Is Ridiculous," in *Queer Looks*, ed. Martha Gever, John Greyson, and Prahtiba Parmar (London: Routledge, 1993), 212.

5. Barbara Hammer, "The Politics of Abstraction," in *Queer Looks*, 72.

6. In 2000, the name was changed to Joanie 4 Jackie, after the Moviola corporation sent Miranda a letter accusing her of copyright violation.

Jesi Khadivi

Artmoreorless

The Early Performances of Asco

A black hole lies at the centre of a photograph. Looking like a gaping wound, brown water appears to trickle from its obscured bowels onto a pile of organic debris before gathering into a fetid pool littered with scraps of plastic and other detritus. Slouching elegantly with their hands in pockets, four figures surround the hole while staring blithely at the camera. Behind them a familiar landscape—of decaying, industrial infrastructure—provides the backdrop to nondescript, overlooked urban terrain.

Harry Gamboa Jr., Gronk, Patssi Valdez, and Willie F. Herrón are the figures occupying this particular frame, individuals who came of age in what Arthur C. Danto describes as the "era of revulsion."[1] After meeting at Garfield High School in East Los Angeles during the late 1960s, they began working together under the name Asco—the Spanish word for nausea or disgust—to produce conceptual performances that unfolded between the street and the printed document.[2] For the work described above, the aptly titled *Asshole Mural* (1975), the precise function and location of the hole in the photograph are unclear and less significant perhaps than Asco's artistic and political responses to such elusive spaces, which eschew direct engagement with identity politics in favour of a politics and practice more difficult to parse, yet still involved with identity. Borrowing an expression from the artists themselves, performance scholar Amelia Jones has used the term "Artmoreorless" to describe the strategically slippery and multifaceted practice of this intermedia collective. Throughout their fifteen years of collective practice, Asco's work both commented on their exclusion from regimes of representation and embraced a "space between," which they carved out for themselves in actions, as in 1972 when Gamboa, Gronk, and Herrón spray painted their signatures on the Los Angeles County Museum of Art (LACMA), effectively appropriating the structure as their own giant readymade in an unsanctioned gesture.[3] Nearly forty years later, LACMA's 2011 retrospective of this complex collective's output, *Elite of the Obscure* (curated by C. Ondine Chavoya and Rita Gonzalez), raised a number of questions about exhibiting performance-based and ephemeral works, as well as the institutionalization of DIY practices.

Like many DIY artist collectives operating adjacent to the circuits of object-oriented production and reception, Asco created works that were difficult to categorize according to the most commonly recognized mediums for art-making. While it can be argued that the sheer range of what they produced—which includes performances, slideshows, drawings, paintings, and ephemera—implies that Asco's work cannot be discussed vis-à-vis medium-specific histories, I would like to argue that obscuring Asco's contributions to the medium of performance in favour of exhibiting the multimedia breadth of their work, as the LACMA retrospective did, fails to capture the nuances in their variegated strategies toward performance and in the questions of representation that their work critically raises. Looking back on Asco's early projects, one finds at least two distinct forms of performance: one that engages the *body* and the urban landscape of 1970s Los Angeles and another that engages the *image* and its networks of distribution. A third, less clearly defined typology combines the two, comprising both live performance and purposefully circulated documentation. Although a dominant discourse within performance art stresses the importance of a live encounter,

Asco's approach to conceptual performance complicates the primacy of *liveness* that this argument presumes.[4] I will analyze the three typologies of Asco's early performances to explore how the collective differently articulates political and social critique through live and media performance, respectively. Moreover, I will consider questions that arise from this analysis, such as "What kinds of challenges did Asco's split focus on live and media performance pose for the curators of *Elite of the Obscure*?" and "How did the exhibition's conceptual framework and methods of display respond to these challenges?"

Taking a multifaceted approach to performance, Asco staged interventions in meaningful sites, including contested urban spaces such as East LA's main commercial thoroughfare—Whittier Boulevard (the site of a series of repressive crackdowns on Chicano youth in the wake of the Chicano Moratorium Riot in 1970)—as well as in performance spaces specifically designed for the camera.[5] In some cases, Asco distributed documentation of their carefully orchestrated scenarios via mail-art circuits, while other performances took the form of unsolicited media interventions. Asco's activities in the margins were perhaps a function of both exile and activism, and the collective used the exclusion of Chicano artists from mainstream exhibition venues in Los Angeles to their advantage. Its members chose to create interventions within their own neighbourhoods instead of seeking institutional validation, enacting a physical and conceptual space for the direct engagement of localized social concerns such as police brutality, drugs, gang violence, and discriminatory urban planning practices. To this end, the collective deployed the power of printed matter, conversation, and rumour, circulating their genre-bending brand of performance art through mail art and popular media channels alike.

The Chicano Body and the City

The body plays a specific and central role for Asco in agitating the urban landscape of Los Angeles. Unlike body artists such as Chris Burden and Carolee Schneeman who use their bodies to consistently refer to the endurance, vulnerability, and limitations of the corporeal form, Asco brought the body into play as a means for drawing attention to space, and vice versa. In other words, Asco's members interested themselves less in the body as a sensuous physical form and more in the social relations that a body's presence could elicit. In their early performances, the group would stage disruptions in busy urban areas dressed in elaborate costumes that combined the aesthetics of glitter rock with bastardized versions of Chicano symbols and religious iconography. For *Stations of the Cross* (1971), the collective's first public performance, Asco hijacked the format of a traditional Mexican Las Posadas processional to enact a protest against the Vietnam War. On December 24, the last day of the nine-day Las Posadas celebration, Gamboa, Gronk, and Herrón paraded down Whittier Boulevard in white face paint, resembling demented biblical figures, lugging a fifteen-foot cross crudely fashioned out of cardboard and craft paint behind them.[6] The trio amassed a crowd of onlookers who followed the artists' processional down East LA's main shopping artery toward their final destination: an army recruiting office. There, the collective conducted a five-minute silent vigil to protest the high Chicano death rate in Vietnam. After a moment of silence, Gamboa, Gronk, and Herrón blocked the door with the crucifix and then ran away. Their outlandish costumes and disruptive street tactics in *Stations of the Cross* appear comical, but, in fact, the intervention responded seriously to an increasing urgency surrounding the effects of the Vietnam War on Chicano communities in Los Angeles and the escalating circumscription of free speech and movement in East Los Angeles during that time. Writing about this period in an article commemorating the fortieth anniversary of the Chicano Moratorium, collective member Gamboa recalled how *East L.A. was placed under excessive police control during the next few years in a manner that closely resembled a military occupation. Chicano youths were routinely rounded up, harassed, beaten and arrested, without regard to their constitutional rights. I had firm beliefs regarding my activist role as an American citizen who sought change from my cultural perspective. Being shot at by numerous riot police strengthened my sense of purpose.*[7]

What might Gamboa mean by saying he sought change from his cultural perspective? Furthermore, how did this desire for change shape Asco's street performances? Jones writes, "one of the tenets of body art, especially situated within an activist practice, is the enacting and the asserting of the self within the social."[8] By inserting their bodies within the fragmented and segregated urban fabric of Los Angeles, Asco's members deployed activist-artistic strategies in their early works, usually performing in highly charged and symbolic areas within their own neighbourhoods, ranging from gang zones to seemingly innocuous non-sites such as a traffic island at Arizona and Whittier boulevards, where a particularly brutal clash during the LA Riots in 1970 occurred.[9] In an era of almost militaristic standoff between police and Chicano youth, Asco opened a space for dissent that directed itself not only towards the war in Vietnam and the divisive zoning that cut East LA off from the rest of the city via a nexus of freeways, but also towards the iconography of Chicano art, especially muralism. In saying that he sought change from his cultural perspective, Gamboa seems to speak not only *from* the position of a young Chicano targeted by police violence, but also *through* Asco's critical methodology of "making strange" (i.e., taking spaces, forms, and practices familiar to Chicano communities and making them unsettling). Gamboa and Asco's other members thus articulate and seek visibility for an expanded notion of "Chicanoness," one that doesn't conform to prevailing models of Chicano identity.

Asco's relationship to the systems of production, display, and reception of contemporary art and accepted artistic strategies within the Chicano art community, largely dominated by the essentialist and nationalistic narratives of muralism, is one of disidentification. According to José Esteban Muñoz, disidentification scrambles and reconstructs an encoded text in a fashion that both exposes the message's universalizing and exclusionary machinations and recruits its workings to account for, include, and empower "minority" identities and identifications.[10] Gronk and Herrón had already independently established themselves as muralists before working together as Asco. However, the ephemeral nature of the group's artistic production, coupled with their interest in creating self-reflexive spaces to interrogate and pluralize the notion of Chicano identity, prompted them to collectively explore a conceptual approach to muralism that worked against the universal, rooted identity (and identification) promoted in many Chicano murals. Instead, they worked to posit a new framework for muralism that was dynamic, flexible, and performative. By combining elements of street theatre and Mexican processionals, Asco's earliest performances riff on Chicano mural iconography, positing a mash-up of religious and mythical references. Unlike most of the murals found in East LA, Asco's "dynamic" murals used actual bodies dressed in varying forms of queer and punk drag, thus physically inscribing a social space in which to challenge static notions of Chicano-ness.

Public Relations

As their work combining muralism and street theatre indicates, Asco's early performances explore notions of identity formation and its representation, deliberately complicating familiar signs and symbols within their cultural milieu to articulate alternative visions and revisions of the Chicano self. As their practice matured and their work gained increasing layers of complexity, Asco expanded their focus on symbols of Chicano experiences in Los Angeles to include thinking about how these symbols circulate in culture more broadly. While Asco documented the bulk of their performances, the dissemination of performance documentation did not become a vital ideational component of Asco's artwork until around 1974. Around this time, Asco began to work on what they called No Movies—a self-created medium featuring "film stills" from nonexistent movies that the collective scripted, staged, and then photographed with the intention of circulating via mail art and media networks. By purposefully disseminating documentation of their performances, Asco expanded their audience and began shifting their collective energy away from creating urban disruptions to intervening in the world of images. While later works in this genre interrupt the homogeneity of 1970s Hollywood with fictitious Chicano stars embodying and promoting their own form of glamour, works like *Decoy Gang War Victim* (1974) and *Instant Mural* (1974) formed a bridge between Asco's nascent activist work in the public realm and their later, more ambiguously political engagement of the image. The notion of place and context is of particular importance in early No Movies, often reflecting real-life concerns affecting the community or directly engaging Chicano cultural heritage. Works like *Decoy Gang War Victim* address cycles of violence and their representation in Asco's East

LA neighbourhoods, while the performances-turned-No-Movies *Instant Mural* and *First Supper (After a Major Riot)* (1974) took place in sites of bloody conflict between Chicano anti–Vietnam War protesters and the Los Angeles Police Department.

For *Decoy Gang War Victim*, Gamboa photographed Gronk lying in the middle of the road covered in ketchup and flanked by two flares. As a hit-and-run performance most likely seen by only a few people, *Decoy Gang War Victim* can be read as a sort of vigil for those engaged in gang violence or victims of violence in general. In a conversation with curator Phillip Brookman, Gamboa recalls: "We would go around and whenever we heard of where there might be potential violence, we would set up the decoys so they would think someone had already been killed."[11] Through creating a decoy, Asco foreground the centrality of violence both gang related and police generated. After the performance, the collective sent a photograph to a number of news outlets, claiming that the depicted figure died in a gang fight. The grainy, yet nonetheless dramatic, image shows Gronk lying alone in the middle of a dark street, except for three or four figures lurking in the deep background of the image. KHJ-TV subsequently used the photograph to support a news segment on "endemic violence" in Chicano communities.[12]

Part performance, part activism, part media hoax, *Decoy Gang War Victim* illustrates the hybridity of Asco's artistic and political engagement during this period. Not only does the project concern itself with how Chicano images circulate in popular media, positing a dramatic image of a "corpse" in the street, but through the work Asco sought to make an impact on life in the barrio by jamming circuits of rumour that fuel gang retaliation, and in doing so, put themselves at risk. Gamboa, in a roundtable discussion on

LA art published in *Artforum*, explained how *the project was a response to the incendiary tabloid-style journalism of the two major Los Angeles newspapers, which often listed the names, addresses, workplaces, and gang affiliations of victims or their family members in an effort to maintain high levels of reciprocal gang violence, thus selling more newspapers. The desired effect of* Decoy Gang War Victim *was to generate a pause in the violence in order to rob the newspapers of their daily list of victims.*[13] By presenting Gronk's body as an absurd, ketchup-covered effigy, Asco's members very well may have deterred further violence and given actual victims of gang violence and their families a temporary reprieve from media scrutiny. Yet how can we understand the significance of this hybrid gesture? And, does it gain power through its hybridity? Not quite a media hoax, nor strictly a performance, *Decoy Gang War Victim* illustrates Asco's adoption of indeterminacy as a guiding principle. By creating a work that resists easy categorization and calls into question the very movement of an image through media networks as a foundational concept, *Decoy Gang War Victim* creates the conditions of its own visibility, establishing a network for the display of the work beyond the confines of the gallery and museum. Around the same time that Asco were working in Los Angeles, curator Seth Siegelaub reached similar conclusions about the power of circulating images and utilizing networks beyond the static exhibition space to promote and distribute artworks that did not fit neatly within its institutional boundaries.[14] In Asco's case, the expanded context for the presentation of artworks had as much to do with imagining alternative systems of representation as it did with finding novel forms of display that accommodated forms not especially well suited to presentation in a white cube space. In other words, Asco developed this system out of contingency and necessity.

Hollywood cinema had certainly locked out Chicano actors and actresses in the mid-1970s when Asco began their No Movies works. As Rita Gonzalez, co-curator of *Elite of the Obscure*, writes: *Asco lived in the shadow of Hollywood, feeding off of its productions but also striving to create a counter-vision out of their own lived realities. Asco's invention of No Movies, or film stills for non-existent films, allowed the group to appropriate the spectacle of Hollywood even as they critiqued the absence of Chicanos in the mass media.*[15]

Unlike Cindy Sherman's *Film Stills*, an ongoing photographic project roughly contemporary with Asco's No Movies, Asco made no attempt to allude to stereotypical scenes that viewers could have seen in other contexts. In Asco's case, Chicano representation in mainstream American cinema simply did not exist. The No Movies genre was thus an attempt to articulate and approximate what Chicano cinema could look like: a fusion of glam and gore as inspired by *fotonovelas* (comic books) as the Hollywood star system that excluded Chicano people. From its beginnings as a supplement to the politically tinged performances described earlier in this essay, which were circulated through correspondence art circuits, No Movies developed into an elaborate system that included faux publicity materials and an award ceremony. Through this system, Asco articulated a concept of representation that reached beyond the image to implicate its systems of distribution, promotion, and reception. By creating an award ceremony and an intricate, albeit satirical, administrative apparatus to accompany the visual components of the No Movies genre, Asco sought to construct a new system that not only represented but also promoted and rewarded them.

Archive of the Obscure

Asco's ethos of Artmoreorless—a way of working and being at the interstices of art, politics, and propaganda—fulfills Gregory Sholette's description of DIY, improvisational practices and institutions as forms of dark matter. As in astrophysics, dark matter in the arts operates in the shadows, while its activities are essential to the perpetuation of the universe of art. Sholette presciently challenges historians of this "dark matter" to consider how best to work with this material. "Where are the historians of darkness?" Sholette asks. "What tools will they require beyond a mere description of these shadows and dark practices and towards the construction of a counter-public sphere?"[16] In other words, how can we move beyond simply showing and describing these artistic practices towards creating a dynamic form of display that accommodates and amplifies their implicit tensions and ambiguities? Operating on the fringes of—and sometimes in direct opposition to—the densely networked power and taste-making structures of both contemporary art and the expanded social field, dark materials coalesce into their own ecosystems that imagine alternative systems while remaining tethered, however obliquely, to the systems they help perpetuate. All of Asco's performances provide glimpses of dark matter, yet nowhere in their work does this shadowy material coalesce into a coherent system as fully as in the No Movies genre. Indeed the presentation of the range and depth of these works was one of the strongest aspects of the collective's September 2011 exhibition at LACMA. The curators placed the No Movies works, dating from the mid- to late '70s, in their own room and arranged photographs, slide shows, magazines, and publicity materials in separate displays that allowed the viewer to imagine the various permutations that this genre has taken. However, the visceral and aesthetic impact of other performance works repre-sented in the exhibition diminishes when presented along-side a plethora of archival materials. As an archive, *Elite of the Obscure* does an admirable job of documenting fifteen years of collective production, treating each element of the group's production with equal weight and rigour.

Elite of the Obscure encompassed most of the collective's canonical works, along with nearly a hundred and fifty collectively and individually authored objects includ-ing paintings, drawings, and photographs, as well as per-formance documentation and props. Many of the works for the meticulously researched exhibition had never been seen before and the works on view included a num-ber of lesser-known works, as well as pieces authored by peripheral collaborators and later members. The exhibition provided a remarkably clear view into the frenetic produc-tion of the collective and the grassroots ebb and flow of its ranks. In terms of presentation, the exhibition presented a roughly chronological order, with some sets of photographs and objects isolated in subcategories to elucidate certain creative relationships and influences outside of the core collective members that influenced Asco's production.

Although the exhibition provided a sensitive, in-depth view of the collective's ad hoc production it failed to con-sistently illuminate distinctive and innovative aspects of Asco's performances. The three models of performance I describe unfolded within specific historical periods, with some overlap and ambiguity among them, but the distinc-tions among these apparently divergent styles begin to erode when placed within a chronological grouping that elides specific sets of concerns. Gonzalez and Chavoya collapsed three distinct typologies of performance—one that relates the body to the urban landscape, another that explores the relationship between images and their circulation, and a third that combines the two. Elevating the group's history over a focus on the aesthetic and political relationships between their works obscured the development of the group's signature No Movies genre. As a catchall phrase for fake film stills, the term also applies to transitional performances such as *Instant Mural* and *Decoy Gang War Victim*—something that was not brought to light in the exhibition's didactic texts, nor through the presentation of photo documentation within the show. The exhibition's comprehensiveness worked against it at times and ran the risk of negating some of the collective's most sophisticated, medium-specific innovation. Iconic works like *Malibu* (1975), *Asshole Mural* (1975), *Walking Mural* (1972), *Spray Paint LACMA* (1972), and Seymour Rosen's documentation of *Stations of the Cross* (1971) disappear among drawings, Polaroid scrapbook pages, and issues of *Regeneracíon*.[17]

What Asco's former members describe as their "hit-and-run aesthetic" testifies not only to the collective's boundless production and creative energy, but also to some of the challenges inherent in displaying their work beyond the different models of performance that they engage. Asco's work is fuelled by an ethos of making-do, working with whatever materials are at hand, including whichever collaborators are available. However, the exhibition's chronological focus and dense interweaving of wildly divergent materials precludes a thoughtful exploration and consideration of Asco's primary medium: conceptual performance. Can a traditional retrospective approach withstand the pressure that DIY practices like collective authorship, rampant productivity, and vast amounts of intermedia material place on the exhibition format? For that matter, can Asco's intermittently formal and informal production withstand the pressure of a retrospective? Would showcasing a more limited set of practices and concerns develop deeper relationships between an audience unfamiliar with Asco's work and their projects? Or conversely, does focusing on the group's strengths and core members' contributions advance an incomplete and dishonest account of the collective's history, obscuring the dark material that propels the group's artistic production?

Elite of the Obscure went to great lengths to contextualize aspects of the collective's artistic production *within* the city of Los Angeles and the broader realm of Chicano art and politics via wall text and an extensive catalogue. However, the exhibition failed to frame Asco's work in relation to national or international dialogues within the arts and did little to underscore how Asco approached performance in innovative or groundbreaking ways. While the retrospective's curators attempted to address the marginalization of Asco's practice historically, their didactic framing of the exhibition continued to peripheralize through blunt-force. The wealth of material on view left behind matter more obscured than revealed.

1. According to Arthur C. Danto, each generation possesses a distinct attitude or *mentalité*, and he defines the *mentalité* of the late 1960s as one of revulsion directed against the Vietnam War. Gronk and Gamboa echo this sentiment in interviews and each draws explicit links between their activism and their disgust with violent conflicts in their own neighbourhoods and around the world. Gronk recalls: *a lot of our friends were coming home in body bags and were dying, and we were seeing a whole generation come back that weren't alive anymore. And in a sense that gave us nausea…that is Asco, in a way.* See C. Ondine Chavoya and Rita Gonzalez, "Asco and the Politics of Revulsion," in *Asco: Elite of the Obscure*, eds. C. Ondine Chavoya and Rita Gonzalez (Ostfildern: Hatje Cantz, 2011), 40.

2. While conceptual performances formed the bulk of Asco's collective activities, each artist developed and maintained an individual practice spanning illustration, painting, muralism, and publishing. The group's collective activity grew out of their collaboration on the Chicano journal *Regeneración*, a political and literary magazine founded in the early 1900s

by the Mexican anarchist Ricardo Flores Magon, which Harry Gamboa Jr. helped to revive as an editor in 1971. This collaboration marked the first of many projects, both as a foursome and with a rotating cast of collaborators that included Terry Sandoval, Humberto Sandoval, and Jerry Greva, among others. Like many loosely articulated artist collectives, the group shifted between more and less formal modes of production, ranging from spontaneous street performances to carefully scripted theatre pieces.

3. After a curator at the LACMA allegedly told Gamboa that Chicanos "don't make fine art, they make folk art," the members of Asco sought retribution by spray painting their names on the side of the building. The spray paint remained for no more than a day and very few photos of the intervention exist.

4. Performance scholar Peggy Phelan argues that a performance is a singular event and changes in its reproduction or documentation, while both Amelia Jones and Phillip Auslander claim that documentation provides an access point to a performed work and thus forms an integral part of a performance. In his essay "The Performativity of Performance Documentation," Auslander differentiates between two forms of performance documentation/residue: the documentary and the theatrical, arguing that "theatrical documentation" is a performance in and of its own right, since the audience is met not via live encounter, but through the image itself. See Philip Auslander, "The Performativity of Performance Documentation," *Performance Art Journal*, no. 84 (2006), 1–10; Amelia Jones, "'Presence' in Absentia: Experiencing Performance and Documentation," *Art Journal* 56, no. 4 (Winter 1997) 11–18; and Peggy Phelan, *Unmarked: The Politics of Performance* (London: Routledge, 1993).

5. The Chicano Moratorium was a political anti-war activist group that organized a broad coalition of Chicano Americans to protest against the Vietnam War. On August 29, 1970, a riot broke out during a protest organized by the Chicano Moratorium, and police injured a hundred and fifty people and killed four, including award-winning Spanish language journalist and columnist for the *LA Times* Rubén Salazar. Accounts differ regarding whether the protestors or police instigated the rioting. See George Mariscal, *Aztlán and Viet Nam: Chicano and Chicana Experiences of the War* (Berkeley: University of California Press, 1999).

6. Gamboa describes this performance in *Gronk*: *On December 24, 1971, Herrón, Gronk, and Gamboa arrived unannounced on the corner of Eastern Avenue and Whittier Boulevard. Herrón was the representation of Christ/ Death, dressed in a white robe that bore a brightly coloured Sacred Heart, which he painted in acrylic. His face had been transformed by makeup into a stylized calavera. Gronk personified Pontius Pilate (aka Popcorn): he wore a green bowler hat, flaunted an excessively large beige fur purse, and carried a bag of unbuttered popcorn. Gamboa assumed the role of a zombie altar boy and wore an animal skull headpiece to ward off unsolicited communion.* Harry Gamboa Jr. quoted in Max Benavidez, *Gronk* (Los Angeles: Chicano Studies Research Center, 2007), 41.

7. Harry Gamboa Jr., "Against the Wall: Remembering the Chicano Moratorium," *East of Borneo*, November 16, 2010, http://fillip.ca/wjm9.

8. Amelia Jones and Tracey Warr, *The Artist's Body* (London: Phaidon Press, 2006), 43.

9. For more detail see C. Ondine Chavoya, "Internal Exiles: The Interventionist Public and Performance Art of Asco," in *Space, Site, Intervention: Situating Installation Art*, ed. Erika Suderburgh (Minneapolis: University of Minnesota Press, 2000), 196.

10. José Esteban Muñoz, *Queers of Color and the Performance of Politics* (Minneapolis: University of Minnesota Press, 1999)

11. C. Ondine Chavoya, "Orphans of Modernism: The Performance Art of Asco," *Corpus Delecti: Performance Art of the Americas*, ed. Coco Fusco (New York: Routledge, 1999), 224.

12. Amelia Jones, "Traitor Prophets: Art of the In-between," in *Asco: Elite of the Obscure*, 116.

13. Richard Meyer and Michelle Kuo (moderators), "LA Stories: A Roundtable Discussion," *Artforum*, October 2011, http://fillip.ca/zgk2.

14. See Alexander Alberro, *Conceptual Art and the Politics of Publicity* (Cambridge: MIT Press), 2004.

15. "Asco's No Movies," *Unframed: The LACMA Blog*, published November 9, 2011, http://fillip.ca/a40f.

16. Gregory Sholette, "Dark Matter, Activist Art and the Counter Public Sphere," in *Anti-Catalogue #01*, ed. Amish Morrell (Sligo: The Model, 2010), 64.

17. The exhibition also included sketches for issues of *Regeneración*, a journal that Gamboa, Gronk, Valdez, and Herrón collaborated on, and which also lead to Asco's formation.

Christopher Cozier and Claire Tancons

No More than a Backyard on a Small Island

In the following interview from December 2011, artist, critic, curator, and Alice Yard cofounder Christopher Cozier shares his insights about contemporary art practice in Trinidad and Tobago and the Caribbean with curator Claire Tancons. An artist collective recently incorporated as a nonprofit organization under the laws of Trinidad and Tobago, Alice Yard formed in 2006 around the backyard of a downtown Port of Spain house, once home to the great-grandmother of Alice Yard cofounder and architect Sean Leonard. At Alice Yard, Leonard and Cozier, along with its other cofounders, writer Nicholas Laughlin and musician Sheldon Holder, run artistic, literary, and music programs and, since building a small exhibition space in 2007, have mounted exhibitions and screened films, growing their network of creative collaborators on site and online along the way. More than an exhibition space, Alice Yard is a platform for creative practice and critical dialogue about the arts that builds upon the various languages and methodologies of its collaborators' disciplines. Continuing an ongoing discussion between Cozier and Tancons initiated in 2004, this conversation circumscribes the Caribbean as a critical space, addressing issues pertinent to artist-run spaces in general and to the small insular setting of Trinidad and Tobago in particular.

Claire Tancons: When we last spoke in Port of Spain in early 2010, you were considering converting Alice Yard from an art collective into a nonprofit arts organization in order to seek funding from international agencies.[1] This year, in 2011, the *Global Africa Project* at the Museum of Art and

Design (MAD) presented for the first time in New York a sample of Alice Yard's creative processes and practices. Given these recent developments and the fact that Alice Yard just celebrated its fifth anniversary, do you feel that institutionalizing tendencies are ineluctably setting in? Do you welcome or wish to avoid these tendencies, and, if so, how?

Christopher Cozier: Alice Yard is very much a response to local institutional deficits. There is no interest or support here for experimental investigative contemporary work. This interest in initiating, hosting, or simply taking seriously projects at their start-up or development stages has now expanded beyond the island to artists living in other places—many with Caribbean connections or interests—who began to ask similar questions and wanted to visit the Yard and engage its processes.

We are a small entity so when funders look at us they have to appreciate our independence, our flexibility, and our openness, all of which allows us to respond to how creative people would like to use the space and collaborate in diverse ways. In this sense, Alice Yard is not just a space, but a relationship. Currently a lot of young music bands rehearse there; we do readings by new and established writers and poets; artists and designers meet there or give talks or develop works together. For us, becoming a not-for-profit is very much about building capacity, our capacity to be able to respond in ways that are commensurate with the questions asked of us. At their simplest, these questions take the form of an artist approaching us with an idea we would like to help develop further. A lot of personal financial resources and time have gone into this process so far. It has been very difficult, but enjoyable when something critically interesting occurs, or someone from our audience and community says, "that was fun," or "now I understand why you are doing this," or just "thanks" and "keep going."

Our presence in *Global Caribbean* (2009–10) at the Haitian Cultural Center, Miami, and other locations, as well as in the *Global Africa Project* at MAD in New York is an acknowledgment, but it also challenges our capacity and sense of what we are about. We are still thinking this through along with our networks.

Tancons: That's interesting because arts funders themselves acknowledge that the nonprofit model is in crisis and foundations' granting capabilities have been steadily downsizing. Speaking for the United States at least, some of the most progressive foundations are encouraging arts organizations and artist collectives to think outside of the box in terms of their funding revenue. There is nothing really new here, but I wonder how you think about sustainably financing Alice Yard outside of the grant-making circuit and using your own resources?

Cozier: We are constantly trying to resolve these questions as we encounter them. Over time we would prefer to be acknowledged and engaged for what we are doing rather than just having credibility simply through being a funded entity. We seek, also, to open a debate about the value of experimental investigative work. We are trying to build a community and a dialogue about imagining in a place such as this. Searching for ways to create meaningfully in what, from our perspective, have become very aggressive, shrewd, utilitarian, and mercantile-driven Caribbean societies is quite a challenge. Compared to other neighbouring Caribbean countries, Trinidad is a relatively wealthy country with oil and natural gas reserves, yet too often the local community and the state are more than happy to leave it to international agencies to fill the gap in funding for arts and culture—all of which I find deeply ironic in a country that once sought to assert its independence from Britain and to find its own voice while being so close to the United States.

Tancons: Can you tell us more about the institutional deficit in the arts in Trinidad? Perhaps you can give us a quick genealogical recap of artist-led initiatives that preceded Alice Yard and tell us how Alice Yard distinguishes itself from them? I am thinking about Contemporary Caribbean Arts (CCA7) (1997–2007) of which you were a founding member and at which I was briefly a curator-in-residence in 2004. Also, could you speak about the more recent city-wide art project known as *Galvanize* from 2006?[2]

Cozier: Well, on the one hand we have a local art market through which a lot of money flows towards traditional and established art forms such as painting. On the other hand, there is a lack of funding and support for experimental and critical art practices from a younger generation of artists who engage Alice Yard. This younger generation—born in the late 1970s and early 1980s—circulates quite a lot internationally, but remains invisible at home as there are no serious collectors here and only a dysfunctional, underfunded museum, the National Museum of Trinidad and Tobago.

CCA7 was founded in 1997 to address and respond to contemporary art practice in Trinidad. Interesting stuff started to emerge in the field of contemporary art in Trinidad during the early 1980s but remained unsupported and misunderstood until the 1990s when a new generation of artists, including myself, began to show work internationally but continued to be rejected or ignored by the local market and institutions. There is a myth that contemporary art practice in Trinidad began with CCA7 or the people it imported, but it really began with the dialogues of the early 1980s around the work of people like Peter Minshall, Johnny Stollmeyer, Wendy Nanan, and Francesco Cabral, who came before. This collectively created the rationale for CCA7. In 2000, CCA7 became a large facility, with two galleries and thirteen residency studios, and was courted by various funding agencies like the Canada Council for the Arts, the Reed Foundation, the Prince Claus Fund, and networks like the Triangle Art Trust. But there was still very little local support and CCA7 eventually became both politically fraught—with resentment from local art advocates and the government about the centre's international attention—and financially challenged with very high overhead and scant resources left for actual projects. In some ways, the building became the project, and CCA7 began to fall short of its original purpose to support contemporary art practice in Trinidad. In the long term, CCA7 simply provided an entry point for foreign artists with solid connections to the international art market but did little to develop the visibility, critical understanding, and access to that international art world economy for the local artists in whose name it was developed. The ultimate demise of CCA7 in 2007 provided a lesson in local developmental politics and seriously questioned the ongoing tendency in the postcolonial Caribbean to emulate metropolitan organizational models to gain visibility and legitimacy even when they may not be adaptable to the local context and become nonfunctional and burdensome. CCA7 may be a good case study in how globalization casts a wide net while failing to seriously alter very old social and economic relations—paradigms that we know all too well in the Caribbean. I am of course referring here to the "other side" of capitalism and modernity otherwise known as colonialism and its ongoing aftershocks.

Galvanize was an attempt, initiated by a younger artist, Mario Lewis, to get back to building our context—i.e., to support our artists and create a dialogue and understanding, locally, of contemporary art practice and also to raise the low expectations international audiences might have of art from the Caribbean, to move ahead with the positive legacy of CCA7 in fostering international exchange among artists, and to take creative practice out of the building and into the public domain. The local art community responded to Lewis's proposition to work together and seek new places to show our work and win the public back. For example, much of the scheduling of the myriad events and projects that took place in the street and in non-art-spaces, as well as the blogging of critical conversation that drove *Galvanize*, was assembled and edited by Nicholas Laughlin (writer and Alice Yard cofounder) in collaboration with people like myself and many others. Interestingly, Alice Yard was first used as a space to show a video installation by Jaime Lee Loy, assisted by Marlon Griffith and Nikolai Noel, who went on to form the artistic collective the Collaborative Frog. So, a series of networks and dialogues began to take shape, all based on the lessons learned through our experience with CCA7, which later developed into what would become Alice Yard. In some ways, we have actually returned to where we were before CCA7, as the need to support and promote contemporary art practices at home and abroad remains, but in a more informed and pragmatic way.

Tancons: Gregory Sholette talks about the emergence of the "mockstitution" trend among artists' collaboratives that organize themselves, mimicking institutions as a response to being rejected by them. Alice Yard is not a mockstitution and yet it also seems to respond to a distinct history of rejection and exclusion both within the national Trinidadian institutional landscape and the framework of the wider global art world. How much has changed in terms of Caribbean artists' ability to show and share their work with wider audiences since the days of Octavio Zaya's *Caribe Insular: Exclusión, Fragmentación y Paraíso* (Museo Extremeño e Iberoamericano de Arte Contemporáneo, Badajoz, Spain, 1998) and the announcement of *Caribbean: Crossroads of the World*, a collaboration between the Studio Museum in Harlem, El Museo del Barrio in Manhattan, and the Queens Museum of Art, set for 2012?

Cozier: Today, we are simply doing our own thing in terms of producing and presenting work so we cannot be excluded, especially from what is ours or from our own imaginings. Of course, we are responding to our location culturally and historically, but to me there is no "them" out there. I have been "included" in many Caribbean art surveys, but most importantly, my colleagues and I at Alice Yard hope others on the purported periphery of the market-driven art world will join or compliment our efforts in generating their own dialogues, spaces, and processes as well. About the Caribbean surveys in museums outside the region—well…one can say, back then, when they occurred, that many of us got to meet each other in the flesh and also to see each other's work firsthand. Otherwise this would occur mainly at the Havana Biennial for those of us invited. In general I would like more of these encounters to happen within the region more regularly and in more varied ways.

Tancons: How do you feel, retrospectively, about the questions of periphery and exclusion, which dominated the discourse of the 1980s and 1990s even in the context of what many believed to be a multicultural boom? Do you feel that the myth of multiculturalism has and continues to produce further marginalization? Do you feel that the exclusion of artists living in what was formerly referred to as the periphery has been institutionalized? Can transnational artistic collaborations of the kind established at and through Alice Yard help fill in the blanks perpetuated by dominant, institutionalized, and marginalizing discourses?

Cozier: The politics, or "politricks," of visibility are myriad. I initially left the United States in the late 1980s to get away from how multiculturalism demanded that I become something already known, fixed, and prepackaged in order to be recognized and included as a marginal underfunded subject and given a little money and attention to operate on the sideline, outside of the mainstream art discourse. I returned to the Caribbean to see if there was another way to be and to function as an artist.

I am a bit horrified to see the same language of multiculturalism, which was constructed by the Euro-American mainstream, arrive here in Trinidad about twenty years later under the government of Prime Minister Kamla Persad-Bissessar, who, when elected in 2010, established the Ministry of Culture and Multiculturalism. But the world is funny in the way in which it retools old notions as new. I recall being in Canada on a panel in 2004 where people were talking about "creolization" as if it could be a new and improved multiculturalism. My earlier work dealt with how constructions of nationhood require an ideal, an approved subject or citizen. To me the concept of nation in the anglophone Caribbean context is the smallest moment of our larger history since the alleged "discovery" by Columbus in 1493. Trinidad, for example, became independent from the UK in 1962. Also, the island state is the smallest location on the Caribbean map, physically and mentally—perhaps an immature and very aggressive guarded territory that belongs to politicians and their funders. Our populations continue to travel between these bordered territories, be they other Caribbean islands sharing a similar history, former metropolitan colonial powers in Europe, or other places of migrations like the US and Canada. What we do at Alice Yard is very much a response to these questions of sovereignty through the dialogues we instigate between artists about what they do both regionally and internationally.

Tancons: Institution-building is a form of history-making, which calls for the preservation of institutional archives. What is Alice Yard doing to make sure that the alternative history it is essentially writing is preserved beyond its artists' documentation of their own material production and actions? Or is this archival preservation less important than the moment and the memory that Alice Yard impresses upon the feelings and experiences of those associated with it?

Cozier: First, perhaps we have to shift our understanding of the concepts of "archive," "institution," and also "alternative." To me, Alice Yard is actually a very traditional space, almost archetypal in Caribbean terms as it is literally a yard—the backyard of a modest 1930s Port of Spain home, a place where generations of the family of the architect Sean Leonard, one of Alice Yard's cofounders, played as children and a place where people built and took to the streets in their costumes during Carnival. If you are familiar with early regional literature, theatre, the story of Carnival, and the steel band yards, you will know that the yards were communal spaces where people lived, dreamed, and collaborated. So using the yard as a site for our activities is an investment in the future built on traditions from the past. The word "alternative" takes up epistemological references of other places and narratives and conversations that I left behind in art school in the United States. To some degree the yard, as a space, is only an alternative to accessing forgotten aspects of our living past. Artist Charles Campbell has recently written a text on his experience working in Alice Yard in which he talks about "failure" and deficits becoming assets. We are about to publish a small monograph of that essay. So our whole dialogue and process is becoming almost like a collaborative conceptual project in development about creating work in places like this. Through our actions we discover and produce our past and futures simultaneously, both virtually and physically. Nicholas, as a writer and publisher, is, of course, concerned with these questions; so, apart from blogging and posting to Flickr and its networks, he has made an arrangement with the University of the West Indies to catalogue and store our archival material.

Tancons: Don't you think that the concept of "alternative" applies to Alice Yard in the sense that the kind of practices it enables, although in a genealogical continuum with past practices, are also distinct, at least in terms of the critical outlook they offer? Specifically, the notion of "alternative history" is a critique of hegemonic histories and discourses that erase or fail to account for what does not fit within its agenda of maintaining political power or status quo.

Cozier: Maybe, but I am always looking for options. I wanted to distance the use of the word "alternative" from the cool, urban, romantic languages I left behind in New York in the 1980s. I do not want to construct a historical allegory of sorts, as if we want to have "alternative" as a brand too.

Tancons: You speak of both Alice Yard and the Caribbean in a larger sense as a "critical space." You and your collaborators see yourselves as elaborating a distinct creative genealogy for the region's discursive and exhibition practices in the tradition of the yard space where Trinidadians grew up honing their creative skills, playing ball as children, batting and bowling as cricketers, crafting verses as calypsonians, and building costumes as masmen (carnival costume builders). Presumably, this familiar space should be inviting to the wider public outside of the artistic community. Yet, in my admittedly rather infrequent experience, I found that those who were in attendance at Alice Yard's events and projects were for the most part creative practitioners from the arts, architecture, design, and literature. It thus seems that for all its familiarity and grounding in a local genealogy of creative practices, Alice Yard remains a threatening space to many, as if the apparatus of criticality inherent in "contemporary art" poses particular challenges of inclusion and exclusion. The adjacent creative field of Carnival was once a critical space in which a dialogue about art and politics emerged in the popular debate. And yet, masmen, even from the Callaloo Company (the carnival production company of Peter Minshall), are wary of crossing the threshold that separates contemporary art and Carnival as if the bridges built between the two by Peter Minshall in the 1980s have crumbled. Is Alice Yard first and foremost, by artists and for artists, strictly defined as "contemporary"?

Cozier: Alice Yard has at least two events a month, attracting very different groups—not everything is publicized on the blog. Sometimes people just use the space to meet and talk privately every other day or so. It has a very diverse following, including musicians, writers, designers, and a few artists. "Adjacent" is an interesting word in considering the relationship between Carnival and contemporary art. Rudolph "Murphy" Winters, a master carnival costume builder from the Callaloo Company, built my *Made in China* box (2009), in fact. There are some assumptions being articulated here about "community" and "public" as relates to Carnival. The era of Carnival as community-driven that is so romanticized has long passed. The Callaloo Company is basically a workshop with a community built on common skills and labour relations. It began in the mid-1980s with a committee of investors to support the interests of one artist, Peter Minshall, up until the early 2000s. Even Carnival, especially now, is removed from the public and is controlled by new investor groups and cultural ministries, not by grassroots community groups. Also, "the public," in the domain of popular expression, does what it wants over time: you cannot force it to participate in either a carnival band or a contemporary art event, unlike "the audience," which you can build around similar interests. Carnival is not only about art, it's first and foremost about competing social groups and their visibility. In this sense we must never confuse "audience" with "public," and this critical difference whose significance extends beyond the context of Alice Yard is certainly not just relevant to Trinidad. So, yes, we aspire to have a wider dialogue, but our audience consists of creative people with similar interests, for the moment. The "critical space" is not a stable geographic location or critical position—it is rather the constantly shifting space in which we are able to have this kind of conversation at a certain point in time. For us, Alice Yard is providing that time and space—for now.

Tancons: I follow the line you're drawing between public and audience, but I am more concerned with demystifying assumptions regarding what constitutes "the general public" or "an audience" in the first decade of the twenty-first century in Trinidad and Tobago—even if there is no "them" as you pointed out earlier. Do you feel that this yearning for a local audience and outreach to a wider public actively informs the work of creative practitioners collaborating with Alice Yard? Or do you feel that the flattening out of difference heralded by the age of globalization makes these distinctions of locality moot?

Cozier: I think we are all simply proceeding—reacting to what artists want to do in and with the space, the actual yard, and also now online. For example, we see *ARC Magazine*, a Caribbean art journal founded by artists Holly Bynoe and Nadia Huggins, as part of our network. Bynoe and Huggins have very actively and fastidiously taken up the challenge of expanding and driving the information flow online in ways that have directly benefitted us.[3] In my writing, I have always argued that the critical space is larger than the geographic island and nation. It is diasporic, meaning it exists in many places at once—New York, London, Amsterdam, Toronto, etc.—wherever Caribbean people have settled and continue to imagine and respond to the world around them.

ARC Magazine as well as the *Draconian Switch*, an art and design e-magazine produced by designer Richard Rawlins in collaboration with Alice Yard, have significantly affected the space in which we operate as it has expanded the speed of information flow to and from the organization as well as the demographic scale we reach in terms of audience.[4] I hear some rumblings about the real and virtual engagement of the Caribbean and about the artwork as well, but I do not think it is fair to compare actual and virtual encounters. New ways of interacting and creating experiences are also happening online, which necessitates an expansion of our understanding of agency. People are now communicating across what were once major divides in both time and space.

Tancons: I agree with you that an understanding of space is not predicated solely upon physically visiting it. Critical engagement across geographic and ideological boundaries is far more important. Recently, we were discussing the impact of the exhibition Caribbeanists love to hate: *Infinite Islands* (2007) at the Brooklyn Museum of Art. Curator Tumelo Mosaka travelled to many of the countries represented in the show, discovering first-hand local creative practices and discussing them one-on-one with artists, but this engagement didn't prevent the show from being most problematic in its use of hackneyed anthropological categories, exhibition of works instrumentalized to serve those categories, and the exoticization of regional artistic practices. How much might the advent of *ARC Magazine* or other boundary-breaking platforms such as the *Draconian Switch* help do away with such geographically contingent categorizations?

Cozier: Well, the "SX Space," which I initiated for the website of *Small Axe: A Caribbean Journal of Criticism*, was my initial attempt at addressing these divides.[5] It may just be a generational thing. I am older and slower than the new players and more concerned with following critical ideas and paths that interest me personally than with promoting new art trends. *ARC* is a glossy art magazine that is about publicity and building a brand—they made a big market-investment, as well as perhaps an investment in volume and speed, which is of course important to their survival in terms of expansion and positioning, all of which is good. I wish I had had a vehicle like *ARC* or even my current internet networks when I first came back to the Caribbean at the end of the 1980s.

I have never been particularly interested in the arguments around *Infinite Island*. The show, for all its stated failings, made the region and a few of us a little more visible even though it was compromised in other ways. I have always been surprised by the force with which people chose to go after Mosaka rather than Holland Cotter, whose review in the *New York Times* showed even more problematic assumptions about art and artists in the Caribbean. Cotter, even if baited by some of the conventional thematic categorizations of the show, offloaded some astonishing judgments. His review of the show brought to light the assumption that a Caribbean exhibition is about identity display and the idea that the Euro-American construction of Blackness was a set standard. He even suggested that getting a green card was more important to Caribbean people than showing art in New York.

The long-term impact of *Infinite Island* will be determined by the degree to which the institutions who receive funding for the next survey respect our work and the context in which it functions and will be willing to collaborate with us in the curatorial process. I have the feeling that Mosaka may have sincerely tried to do this only to find himself embroiled in institutional politics and funding difficulties. Ideally, as an artist I want to get my work and ideas across to a public. I am not interested in the internal politics of the New York art world. I also do want to have curatorial agency to ensure that my work and the work of the artists we support at Alice Yard and throughout the Caribbean receive appropriate presentation and contextualization.

Tancons: Over the last year, you co-curated *Paramaribo SPAN* (2010) in Suriname at various venues and *Wrestling with the Image: Caribbean Interventions* (2011) in the United States at the Art Museum of the Americas in Washington, DC.[6] Recently, you also participated in *Dislocating the Studio*, an artist residency in Johannesburg, South Africa. Is this geography of mobility—the Caribbean, the United States, South Africa—representative of your and Alice Yard's network? And how do you seek to expand it? In many ways, it is very much a south-south network mediated by the United States and Europe.[7] Do you feel that the United States and Europe are mediating south-south relationships, even if indirectly, as a relic of a colonial past, or that they are happening on their own terms? Do you and Alice Yard proceed according to what could be called group affinities, to employ a rather of-the-moment term?

Cozier: As I keep saying: we are simply proceeding. We are trying to build relationships with groups of artists and thinkers who are faced with similar challenges and are seeking creative solutions. We are all talking with Popop Studios in Nassau, Bahamas; Tembe Art Studio in Moengo, Suriname; Projects & Space in Barbados;[8] and with *ARC Magazine* and others outside the Caribbean.

My grandparents and parents lived in a colonial world in which one could do teacher training in Port of Spain and end up teaching in a school in Colombo, Christchurch, or Lagos. This kind of mobility ended in the early 1960s after independence, when Jamaica, Trinidad, and other British colonies became national states and granted their citizens passports, establishing boundaries in what was a previously unbounded colonial territory. Again, the question of mobility and the challenge of establishing exchanges among Caribbean countries divided by geographic and national boundaries brings us back to who is willing to fund these conversations. Unless we can solve these questions ourselves, the problem of the distracting and sadly entertaining conversations about inclusion and exclusion will always linger.

Tancons: The title of Alice Yard's fifth anniversary project was *ACT5: The Performative Moment* (2011), for which you featured the work of some of the Caribbean's most exciting young artists in an exhibition and hosted discussions and performances over a three-month period. As an artist, your practice of drawing, printmaking, and note-taking externalizes itself most when you travel and engage in residencies and exhibitions where you are almost always a co-curator of your own work in collaboration with a curator who invited you to participate. As a curator you are intent on breaking authoritative and hierarchical methodologies inherent in traditional artistic and exhibition-making practices by instigating participatory actions aimed at the audience, which may be a way of circumventing the challenges articulated earlier in our conversation. In this sense, we could think of your work as conceptually if not formally performative, in that it establishes tangible connections between art practitioners and audiences. Can you talk about the performative artistic traditions in the region and the way in which they inform their own curatorship and the curatorship of other visual art forms, specifically as they relate to participatory modes of engagement?

Cozier: Well, in the beginning, I experimented with performance outside of playing mas' (i.e., participating in Carnival) with my *Conversation with Shirt Jac* performance in 1991 and in *System of Control* (1992) where I used a primary-school whip or switch, which later evolved into the slightly theatrical *Blue Soap* video shown at the 1994 Havana Biennial. My interest in performance came in part out of my thinking about Peter Minshall's *Mancrab* (1983) and how objects and actions can function with equal agency.[9] I am very interested in the distinction between the public and the private domain, as well as between public and audience. I think that all art that is serious carries a critical, sometimes curatorial objective, which is like a visual or critical DNA. My retreat to drawing or my return to the drawing board has been an investigation of narrative and the time-based action of a line moving between points as well as the way in which the viewer has to become active in making sense of things encountered, the way in which the viewer produces the experience and, by extension, the work itself. Also, for me works on paper imply a speculative or investigative feeling, which is like thought, ephemeral and fleeting.

To my mind, critical dialogues and curatorial purpose can come into being through experiencing the work itself. The work asks the questions or declares the intentions of the artist. The informality of Alice Yard and the openness of the architectural space alter how we encounter visual objects or actions. I see some interesting connections between the documentation of a performative action and the actual performance in real space and time coming out of *4x4: Shot in Kingston* (2010), a small survey of digital photography and video by young artists from Kingston. Think of Marlon Griffith's *Runaway/Reaction* shot in video by artist Caecilia Tripp as part of *SPRING*, the art procession you curated for the 7th Gwangju Biennale. This connection between the performative action and its video or photo documentation also came up, albeit in a reverse fashion, with Charles Campbell's ongoing re-creation of *Actor Boy*, in which an early post-Emancipation form of masking depicted in a well-known topographic illustration is now documented buying a phone card; Hew Locke's eccentric and playful heraldic adornments; and of course Ebony Patterson's recent staged and altered images of dancehall posses, to name a few examples. Through masking and re-creation they are producing or becoming new presences that both obscure and produce identities and ways of being that also entwine the past with the present. Similarly, James Cooper's temporary sculptures and Ivan Monforte's performances, which he defines as emotional sculptures, manifest a diversity of ways of understanding the performative. So, within each of these moments there are a range of proposals—manifestos, so to speak—all happening at Alice Yard, in a space that is no more than a backyard on a small island.

Tancons: You mentioned *SPRING*, the procession project that I curated for the 7th Gwangju Biennale (2008), which linked the resistant ethos of Black Atlantic carnivals with South Korea's democratic history. We were also more recently discussing my essay for *e-flux journal*, "Occupy Wall Street: Carnival Against Capital? Carnivalesque as Protest Sensibility," which compares carnivalesque strands in current protest movements with contemporary resistant practices in the New Orleans and Trinidad carnivals. In an older essay, "Curating Carnival? Performance in Contemporary Caribbean Art and the Paradox of Performance Art in Contemporary Art," I question the Eurocentric notion of performance art.[10] Provocatively, I'd like to ask: can Carnival be an antidote to performance art? Isn't performance art a sort of commercial capitalization of an intangible medium whose immaterial economy is being objectified in order to be sold? If so, given Alice Yard's position at the critical junction of the visual arts, performance art, and Carnival, how do you navigate such potentially fraught territory?

Cozier: Our conversation about the carnivalesque is taking place at a time in which Carnival has become grand and highly commodified, much like a Hollywood lot in the 1930s. This happened in my lifetime during which artists began to look more at the process rather than focusing on the actual form and festival in order to find their way. I think that it is very fertile to tease out the question of the relationship between Carnival and performance art. A similar debate came up years ago about the differences between Latin American conceptualism and that of the United States and Europe. However, coming from the Caribbean, and the little I know about our colonial past, naming is claiming. Fresh out of art college, I recall once saying that our Cabaret Voltaire was in the 1860s with the Jamette riots (uprisings of the underclass against British rule during Carnival). Then I realized how language and terminology entrap and that we might have nothing to gain from claiming a language that is not our own and applying it to our practices. I think there are certainly claims to be contested—many were made before there was the information flow of the internet and before there was any need to be more globally aware or discreet—but those were not our claims. What I continue to learn from living in a place like Trinidad before and after an art education in the US is that people here just do things. They are always processing, almost indiscriminatingly, anything they find useful and casually applying their own meaning and value to these actions. It's another education—one that we often take for granted.

Tancons: It seems to me that we have come full circle. On the one hand we have been advocating for the necessity of acknowledging place and site, and on the other hand, the need to extend ourselves beyond locality, embracing digital technology as a means to achieve boundarylessness. Of course, there are fantasies in both discourses, but how do you see them played out in the contemporary Caribbean imaginary in all its global connectedness?

Cozier: We have always been global. We are a mobile transplanted people. We either dream or travel. The internet is just a new device. Even though we are witnessing its effects, it is still too early to be definitive about what is actually being created. But isn't this what we always say in the process of becoming?

1. Alice Yard's website is at http://aliceyard.blogspot.com. Christopher Cozier's website, Visual Matters, is at http://christophercozier.blogspot.com.
2. Described as "a contemporary arts programme based in Port of Spain, Trinidad and Tobago," *Galvanize* ran from September 14 to October 26, 2006, and was supported by CCA7. See https://fillip.ca/85ja.
3. *ARC Magazine*'s website is at http://arcthemagazine.com/arc/.
4. The *Draconian Switch*'s website is at http://www.artzpub.com/home.
5. The website for *Small Axe*'s "SX Space" is at https://fillip.ca/9zcx.
6. *Paramaribo SPAN*'s website is at http://paramaribospan.blogspot.com.
7. *South-South* is the title of an exhibition that was held at the Justina M. Barnicke Gallery of the University of Toronto (2009) to which Cozier contributed a critical essay on the work of fellow Trinidadian artist Marlon Griffith.
8. Popop Studios International Center for the Visual Arts is an artist residency founded by artist John Cox in Nassau, Bahamas. See https://fillip.ca/zc8o. The Tembe Art Studio is an artist residency and art centre initiative lead by artist Marcel Pinas in Moengo, Suriname. See http://www.tembeartstudio.org. Projects & Space was founded by the artist Sheena Rose. It seeks spaces to realize projects throughout Barbados. See http://projectsandspace.tumblr.com.
9. *Mancrab* is the name of the King's character and costume in Peter Minshall's *River* mas' band of 1983. A competitive art form, Carnival involves several juried categories, of which the King costume is one. Peter Minshall (born 1941) revolutionized mas' by bringing a conceptual outlook more commonly associated with the visual arts and a sophistication in costume design learned from his training in theatre at London's Central Saint Martins in the mid-1960s. Minshall's work played an important role in shaping the conversation around contemporary art in Trinidad during its heyday in the mid-1980s to the mid-1990s. Although under-recognized in the realm of contemporary art, Minshall's influence on creative

practice in the Caribbean and beyond is enormous. For instance, he was a recipient of a Guggenheim Fellowship in carnival design and kinetics in 1982 and a Prince Claus Fund Award in 2001. Minshall organized the opening ceremonies of three Olympic Games (Salt Lake City, 2002; Atlanta, 1996; Barcelona, 1992) and designed performances for Jean-Michel Jarre's concert-spectacles in the 1990s (among many other contributions to international theatrical, music, and sporting events), in addition to producing large-scale costumed bands for the annual Trinidad carnival from 1976 to 2006. 10. Claire Tancons, "Spring," in *The 7th Gwangju Biennale. Annual Report: A Year in Exhibitions*, ed. Okwui Enwezor (Gwangju: Gwangju Biennale Foundation, 2008), 334–63, https://fillip.ca/dco4; Claire Tancons, "Occupy Wall Street: Carnival Against Capital? Carnivalesque as Protest Sensibility," *e-flux journal*, December 2011, https://fillip.ca/y8vr; Claire Tancons, "Curating Carnival? Performance in Contemporary Caribbean Art and the Paradox of Performance Art in Contemporary Art," in *Curating in the Caribbean*, eds. David Bailey, Alissandra Cummings, Axel Lapp, and Allison Thompson (Berlin: Green Box, 2012), 37–62.

Christopher Régimbal
Institutions of Regionalism

Artist Collectivism in London, Ontario

1024 great great great great great great great great grandparents
512 great great great great great great great grandparents
256 great great great great great great grandparents
128 great great great great great grandparents
64 great great great great grandparents
32 great great great grandparents
16 great great grandparents
8 great grandparents
4 grandparents
2 parents
One Child

—James Reaney, *Colours in the Dark*[1]

Writing in *Art in America* in 1969, Barry Lord called London, Ontario, "one of Canada's four major art scenes," declaring the city to be "younger than Montreal, livelier than Toronto, vying with Vancouver in variety and sheer quantity of output,…in many ways the most important of the four."[2] From the 1960s through to the end of the 1980s, the unlikely city of London in southwestern Ontario drew the attention of the national and international art media for its energetic community of artists, filmmakers, novelists, poets, musicians, and activists who collectively became known as the London Regionalists, or more often and more simply, as the Regionalists.[3] Regionalism in London was the subject of articles in popular and art-specific magazines in the 1960s and 1970s and of a major touring exhibition organized by the National Gallery of Canada in 1966. Despite its name, Regionalism developed a profile of international significance when many artists from London began showing across Canada and around the world, including at the São Paulo Biennial in 1969 and 1987,[4] the Biennale des Jeunes in Paris in 1969,[5] and the Venice Biennale in 1972, 1976, 1978, and 1982.[6] As a testament to the influence of Regionalism in London, half of the artists represented in the contemporary Canadian art section when the National Gallery of Canada opened on Sussex Drive in 1988 had spent important parts of their careers working in that city.[7]

Scholars of art history and literature in Canada have often applied the idea of regionalism to the study of Canadian culture with the understanding that because of the vast size of the country, and the distances between its urban centres, artistic and literary movements have often fermented in relative isolation from one another.[8] In these cases, regionalism signifies the location of production, and often the relationship of that locality to centres of influence where the presentation, circulation, and reception of art takes place. More specifically, art historians such as J. Russell Harper, Charles Hill, and Dennis Reid have all used the term "regionalism" to describe Canadian painting in the 1930s and 1940s.[9] Harper, for example, discusses this era in the context of American regionalism, which itself developed as a refutation of European painting traditions in favour of American subjects and styles. Like their American counterparts, Canadian regionalists in the 1930s, such as Carl Schaefer and Charles Comfort, privileged scenes and subjects in their paintings that depicted the ordinary and local over the extraordinary,[10] articulating a relationship to a specific locality in the content of their work.

Later, in the 1960s and 1970s, Regionalism in London found similar expression in terms of artistic content *and* a local context, but it is difficult to discuss in consistent stylistic terms since the output of the movement was as varied as the personalities of its practitioners. What brought these artists together was, therefore, not a particular approach to art-making but instead a shared desire to produce work out of personal and local experiences. For Vancouver poet George Bowering, London Regionalism was the "performance of a social consciousness," suggesting that its artists heard Toronto "speak of the Souwesto experience as regional and they cheerfully adopted the word, from inside their space, changing it from a mild insult to an affirmation of their cohesiveness."[11] Such characterization situates Regionalism as a resistant response to the global phenomenon theorized by Australian art historian Terry Smith as the "provincialism problem"; that is, the perpetuation of an artificial centre-periphery relationship that reinforced New York's hegemony over the rest of the art world. In his landmark 1974 article, Smith argues that provincialism binds non–New York artists within a cycle that dominates not only the reception of their work but the conditions of its actual production as well.[12] Being doubly provincial, not only vis-à-vis New York but Canada nationally, London artists embraced the provincialism that other art scenes within the country struggled against and assumed it as a practice.

One vital component of the ideology of Regionalism identified by Bowering was collectivism, about which he wrote: "I do remember the eager hubbub of those London, Ont. Regionalists, their homemade art galleries, ironic picnics, theatre workshops, their gladsome business. They *gathered*."[13] In fact, London artists were among the earliest and most enthusiastic innovators of artist cooperatives in Canada due in part to the city's small size, relative isolation, and conservative art establishment, which gave young artists few professional options to publish and exhibit their work at the start of the 1960s. In response to such limitations, a small group of London artists self-organized by founding three magazines (*Alphabet*, *Region*, and the *Embassy Cultural House Tabloid*), four cooperative galleries (Region Gallery, 20/20 Gallery, Forest City Gallery, and the Embassy Cultural House), a theatre workshop (the Alpha Centre), a pseudo–political party (the Nihilist Party of Canada), a film distribution cooperative (London Film Cooperative), and a national arts advocacy group (CARFAC), all within the thirty years covered by this essay. Significantly, London artists developed new cooperative structures around the ethos of Regionalism and in so doing gave form to a type of collectivism particular to London that artists across the country embraced and that contributed significantly to a reordering of the institutional landscape during the artist-run gallery movement of the 1970s in Canada.

Jumping off from Bowering's idea of Regionalism as a performance of a social consciousness, this discussion explores the correlation between London's artist cooperatives and the ideology of Regionalism to reveal how these two entities grew together out of local tactics to subvert provincialism into internationally significant movements. This assessment will consider the specific contributions of London artists to Canada's larger artist-run movement, reflecting on how each artist brought Regionalism to bear on his or her own artwork and involvement in cooperatives. It will become apparent that in each case the artistic and bureaucratic roles of these artists coexisted to cultivate the Regionalist movement and influence the direction of modern artist collectivism in Canada.

A Very Locally Coloured Tree

In the first half of the 1960s, London's cooperative galleries and publications were small and dedicated to decidedly local subject matter. The artists who administered them were young, and their limited means and boundless energy shaped the early direction of their institutions. *Alphabet* (1960–71), *Region* (1961–90), Region Gallery (1962–63), and Alpha Centre (1966–69) were where London artists first articulated the aims of Regionalism and put them into action. Analyzing the work and involvement of poet and playwright James Reaney and artist Greg Curnoe in these four organizations reveals an early version of Regionalism whose subscribers sought to use local materials and influences to produce art that transcended local significance—a transcendence they themselves called universality. In fact, the desire for universality was a primary concern of Reaney's, who rejected the notion that Regionalism was parochial in a 1962 *Alphabet* editorial, which read: "I don't believe that you can be world, or unprovincial or whatever, until you've sunk your claws into a very locally coloured tree trunk and scratched your way through to universality."[14] Here, Reaney draws a deliberate association between the ideology of the Regionalist movement and a perceived need to surmount a provincialism trap.

The chosen platform for Reaney's Regionalism was *Alphabet*, a semi-annual literary journal published between 1960 and 1971 from a small print shop in the Cities Heating building in downtown London. An early champion of poets such as Margaret Atwood, Michael Ondaatje, and Margaret Avison, Reaney published these then burgeoning writers in the journal, putting into practice an approach he articulated in its first editorial, writing: "Let us make a form out of this: documentary on one side and myth on the other: Life & Art. In this form we can put anything and the magnet we have set up will arrange it for us."[15] For each instalment of *Alphabet*, Reaney structured the issue around a guiding myth, such as Narcissus, Icarus, or Job, to which writers could respond creatively, as if inside Reaney's magnet. For Bowering, Reaney's editorial represented "the shortest and best definition of the regionalist's art."[16] Moreover, it launched his activities at *Alphabet*, and later the Alpha Centre, in practical terms while opening a way to reconcile his promotion of Regionalist myth and documentary with a desire to stimulate a corresponding social consciousness stretching beyond local concerns.

Building on his experiences with *Alphabet*, Reaney founded the Alpha Centre in 1966 above a former legion hall on Talbot Street. There he ran the Listeners' Theatre Workshop, which met regularly on Saturday mornings. Out of their improvisations, he wrote several plays including *The Donnellys* trilogy (1975/1977), which told the story involving the mass murder of an Irish Catholic family by their neighbours in 1880 in Biddulph Township, eighteen miles northwest of London.[17] Reaney meticulously researched the details surrounding the murders and consequently developed a series of plays using a style that emulated the collective improvisations that took place at the Listeners' Theatre Workshop. *The Donnellys* recounts the story of the eponymous family over their thirty-six years in Canada, ending with their gruesome murder, and presents the family as victims of systemic racism and violence who struggled to overcome a land ownership system that disadvantaged the immigrant farmers settling the region.

Reaney's perspective on the folk story, well known in southwestern Ontario, varies from the usual telling of the "Black Donnellys" and casts the family in a struggle against the social oppression and irrationality of the institutions that dominated rural life. This perspective places his account within the Southern Ontario Gothic literary tradition, which often explores the hidden suffering beneath the outward dullness of rural life in the region.[18] His interest in myth drew him to explore the stories he would have heard growing up in southwestern Ontario while his interest in documentary compelled him to research those myths and present them in a historically informed way. Reaney's Regionalism, outlined in the pages of *Alphabet* and put into action at the Alpha Centre, found its expression in the structure and story of the Donnellys. Despite Reaney's anchoring of the story in local history and context, his telling of it is much greater in scope as a tale of human tragedy and community shame.

Like Reaney, Greg Curnoe's early involvement with artists' institutions explicitly charted the early doctrine of Regionalism in London and in his own practice. In fact, Curnoe is the artist most directly associated with the Regionalist movement. Upon returning to the city after failing out of the Ontario College of Art (OCA) in 1960, he became an early advocate of Regionalism. He cofounded the Nihilist Party of Canada, a pseudo–political group that organized annual picnics, and the legendary Canadian noise band the Nihilist Spasm Band, and was the driving force behind *Region* magazine and Region Gallery. Describing *Region* magazine as "chock full of items of interest from the forest city,"[19] Curnoe imagined the publication as a forum for London's young artists and writers to publish experimental writing about local subjects, not always related to art. In its pages, for instance, painter Clark McDougall wrote about a reclusive St. Thomas-area farmer who had amassed a collection of empty Carnation Milk tins and fashioned them into a room-sized sculpture.[20] Through McDougall's article, the work drew the attention of Pierre Théberge, a curator at the National Gallery of Canada, who ultimately showed the assemblage at the Biennial of Native Art in Bratislava, Czechoslovakia, in 1969 as Canada's official entry; the work won a prize at the festival and joined the National Gallery of Canada's collection a year later.[21] Such idiosyncratic and regional cultural expressions were the kind Curnoe championed in the pages of *Region*, which offered a viable way for his work and publishing to valorize everyday life in the region.

Curnoe, along with Jack Chambers, Brian Dibb, Art Pratten, Larry Russell, Tony Urquhart, Bernice Vincent, and Don Vincent, founded Region Gallery on November 3, 1962, taking inspiration from Garret Gallery, a small cooperative run by OCA drawing and painting students in Toronto while he was a student there. Employing a DIY approach, Region Gallery's members together sublet the front section of a framing shop at 521 Richmond Street, keeping the small gallery open during regular store hours. They applied to the Canada Council for the Arts for programming funds but were unsuccessful as it did not support cooperative applications at the time. The gallery folded in late 1963 when the framing shop began keeping irregular hours, but despite its short life, the gallery created a space where young artists could experiment with forms of art-making unrecognized and unsupported by the city's main public art gallery, the London Art Gallery (LAG). Not coincidentally, 1962 saw the first of two high-profile run-ins between Curnoe's circle and the LAG. Led by Curnoe, many of the artists who established Region Gallery, as well as Joyce Wieland and Michael Snow, staged a happening that "wrecked" the LAG, as Wieland reportedly described it, making an enemy out of the gallery's curator, Clare Bice.[22]

Opposition to the LAG was a driving factor behind the penchant for collective action in London in the 1960s. Region Gallery's first exhibition featured work by its founding members, who were all in their twenties or early thirties and increasingly frustrated by the work celebrated in London's official art circles, which Curnoe characterized as "completely smothered by out-of-date sophistication."[23] It featured artwork along with objects collected by the artists, such as window frames, railway lights, and umbrella stands, that were meant to relate somehow to the idea of the region. A review in the *London Free Press* described the gallery as a "home [away] from home" where local artists could display "the things they are interested in and which may or may not appeal to people who visit public galleries."[24] Thus, in response to the outmoded art scene sanctioned by the LAG, Region Gallery proposed a short-term and radical alternative, and set the stage for future collective experimentation in London.

While Reaney's approach to Regionalism explored myths and what they meant to the local community, Curnoe's approach, as seen in his writing and artwork over thirty years, involved mythologizing the local through anecdotes about life in London. For example, in a column he wrote for *Region*, Curnoe described going to various places in town with artist Brian Dibb to get vacuum cleaners and vacuum cleaner parts. "I now have 4 vacuum cleaners," he wrote by way of a conclusion to the short piece. "The vacuum cleaners are called No. 1 Torrington electric vac, No. 2 Premier Duplex, No. 3 Beatty Storm Cleaner, No. 4 Royal."[25] Daily observations such as these were often the subjects of his regular columns for another local publication entitled *20 Cents Magazine*, many issues of which featured stream of consciousness reflections, whether on music as it aired on the radio, trips that he took, or reports detailing local events that he attended.

The matter-of-fact documentation of London in Curnoe's writing for *Region* and *20 Cents Magazine* is found in his artwork from the period as well. Early collages and stamp drawings were composed of scraps of life from London—e.g., bus transfers, newspaper clippings, prescription cards, train tickets, and matchbooks—and took inspiration from the artist's immediate surroundings, thoughts, and observations, including boys he knew growing up, words lingering in his mind, a walk through Victoria Park, or the distance from his studio to the post office. By the end of the 1960s, Curnoe began incorporating these details into large, all-text paintings such as *24 Hourly Notes* (1966), a series of twenty-four panels onto which he recorded notes once an hour for a whole day. Some of the entries describe his interaction with friends, such as "Jim is here so is Dave, I called him John by mistake," while others describe commonplace observations of a cold December day—"Sore ass, sirens, they're at the Jack tar, now the fire trucks"—all in a dry tone resembling his *Region* articles.

In both his articles and artwork, Curnoe often took extra care to record the exact locations and the names of the people who inhabited his world, players in London's cultural community, including other artists, members of the Nihilist Party and Nihilist Spasm Band, contributors to *Region* and *20 Cents Magazine*, artists involved in Canadian Artists' Representation, and board members of the Region and 20/20 galleries, but also local residents and childhood friends. Curnoe was, therefore, not only an artist, but also a facilitator and social catalyst who brought people together and also inducted them, as critic Sarah Milroy would describe it, into "his pantheon of local heroes."[26] Viewed and read over time, his artwork and writing created a vision of London through repeated references while *Region* and Region Gallery created a space where his vision of London could be performed. As such, *Region* and Region Gallery embodied more than just physical spaces where regionalist art could be disseminated. They were in fact social spaces where Regionalism could be willed into being.

A Region of the Mind

In the late 1960s and early 1970s, London's cooperative organizations began looking to new audiences and communities, adopting more outward-looking mandates, while cracks began to appear in the idea of Regionalism as a closed system. Where Region Gallery and the Alpha Centre stubbornly clung to their local roots, the 20/20 Gallery (1966–70) and Canadian Artists' Representation (1967–) offered platforms where London artists could participate in the national cultural arena. One of the precipitating factors for these expanded horizons was the exhibition *The Heart of London* (1966), curated by Pierre Théberge for the National Gallery of Canada, which featured the work of eleven London artists and travelled across the country, consequently solidifying London's position on the national scene.[27] London artists began regularly being featured in the pages of *artscanada* and participating in exhibitions in Toronto and elsewhere in the country.

The 20/20 Gallery opened on the second floor of 68 ½ King Street, around the corner from the Alpha Centre, and was helmed by a mix of working artists (Jack Chambers, Greg Curnoe, Rae Davis, Murray Favro, and Tony Urquhart) and art supporters (John Davis, Geoffrey and Goldie Rans, Richard Shroyer, Ross Woodman, and Archie Young). In circumstances similar to those that led to the establishment of Region Gallery four years earlier, the foundation of 20/20 Gallery was preceded by a second high-profile run-in between London's young, and increasingly influential, artists and Bice. In a show of contempt for the LAG curator, Curnoe, Favro, and Bernice Vincent removed their artwork from the gallery mid-exhibition after Bice barred a painting by John Boyle from the 27th Western Ontario Exhibition. The story played out in the local press and London's young artists won popular support in the dispute.[28]

Positioning itself in direct opposition to the LAG, the 20/20 Gallery had a very specific mandate to showcase the work of London's emerging artists, to present major solo shows by Canadian and international artists, and to support experimental works by local and nonlocal artists.[29] In a marked break from the precedent set at Region Gallery, 20/20 Gallery opened with an exhibition by a non-London artist—an exhibition of Michael Snow's *Walking Women* paintings (1961–67). Between 1966 and 1970, the gallery presented important solo exhibitions of local artists Jack Chambers, Greg Curnoe, Paterson Ewen, and Robert Fones, as well as Canadian artists Serge Lemoine, Guido Molinari, and Joyce Wieland. Besides its commitment to support emerging and experimental artists through its exhibition program, 20/20 Gallery was the first gallery in Canada to pay artist fees and the first alternative gallery to receive funding from the Canada Council for the Arts—two significant milestones in the development of artist-run centres in Canada.[30] In this sense, 20/20 Gallery's members sought to operate it as a professional space that could rival established public institutions in terms of its ability to receive legitimacy among artists working within Canada and elsewhere.

In stark contrast to Region Gallery, 20/20 Gallery's members had larger ambitions for the geographic scale and artistic aims of their exhibitions as demonstrated by the presentation of *Swinging London* (1968) and a Bruce Nauman solo exhibition (1970). Organized by Tony Urquhart, *Swinging London* featured the work of twenty-four

London-based artists and toured Ontario for two years, thus providing greater visibility to the exhibition's artists within the larger region. Robert C. MacKenzie, editor of *20 Cents Magazine*, observed that *Swinging London* was an attempt to demonstrate that the cooperative "could mount a show of its own artists without big-gallery initiative, and organize its circulation, and allow the exhibiting artists to be the only ones to benefit financially from its circulation."[31] Nauman's solo exhibition further illustrates the gallery members' ambitions to look not merely inward but toward other contexts for art. Paradoxically, it was one of the only exhibitions at the gallery organized almost entirely by Curnoe himself, who was famously anti-American.[32] Indeed, only one month after Nauman's exhibition at the 20/20 Gallery, Curnoe published a tongue-in-cheek nationalist manifesto entitled *Amendment to Continental Refusal* in the pages of *20 Cents Magazine*. Statement #29 of that document reads: "All American art in Canada to be exhibited in a degenerate art exhibit & then to be auctioned off in the States."[33]

This apparent contradiction between Curnoe's anti-Americanism and his enthusiasm for working with Nauman indicates that his approach to American artists was more nuanced than his hyper-nationalist work at the end of the 1960s and early 1970s would suggest. Some insight into the provincialism trap that Curnoe was reacting against is helpful here for discussing the role that anti-Americanism played in his idea of Regionalism. The world of the provincial artist, Terry Smith argued, is "replete with tensions between two antithetical terms: a defiant urge to localism…and a reluctant recognition that the generative innovations in art, and the criteria for standards of quality, originality, interest, forcefulness, etc. are determined externally."[34] Although Smith's article was written in 1974,

Curnoe expressed this anxiety concerning provincialism as early as 1966 in a short piece for *Canadian Art* magazine: "In the 60s the U.S. influence here is enormous," he wrote. "After all, artists can only record and respond to what they are exposed to. That is why I live in London, Ontario. That is why [Michael] Snow and [Les] Levine have moved to New York. You either go to the source of the main influences or to the roots of your own experience."[35] In this passage, Curnoe lays bare the correlation between the American cultural industry and his drive to Regionalism. In his mind, the provincial artist had only two tactics to resist the provincialism problem: to emulate the centre or to propose an alternative. Regionalism was his alternative.

Curnoe's satirical drawing *Ontario University Fine Art Teachers Manual © 1976 Global Teaching Aids, Des Moines, Iowa* (1980) could very well be a literal illustration of Smith's article. The drawing depicts the mind of an Ontario post-secondary student split between an international awareness fuelled by New York and other American cities and a provincialism fed by global art capitals such as Berlin, London, UK, and Paris. Curnoe portrays Toronto as a supplicant to New York's internationalist hegemony while London and Ottawa appear to exert no influence on the mind of the student. The drawing illustrates Curnoe's anxiety about American influence on Canadian art consciousness and sheds light on the fine balance that the 20/20 Gallery artists strived to maintain between local, regional, national, and international content. *Swinging London* and Bruce Nauman's exhibition signalled a desire to be nationally and even internationally relevant without being part of a global art system that privileged international styles over local expressions.

Writer Ross Woodman addresses the nature of this balance and argues that London's production in the 1960s was no more regional in its outlook than the work being produced in New York, writing: "the expansion of [New York's] regionalism into an international style can no more be attributed to intrinsic aesthetic values than the U.S. presence in Viet Nam can be attributed to intrinsic moral values."[36] The assumption was not that their regional experience was superior to any other, but that London artists should not subvert their local production to international trends that did not reflect their own experiences. In the same article, Woodman addresses the effect of provincialism on Regionalism in psychological terms: "Regionalism in London is essentially a region of the mind.... It subordinates geographical or historical origins to psychic origins, and thus both establishes and communicates a ground free of the fakery of the colonial scrim."[37] Curnoe's nationalist work rejects the soft colonialism of the American culture industry while recognizing it as part of the regional story. The 20/20 Gallery's programming belied the national ambitions of its members who wished to connect their regionalist art to a broader audience while simultaneously having this art seen as equal to movements already recognized internationally.

Painter and filmmaker Jack Chambers, who, along with Curnoe, was instrumental in the Region Gallery and the 20/20 Gallery, sought to apply the innovations of those two institutions to the national stage, specifically in the realm of fair pay for artists. In 1967, the year after the 20/20 Gallery opened and began paying exhibition fees to artists, Chambers received a request from the National Gallery of Canada to reproduce an image of one of his paintings. The request offered no payment and implied that they did not actually need his permission for the project. Chambers replied in a letter, copied to other participating artists, demanding fair payment for the reproduction of their work.[38] The debacle ultimately led to the development of Canadian Artists'

Representation (CAR), a national advocacy group for artists that is today known by its bilingual name, Canadian Artists' Representation/Le Front des artistes canadiens. Chambers, Kim Ondaatje, and Tony Urquhart formed the first CAR executive, and, in 1971, the first CAR national conference took place in Winnipeg, where Chambers was elected president. Four years later, CAR successfully negotiated for payment of artists' exhibition fees in all public museums and art galleries in Canada, an innovation established at the 20/20 Gallery that evolved into the national standard and set an international precedent.[39]

The expansion of London's early-1960s collectivist ideology into a historic national campaign corresponds to Chambers's approach to Regionalism, which used local subject matter to work through ideas and styles that he was exposed to in Europe and the United States. Owing perhaps to his time spent studying painting in Spain in the late 1950s, he was much more open to outside influences and did not share Curnoe's anti-American position, travelling often in the United States before his death in 1978. Chambers's late-career work, which he called Perceptual Realism,[40] was a reaction to American photorealist painting infused with the classicism of his European influences and distilled through intimate documentary-like depictions of his personal life.[41] Almost all of his paintings from this era were created from photographic and film documents, and his objective was to explore the universal phenomenology of perception. His rooting in documentary was a way to investigate the experiences of perception and his focus on a regional subject matter was a means to this end.

Chambers's subject matter was domestic and deeply personal. His wife and children were often the central focus in his work, such as in *Sunday Morning No. 2* (1968–70), but he also turned his attention to London, famously in

401 towards London No. 1 (1968–69) and *Victoria Hospital* (1969–70). His family was perhaps never more intimately portrayed than in his 1970 film *The Hart of London*, which includes long scenes with his wife and two sons. Influenced by the pioneering American filmmaker Stan Brakhage's childbirth films, including *Window Water Baby Moving* (1958), Chambers wove a childbirth scene together with newsreel footage and scenes he shot of London into a seventy-nine-minute meditation on death and rebirth. Brakhage would later call *The Hart of London* "one of the greatest films ever made."[42] While the city of London and Chambers's family are central to this work, his capacity to use local and personal stories to explore the structures of avant-garde film and American and European painting flies in the face of the kind of Regionalism espoused in the pages of *Alphabet* and *Region*, but nevertheless demonstrates that, by the end of the decade, the ideas that had fermented in the city in the 1960s were engaging with broader discourses in contemporary art.

The Shifting Geographies of Regionalism

By the 1970s, a new generation began making art and exhibiting in London, and new cooperative institutions evolved to reflect the changing community. For instance, Montreal-based painter Patterson Ewen moved to London in 1968 and completely reimagined his style. Young artists such as Robert Fones, Becky Singleton, Sandra Semchuk, Spring Hurlbut, and Wyn Gelyense began experimenting with conceptualism, filmmaking, installation, and sculpture in new and interesting ways. Ron Benner and Jamelie Hassan, two artists raised in London, travelled extensively throughout the Americas and the Middle East and continually brought global, social, and political discourses back to the city as new frames of reference for London's artists. Two cooperative galleries, the Forest City Gallery (1973–) and the Embassy Cultural House (1983–90), emerged as venues for the next generation of artists who successfully sought new funding available to artist-run centres. More than any of the London cooperatives before, the Forest City Gallery and the Embassy Cultural House looked to global rather than North American subjects and artists in order to participate in a wider conversation about art. The Regionalism of the previous generation, as a distinctive approach based in local experiences, began to apply less to the work produced by the succeeding generation and to the direction cooperative institutions were taking in their exhibition programs. Still, as the city's artists and cooperatives opened up to global experiences, the ideology of Regionalism continued as an undercurrent in work that often explored how global political issues affected a distinctly local social consciousness.

After the 20/20 Gallery closed in 1970, London was without an alternative gallery to the LAG until 1973, leaving a gap in the community. In the meantime, some artists organized makeshift, one-off exhibitions including *The Warehouse Show*, a cooperative sculpture exhibition held in June 1970,[43] and a week-long solo exhibition by Curnoe, who was by then an established artist, in a rented hotel room in February 1972.[44] Dave Gordon and Jamelie Hassan ran a small independent gallery in the front of a downtown bookstore in 1973, but found that the owner exerted too much control over their programs. After their dispute with the bookstore owner, Gordon and Hassan approached Bob Bozak, Greg Curnoe, Murray Favro, kerry ferris, Robert Fones, Ron Martin, and Raymond Sedge to open the Forest City Gallery in a rented space at 432 Richmond Street.[45] Taking advantage of the new Canada Council for the Arts and Ontario Arts Council support for parallel galleries, the collective's members exhibited the work of many local and Canadian artists throughout the 1970s, and, in 1980 and 1984, they instigated exchanges with galleries in Mexico and Cuba, with Hassan initiating the 1980 exchange after meeting Gildo Gonzalez of the Agora-Fonopas Gallery in Merida, Mexico. To save on costs, all the pieces included in the exhibition were works on paper, and no more were sent than could be carried by a single person on a commercial flight. Ultimately, ten local artists sent work to Mexico and seven artists from the Yucatán sent their work to London in exchange.[46] Like *Swinging London* in 1968, *London/Merida Exchange* demonstrated that the community could produce an exhibition of its own artists, without the support of a museum, and promote local culture to new audiences on its own terms.

By reaching out to other peripheral centres, the members of the Forest City Gallery signalled a new direction in which transnational dialogues eschewed traditional art centres in favour of other regional experiences. In her correspondence with Gonzalez, Hassan outlines why she felt the exchange was important for the Forest City Gallery, writing: "We as an artist directed centre are concerned with the expression of art within our region as well as those areas such as yourselves, whose priorities are the stimulation of protection of culture within a certain geography."[47] The framework for international dialogue that Hassan set up in the *London/Merida Exchange* carries through the rest of her career as an artist and as a facilitator, and represents a significant expansion of London's deep-rooted Regionalist ideology to include a global exchange of ideas as part of the regional ethos.

In *Beyrouth...is war art?* (1980), an installation that Hassan executed at the Forest City Gallery the same year as *London/Merida Exchange*, the artist destroyed the back wall of the gallery in a simulation of a rocket attack and juxtaposed this violent intervention with photographs of actual rocket attacks in Lebanon. In discussing this work, critic Dot Tuer writes: "The disjuncture between the place Hassan speaks from and a sense of being shaped by her travels to her parents' homeland produces an ethical imperative to speak to the experience of war and repression as part of, and not distinct from, a Canadian context."[48] Destroying part of the gallery that she helped to create physically connected Hassan's life in London to her parents' homeland in the Middle East. For Hassan, however, London is part of a global world and not separate from political violence, even if it takes place halfway around the globe.

This desire to connect London to global political issues led Benner and Hassan to later resign from the Forest City Gallery, frustrated by an unwillingness of the artist board to support programs that responded to politically pertinent issues at home and abroad.[49] In response, Benner and Hassan, along with musician Eric Stach, in 1983 founded the Embassy Cultural House (ECH), which became the meeting place for London's post-1960s generation of artists. The idea for the gallery came from Hassan's sister, who owned and operated the Embassy Hotel, a tavern on Dundas Street in the city's east end, when she proposed the idea of operating it out of what was the ground-floor restaurant of the hotel. The artists of the ECH did not apply for operating funds, preferring the flexibility of producing projects through project grants from the Canada Council for the Arts and the Ontario Arts Council instead. Programming at the ECH reimagined and put into practice Regionalism by opening it up to global influence, situating London within the broader social and political world, as Hassan had begun earlier at the Forest City Gallery.

The Embassy Hotel was unlike contemporary artistic hotel projects such as the Drake or Gladstone hotels in Toronto.[50] For instance, unlike the clientele of the Drake and Gladstone, about 60 percent of the residents of the forty-room, $65-a-week Embassy Hotel were on welfare, fixed incomes, or in other financially marginal circumstances and living there on a full-time basis. Instead of facilitating gentrification, the ECH helped the neighbourhood resist it with ECH artists often working as advocates for the disenfranchised communities in the area by participating in a coalition of residents to protect heritage sites and prevent crippling development. The cooperative's exhibitions and programs often examined how the global political concerns of the 1980s related to this economically depressed part of the city and its denizens. Speaking at the Dia Foundation in 1989, Hassan described their approach to programming as involving "an in-depth analysis…of critical concerns relevant to our specific neighbourhood and city, as well as to the national and international contexts."[51] This critical focus on local concerns was manifest in several multi-part projects including a series of site-specific installations in the rooms of many of the hotel's residents, a major exhibition and publication on the topic of the emergent HIV/AIDS crisis, and projects that highlighted work of Indigenous artists and artists of colour. The ECH closed in 1990 after the relationship between the artists and hotel management became strained and Benner and Hassan resigned from the board.

Owing to far-reaching travel and global political causes, Benner and Hassan introduced new ideas of collectivism and forms of alternative institutions to London. Along with these changing institutions came new ways of making global art and politics relevant to local experiences, a reversal of the stated goals of Regionalism at the start of the 1960s. Even with these broadening horizons, the work produced in these institutions and by these artists never ceased to relate back to a local social consciousness. Regionalism's recognition of the primacy of local experience had transformed through Benner and Hassan into a form of social practice concerned with the realities of life in London. Exchanges with South and Central America plugged these realities into a global exchange of ideas that rejected the United States' hegemony in culture and politics. The Forest City Gallery and the Embassy Cultural House both enabled local artists to bring new conversations into the life of the community. And from those new conversations, new local cultural expressions emerged.

Regionalism, Provincialism, and Internationalism

The story of London's collective organizations is part of a moment in Canadian art that saw the establishment of a cross-country system of artist-run centres and galleries, a history that is eloquently outlined in AA Bronson's wide-ranging study *From Sea to Shining Sea*.[52] Bronson describes a scene in Canada at the end of the 1960s where museums and magazines were openly hostile to the work of young artists. "Knowing the impossibility of an art scene without real museums (the Art Gallery of Ontario was not a *real* museum for us)," he wrote in 1983, "we laboured to structure…artist-run galleries, artists' video, and artist-run magazines. And that allowed us to allow ourselves to see ourselves as an art scene."[53] The reordering of Canada's cultural ecology in the 1970s was a grassroots phenomenon that took place across the nation as artists came up against rigid institutional structures that could not adapt to the rapidly changing nature of the visual arts. The unique brand of collectivism that developed in London in the 1960s predated that history by a decade and contributed to the national development of artist-run centres in two measurable ways. First, London collectives established a relationship with the Canada Council for the Arts that would set the model for how the first generation of artist-run centres in Canada were funded, and second, London artists introduced the idea of exhibition fees and fought to have them instituted across the country.

Similarly, London's Regionalist movement evolved as part of a wide range of regional movements in Canada. In the 1960s, artists in cities like Vancouver, Halifax, and Regina began contributing to a national conversation that had previously been dominated by Montreal and Toronto. Unlike regional movements in these other cities, Regionalism in London did not have a unifying aesthetic form; instead, London's experimental artists pursued a wide range of styles and subjects. Distinguishing itself from an earlier American and Canadian regionalism in the nineteenth and twentieth centuries, Regionalism in London was less focused on simply representing local subjects than it was on creating new forms from the foundation of local experience. London artists embraced provincialism as a way of subverting its power, but that in itself does not make a movement. As curator Philip Monk writes, "Internationalism is a regionalism that people pay attention to."[54] What made London's Regionalist movement a regionalism that people paid attention to is that London artists went beyond simply embracing their provincialism and explored how their own imposed marginalization positioned them in an increasingly connected world. Their cooperatives gave them the means to do so.

This essay has outlined how London's collective organizations were integral to the shaping of an ideology of Regionalism in the work of several of its artists across generations. It reveals how these artists set up cooperatives as incubators to foster ideas of Regionalism and how these institutions acted as social spaces where the community could perform itself. The structures of collectives in London evolved alongside the ever-changing ideology of Regionalism as new artists became involved and more interest began focusing on the community. As the ideas of Regionalism began reaching wider audiences at the end of the 1960s, London's collectives influenced the direction of artist cooperatives in Canada, helping to shape the parallel system of galleries in the 1970s. In this way, these two unique and interrelated manifestations of local culture in London in the 1960s grew together to influence the national conversation.

Through their work and through their cooperative institutions, London artists willed their community into being; they created an image of themselves and transformed that image into reality. This process is what George Bowering was referring to when he called Regionalism a performance of a social consciousness. London's collective institutions and publications were more than just meeting places that enabled this local movement to flourish; in a movement defined, as I've argued, by community involvement, they became transformative spaces. The discussion of Regionalism in London is therefore enriched when we consider the way that collectivism brought these aesthetically individual artists together to shape and be shaped by the priorities of the movement. This generative process is the most remarkable contribution of the London Regionalists to the Canadian and international history of artist institutions.

1. James Reaney, *Colours in the Dark* (Vancouver: Talonbooks, 1969), 90.

2. Barry Lord, "What London, Ontario, Has That Everywhere Else Needs," *Art in America*, September/October 1969, 103.

3. Robert McKaskell, *Regionalism in London: Art in the 60s*, exhibition brochure (London: McIntosh Gallery, 1983).

4. Greg Curnoe in 1969 (with Robert Murray and Iain Baxter) and Wyn Geleynse in 1987.

5. The Nihilist Spasm Band played a series of concerts in Paris in October 1969, including three during the opening of the Sixième Biennale des Jeunes and one at the Galerie de France. The following week they performed two concerts at the Institute of Contemporary Art in London, UK. See Pierre Théberge, "Confessions of a Nihilist Spasm Band Addict," *artscanada*, December 1969, 67–68.

6. Walter Redinger in 1972 (with Gershon Iskowitz); Greg Curnoe in 1976; Ron Martin in 1978 (with Henry Saxe); and Paterson Ewen in 1982.

7. Mary Malone, "Portraits of Three Artists," *London Magazine*, November 1988, 46.

8. A recent and significant example of this type of scholarship can be found in *Traffic: Conceptual Art in Canada, 1965–1980*, an exhibition and publication that explores conceptualism in Canada by focusing on regional manifestations in Vancouver, Calgary, Winnipeg, Edmonton, Toronto, London, Montreal, and Halifax. See Grant Arnold and Karen Henry, eds., *Traffic: Conceptual Art in Canada, 1965–1980* (Vancouver: Vancouver Art Gallery; Edmonton: Art Gallery of Alberta; Toronto: Justina M. Barnicke Gallery; Montreal: Leonard and Bina Ellen Art Gallery; Halifax: Halifax INK, 2012).

9. A discussion of how regionalism is applied by these three authors can be found in Virginia Nixon, "The Concept of 'Regionalism' in Canadian Art History," *Journal of Canadian Art History/Annales d'histoire de l'art Canadien* 10, no. 1 (1987), 30–40.

10. J. Russell Harper discusses Carl Schaefer and Charles Comfort's work in his chapter "Regionalism in the 1930s," in *Painting in Canada: A History*, 2nd ed. (Toronto: University of Toronto Press, 1977), 304–13.

11. George Bowering, "Reaney's Region," in *Approaches to the Work of James Reaney*, ed. Stan Dragland (Toronto: ECW Press, 1983), 3.

12. Terry Smith, "The Provincialism Problem," *Artforum*, September 1974, 54–59. Reprinted in the *Journal of Art Historiography*, no. 4 (June 2011).

13. Emphasis in the original. Bowering, "Reaney's Region," 13.

14. James Reaney, "Editorial," *Alphabet* 4 (June 1962), 3.

15. James Reaney, "Editorial," *Alphabet* 1 (Sept 1960), 3.

16. Bowering, "Reaney's Region," 6.

17. The three plays that make up *The Donnellys* trilogy are *Sticks & Stones* (1975), *The St. Nicholas Hotel* (1976), and *Handcuffs* (1977). James Reaney, *The Donnellys* (Vancouver: Porcepic Books, 1983).

18. William Toye, ed., "Southern Ontario Gothic," in *The Concise Oxford Companion to Canadian Literature* (Oxford: Oxford University Press, 2001), 455–56.

19. Greg Curnoe, "Editorial," *Region* 8 (c. 1964–65).

20. Clark McDougall, "Dan Patterson's Carnation Milk Tins," *Region* 5 (February 1963).

21. County of Elgin Women's Institutes Tweedsmuir Histories Archive.

22. Nancy Geddes Poole, *The Art of London* (London, ON: Blackpool Press, 1984), 131.

23. Greg Curnoe, letter to Helen Hodgson, c. March 1963. Greg Curnoe Fonds, Art Gallery of Ontario.

24. Lenore Crawford, "Artists Find a 'Home from Home' at London's Latest Art Gallery," *London Free Press*, January 19, 1963.

25. Greg Curnoe, "Saturday 4:00," *Region* 4 (c. 1963–64).

26. Sarah Milroy, "Greg Curnoe: Time Machines," in *Greg Curnoe: Life & Stuff*, eds. Dennis Reid and Matthew Teitelbaum (Toronto: Art Gallery of Ontario; Vancouver: Douglas & McIntyre, 2001), 46.

27. Participating artists in *The Heart of London* were John Boyle, Jack Chambers, Greg Curnoe, Murray Favro, Bev Kelly, Ron Martin, David Rabinowitch, Royden Rabinowitch, Walter Redinger, Tony Urquhart, and Ed Zelenack. See Pierre Théberge, *The Heart of London*, exhibition catalogue (Ottawa: National Gallery of Canada, 1966).

28. See "Three Artists Intend to Withdraw Exhibits in Gallery Dispute," *London Free Press*, May 10, 1966, and "Three Artists Quit Show," *Toronto Daily Star*, May 11, 1966.

29. 20/20 Gallery press release, April 27, 1970. 20/20 Gallery Fonds, London Public Library.

30. Greg Curnoe, "Five Co-op Galleries in Toronto and London from 1957 to 1992" (paper presented at an unknown conference, Montreal, October 1992). Transcript from Greg Curnoe's artist file at the London Public Library.

31. Robert C. McKenzie, "20/20 Gallery Closes," *20 Cents Magazine*, September 1970.

32. The "Correspondence" file in the Greg Curnoe Fonds at the Art Gallery of Ontario contains several letters and postcards between Curnoe and Nauman from 1969 and 1970 outlining the coordination of the exhibition.

33. Greg Curnoe, "Amendment to Continental Refusal," *20 Cents Magazine*, April 1970.

34. Smith, "The Provincialism Problem," 3.

35. Greg Curnoe, as part of "Ten Artists in Search of Canadian Art," *Canadian Art*, January 1966, 64.

36. Ross Woodman, "London (Ont.): A New Regionalism," *artscanada*, August/September 1967.

37. Ibid.

38. Poole, *The Art of London*, 143.

39. "CARFAC History," Canadian Artists' Representation/Le Front des artistes canadiens, accessed January 7, 2012, http://fillip.ca/car5.

40. Jack Chambers, "Perceptual Realism," *artscanada*, October 1969, 7–13.

41. Mark A. Cheetham, "Past the 401: The International Classicism of Jack Chambers," in *Jack Chambers: Light, Spirit, Time, Place, and Light*, ed. Dennis Reid (Toronto: Art Gallery of Ontario, 2011), 130–31.

42. Stan Brakhage, "The Hart of London: A Document of the City," in *The Films of Jack Chambers*, ed. Kathryn Elder (Toronto: Cinematheque Ontario; Bloomington: Indiana University Press, 2002), 123.

43. The exhibition featured sculptures by Don Bonham, Bob Bozak, Michael Durham, David Gordon, Robin Hobbs, Terry Hughes, Steve Parzybok, and Jeff Rubinoff. See Stephen Joy, "The Warehouse Show, June 1970," *artscanada*, August 1970, 63.

44. Victor Coleman, "Knowing the Surface," *artscanada*, February/March 1972, 71–72.

45. The story of the founding of the

Forest City Gallery is told by Bernice Vincent in "Bernice Vincent on the Origins of the Forest City Gallery," in *Forest City Gallery 1973–1993, 20th Anniversary Issue* (London, ON: Forest City Gallery, 1993), 12–16.

46. The participating London artists were Ron Benner, Greg Curnoe, Christopher Dewdney, Lise Downe, kerry ferris, Jim Gillies, Jamelie Hassan, Sam Krizan, George Lagrady, and Bogdan Zarski.

47. Jamelie Hassan, letter to Mr. Gildo Gonzalez, April 3, 1980. Forest City Gallery Fonds, McIntosh Gallery, University of Western Ontario.

48. Dot Tuer, "At the Far Edge of Home," in *Jamelie Hassan: At the Far Edge of Words* (London: Museum London; Vancouver: Morris and Helen Belkin Art Gallery, 2009), 22.

49. In a 1993 interview Hassan stated: "I felt that the kind of political/activist work that I was doing—and wanting to see more support for it in the Forest City Gallery—that there was not a particularly good reception to that kind of work and that any kind of programming that had been done at the Forest City Gallery, throughout the seventies, around these issues had been brought in mostly by myself and Ron Benner." See Jamelie Hassan, "Interview with Jamelie Hassan," interview by uncredited interviewer, November 25, 1993, transcript, Embassy Cultural House Fonds, London Public Library.

50. In 2010 I published an article in *FUSE Magazine* about the Embassy Cultural House. See Christopher Régimbal, "A Fire at the Embassy Hotel," *FUSE Magazine*, Summer 2010, 12–15.

51. Jamelie Hassan, "Planning: Power, Politics, People," Dia Art Foundation discussion, in *If You Lived Here: The City in Art, Theory, and Social Activism. A Project by Martha Rosler*, ed. Brian Wallis (Seattle: Bay Press, 1991), 247.

52. AA Bronson, *From Sea to Shining Sea* (Toronto: Power Plant, 1987).

53. AA Bronson, "The Humiliation of the Bureaucrat: Artist-Run Centres as Museums by Artists," in *Museums by Artists*, eds. AA Bronson and Peggy Gale (Toronto: Art Metropole, 1983), 30.

54. Philip Monk, "Five Questions of Regionalism," *Open Letter*, series 11, no. 5 (Summer 2002).

Sarah Lowndes

Learning to Get Along with People We Don't Like

Artist-Led Projects in Glasgow

When Jeff Khonsary, the Artistic Director of Fillip, first wrote to me about participating in International Artist Initiated at David Dale Gallery, Glasgow,[1] he posed a single question that might shape my response, which was, "Should artists professionalize?" I think that question has very interesting resonances in Glasgow today.

I will start with a few general comments about DIY practices and then relate that to the current situation in Glasgow in the mid-2010s, focusing on three examples of artist-run institutions from the local area that were founded in the 1980s: Glasgow Women's Library (GWL), Transmission Gallery, and the Free University. I have chosen these examples in part due to their longevity, as both GWL and Transmission are still in operation, and the Free University, while no longer extant, lives on as a model for similar local organizations today. All three examples can be considered as having implemented "best approaches" in their development and continuance as sustainable and independent creative enterprises. I will consider three possible theoretical and developmental models in relationship to my examples—governmentality theory, deliberative democracy, and agonistic pluralism—as further ways of thinking through what we might consider to be best practices for artist-led projects.

I feel that artists should not necessarily professionalize but should instead organize in such a way that they can access public funding, secure documentation and longevity for their projects (if appropriate), and ultimately influence decisions about how their local community is run. Securing public subsidies to support such things as operating costs and materials also allows an artist to retain the positive aspects of amateurism in relation to their practice, meaning that a given path can be pursued for the love of that pursuit without full recourse to monetizing that activity. Of course, the avant-garde model of the "bedroom producer"—who works alone on small-scale, esoteric, and self-limited projects with low operational costs, such as composing electronic music or writing a blog—obviates the risk, outlined by critic Peter Bürger in *Theory of the Avant-Garde*, of how engagement with the existing art world may entail a compromise that neutralizes the work. However, those artists who also seek to engage with "official" cultural organizations such as governmental bodies have increased possibilities to secure both a physical civic space and the possibility of documenting and circulating their work. Through that engagement, they may also be considered as having taken responsibility for the tenor of the wider society in which they operate. These may be aims inconsistent with self-limiting artist-led projects that are informed and defined by their ephemerality.

As an independent writer and curator, my practice often concerns documenting work that is ephemeral, process-based, and performative, perhaps in part to try to save something of that work for the future. I was very struck recently by a line in art historian Kenneth Clark's book *Civilisation*, in which he describes how early Norsemen felt so under threat due to fear of war, fear of invasion, and fear of plague and famine, and so undermined by energy-sapping meaningless rituals and mystery religions, that they lacked the confidence to act—it simply wasn't worthwhile to construct things or to plant trees: "And for that reason it didn't occur to them to build stone houses or to write books." He continues, "Of course civilisation requires a modicum of material prosperity—enough to provide a little leisure. But far more it requires confidence—confidence in the society in which it lives."[2] He further writes about the importance of a sense of permanence, pointing out that, whereas the early Norsemen lived in a permanent state of flux, others who were able to produce more lasting artifacts of their time—like the monks on the Scottish island of Iona who made the Book of Kells—had the prerequisite of a more settled situation in which to work. Clark's words resonated for me in terms of the Glasgow art scene, which emerged with great difficulty and with very little public support. Confidence, a modicum of material prosperity, and a settled place to work have been hard won and hard defended in a civic atmosphere that until relatively recently was, if not threatening, then certainly unreceptive. Those artist-initiated projects that have stayed the course since their inception in the 1980s were powered by more than the energy, will, and creative power of individuals. In every instance, their continuance was secured by the collective energies of a group who reached out to find support from other likeminded groups both within Glasgow and in other cities.

Today its labelling as a "creative city" is viewed as a driver of tourism and regeneration in Glasgow, as it is in many other post-Fordian cities, and so the terms of the struggle have changed. The central issue concerns how individuals and organizations might not only operate sustainable, independent, locally owned creative enterprises but also crucially be in a position to re-invest in the creative and educational possibilities of their local communities. Tonight's discussion is framed in terms of "artist-initiated projects," although I tend to see the issue within the wider context of DIY activity. Sociologist Kevin Wehr, in his book *DIY: The Search for Control and Self-Reliance in the*

21st Century, uses philosopher Jürgen Habermas's notion of the "colonization of the lifeworld" as a frame and mobilizes Karl Marx's concepts of "alienation" and "mystification" to examine "how social behaviors can be a conscious reply to a complex and fast-moving world, a nostalgia for simpler times past, or a just an economic impulse."[3] DIY-methodologies grew out of a desire for both thrift and self-reliance in the post–World War II years, which presaged a wider shift in the 1950s and '60s from the dominant top-down cultural model toward self-directed and self-realized modes of expression.

The American writer and anarchist Bob Black argues in his 1985 essay "The Abolition of Work" that "no-one should ever work," because work—defined as compulsory productive activity enforced by social or political means—is the source of most of the unhappiness in the world, eating up as it does time and inclination for friendship and what he calls "meaningful activity."[4] In contrast, DIY can be understood as a voluntary productive practice, resulting in meaningful activity that is not for profit, artist led, and supported by independent galleries, independent record labels, and independent publishers. How can we relate or reconcile that definition with the earlier question of "Should artists professionalize?" Does this entail a problematic combination of two approaches: the voluntary meaningful activity becoming compulsory and enforced? Is there a way to understand and negotiate a compromise without neutralizing the work?

In *Club Cultures: Music, Media and Subcultural Capital*, cultural sociologist Sarah Thornton outlines a pragmatic interconnectedness between youth and parent cultures, and suggests that the earlier writings of subculture theorists Stuart Hall, Tony Jefferson, and Dick Hebdige rely upon unsustainable binaries such as mainstream/subculture, resistance/submission, and parent/youth. The post-subculture city art scenes that have risen to global prominence since 1995, amid the rise of digital and internet technologies, such as those of Berlin and Glasgow, provide a means of exploring the repercussions of those advances for independent practitioners. In particular, these city's art scenes allow us to examine sociologist Chris Baker's theory that, following the rise of globalized culture facilitated by digital and internet technologies, "youth cultural difference is not necessarily a form of resistance but is better grasped as cultural capital or distinctions of taste."[5] Such distinctions of taste translate into trends for manufactured goods promoted through mass-media channels. This understanding of subculture—as an incubator for market-stimulating crazes—is accepted by most subsequent literature relating to "alternative" cultural activity, for example in the 2012 book *DIY Style: Fashion, Music and Global Digital Cultures* by sociocultural anthropologist Brent Luvaas. He writes: *The actual practice of DIY production, no matter how countercultural DIYers imagine it to be, poses no structural threat to the smooth running of a free market capitalist economy. Instead, DIY fuels entrepreneurship, contributes to economic growth, provides sources of income and labour to youth, as well as useful training in business and management skills, and of course, increases the total number of goods available on the market. In other words, the activities of DIY production further the ends of global capitalism even when the DIYers themselves stand against those ends.*[6]

My contention is that "alternative" activity is here being described as a style of production rather than an experiential process rooted in a particular time and place. Luvaas's understanding of DIY is rooted in production rather than in the process-based activity so central to many alternative scenes, which may not necessarily yield any tangible "goods" that can be sold. The processes associated with DIY are also discussed in curators Stine Hebert and Anne Szefer Karlsen's reader on recent art practices, *Self-Organised*, from 2012; however, Hebert and Szefer Karlsen describe these processes in a way that seems antithetical to an understanding of DIY as a movement rooted in resistance to capitalism. They write: *Our investigations have focused on self-organisation beyond the limiting labels of "alternative", "non-profit" or "artist-run", which have been the prevailing terms dominating discussions of both the subject and its history in recent times.… The field of self-organisation is therefore more complex than the conventional separatist approach entails. It has moved beyond a process of simply dissolving boundaries between institutional and non-institutional platforms to creating new possibilities.*[7]

"Non-profit" and "artist-run," as described by Hebert and Szefer Karlsen, are "limiting labels," but I understand these as guiding principles of the recent history of do-it-yourself practices. DIY strategies have transitioned from being marginal, to emergent, to their current position: co-opted by global capitalism, embedded within "official culture." As DIY strategies have travelled both geographically and through time, their application has changed according to each locale, each specific set of circumstances. What are the commonalities that link the examples together? That is, how can we trace a template of best approaches for sustainable, independent, locally owned creative enterprises? These include, but are not limited to, a comparative lack of economic pressure, the importance of art schools, and the significance of independent spaces that facilitate research, production, and distribution, such as libraries, bookstores, rehearsal and recording studios, workshops, galleries, bars, nightclubs, and online meeting places.

My overarching argument is that DIY is rooted in a form of democratic socialism, and therefore it's intrinsically motivated not by profit but rather by increasing the well-being of the participants through self-actualization. In most cases, DIY activity is in some way associated with disenfranchisement and often arises when conventional pathways to effect change are blocked. DIY can be characterized as the urge not only to create a new cultural form but also to transmit it to others on your own terms: as a means of engaged critical making that is informed by a resistance to consumer culture and motivated by a desire for empowerment. Unlike other creative practitioners, such as, for example, fashion designers, software engineers, and interior decorators, who usually produce work in consultation with and for sale to clients, the DIY practitioner is self-directed and produces something that may have an audience but not necessarily an intended end market. Indeed, the artist may decide not to sell, document, or disseminate their work, but rather to give away their work or destroy it. However, we must also keep in mind the relationship between DIY and entrepreneurship and explicitly address the importance of small-scale commerce in DIY cultural production since the 1980s, and in particular what we could describe as a convergence between an ideology based on autonomy and thrifty business practices, emblematic of 1990s independent and underground music scenes and aptly summarized in the punk band the Minutemen's slogan "We Jam Econo."

However, we can draw an important distinction between conventional business and DIY models followed in the UK by, for example, a major record label such as Virgin, as opposed to an independent label such as Rough Trade. Rough Trade publicly experimented with the business model of running a record label by offering its signed artists complete artistic control and a 50-50 split of all profits after costs. The more equitable relationship between artists and label established by Rough Trade, and later adopted by Factory Records in Manchester, among others, was indivisible from their nonprofit approach, by which the interests of the artistic community took precedence over wholly commercial concerns.

Although DIY activity is not motivated by profit, it may still generate profit. However, these funds are typically re-invested back into the relevant artistic community, as in the case of Dischord Records, founded in Washington, DC, in 1980. As founder Ian MacKaye explains in a history of the label: *In the beginning it was basically a volunteer arrangement as there was no money to pay anyone, but by the early '90s we were not only able to pay everyone, but also able to provide them with health insurance and other benefits. I've always considered this one of our most important achievements. Most businesses, including record labels, have used profits (or at least the fear of losing profits) as their guideline for operations. Because we have tried to approach the label as a mission of documentation as well as a community-based entity, we have managed to avoid many of the industry-standard practices. The fact that we are able to help support the people who work for us as well as pay royalties to the bands seems to be proof that such an approach is possible.*[8]

In Glasgow, projects that have resisted the values of neoliberalism since the 1980s have tended to apply similar approaches to those outlined by MacKaye, such as profit-sharing, community activism, collective working, and free educational initiatives.

Most of Glasgow's artist-initiated projects grew out of a frustration with the existing cultural provision. As artist Merlin James observes in his article on artist-led spaces in Glasgow for *Art in America*: *Bits of support for all this activity come from an intermittently sympathetic city council, and grants from the arts administration body Creative Scotland (formerly the Scottish Arts Council). But funding is often meager and the criteria for awarding it are frequently dubious. The best efforts rely on the energy and inventiveness of individuals and the proverbial shoestring budget.*[9]

The city's subcultural scene has grown incrementally, following the model of the avant-garde: nineteenth-century Parisian salons reimagined as exhibitions in rented tenement flats. But as many of the participants were and are without private income, it continues to be a scene largely funded by goodwill and income derived from benefits and non-art-related jobs in "semi-routine" occupations, such as manual work, cleaning, temping in offices, and bar and shop work, often on a temporary or part-time basis, or through art-related employment such as arts administration, gallery installation and invigilation, art therapy, and art instruction. Such projects are also buttressed through small-scale commerce: via sales (of books, recordings, artworks, tickets for live events, merchandise) or crowd-sourced funding streams such as subscriptions, membership fees, and donations.

At its heart, the scene that developed from Glasgow's first grassroots organizations—such as the artist-run gallery Transmission Gallery (est. 1983), Women in Profile (est. 1987, becoming the Glasgow Women's Library in 1991), and the Free University (est. 1987)—was not motivated by profit, but instead rooted in a desired social experience: one that relied on people investing time in supporting one another through social cooperation, collectivism, and conviviality. All these organizations were galvanized into action by their opposition to the Thatcher governments (1979–90) and the desire to establish an arena in which political participation could be enacted through the medium of talk and that was conceptually distinct from the state. As I mentioned in my introduction, I'm going to here focus on the Glasgow Women's Library, Transmission, and the Free University, as all still offer models for how artist-activists can move beyond the Marxist position outlined by earlier cultural studies theorists such as Raymond Williams. Williams's position came down from Antonio Gramsci, who thought that the overthrow of capitalist hegemony should come about not by violent revolution but through the rise of "counterhegemonies"— alternative cultures developed by disenfranchised groups. He believed that through self-education, self-organization, and the creation of its own institutions, a proletarian culture might someday become powerful enough to displace the bourgeois culture of modern, industrial society.

I will consider three possible theoretical and developmental models in relationship to my examples: governmentality theory, deliberative democracy, and agonistic pluralism. My three examples differ in key ways, but all, I think, sprang from a period in which artists began to consider self-organized public meetings as a necessity and worked to establish places where some of the divisions and contradictions of communal, lived politics could be expressed.

Governmentality theory, developed by philosopher Michel Foucault, delineates the formation of new ensembles or apparatuses as a means of allowing the voicing of identity positions previously unheard. A good local example of this approach is Glasgow Women's Library, which began life as an artist-led group called Women in Profile in 1987. In 2013, GWL moved into a permanent home in the Bridgeton neighbourhood, but prior to that the library's history was one of ongoing struggle for a space in which to operate and funds to stay afloat. As Adele Patrick, a GWL cofounder and its lifelong learning and creative development manager, explained in a 2009 talk reviewing the history of Women in Profile and GWL: *Glasgow Women's*

Library has been variously critiqued as not a real library, not a real artwork or art space, as not living in the real world (principally for focusing on women and not men). Despite or because of this liminal, unsettling, and indeterminate status, GWL has been open to and uniquely positioned to develop work that responds to the heterogeneity of women's experiences from different worlds, often using the agency of art and artists. The group of women who gave rise to Women in Profile (mobilized around the announcement in the late 1980s that Glasgow was to be European City of Culture in 1990) were largely women trained in the visual arts. The group grew into a project to be called Women in Profile that established a less-than-modest base in Dalhousie Lane. Their work culminated in a program of women's art and culture during September 1990. The festival in 1990 was indicative of the hybridity that has characterized the future Glasgow Women's Library and its anomalous positioning straddling academic and real-world concerns, exploring issues of hidden histories, representation, and women's access to cultural capital.[10]

After 1990, and inspired by visits to the Women Artists Slide Library in London and exchange visits to the Kunstlerinnerarchiv, then in Nuremberg, Glasgow Women's Library opened in a former secondhand clothes shop on Hill Street, in the Garnethill neighbourhood, in 1991. The founders—who worked on a voluntary basis, as no public funding was forthcoming to support the library—endeavoured in those early years to engage with and learn from the example of the women's library and museum movement by visiting arts libraries and archives in Europe, such as the Hidden Museum in Berlin. In 2004, GWL moved to new premises behind King Street, at 109 Trongate. There was still no core funding for the library, but volunteers, donations from supporters, and sporadic allocations of cash from the Scottish Office, city council, and charitable organizations kept the library running. GWL continued to draw support from the wider network of global women's libraries through the KnowHow project, attending Know-How gatherings in Amsterdam in 1998 and in Mexico in 2006. In 2001, a decade after the library first opened, GWL had amassed over twenty thousand volumes and was also able to recruit their first librarian, who developed a specific feminist-informed classification system for what now is the largest collection of information on women in Scotland.

In 2007, GWL was forced to move, in order to make way for the Trongate 103 development, an initiative funded by public bodies that sought to modernize and rationalize the six-storey former Edwardian warehouse where many other local independent organizations, including Transmission, were based, into "an arts resource for the city of Glasgow."[11] The enforced move to Parnie Street proved short-lived, as GWL was soon being served notice to move again—this time to make way for a new Workshop and Artists Studio Provision Scotland studio complex. In 2010, GWL took up residence in a vacant space in the Mitchell Library in the city centre, where it had its own space, albeit one that was still not fit for purpose. At this point, GWL still had no revenue funding but had gained charitable status, and after nearly twenty years in operation, was able to employ twelve staff. Now, four years later, GWL is a member of Museums Galleries Scotland and has a learning program that works with over a thousand women a year. However, as Adele Patrick points out, "for the women's library to survive and develop a meaningful practice, negotiations, interventions, and partnerships have had to be created, bridging and traversing discrete territories and cultures, including the communities of women in Glasgow and the visual arts, libraries, archives, and museums sectors."[12] This year, in 2014, the Library received financial assistance in the form of "ring-fenced" grants for specific projects from many sources;[13] however, the library still does not receive any funding for core costs and needs to constantly fundraise to meet day-to-day expenses such as utility bills.[14] The library continues to have no budget for materials, and GWL's collections have grown through the generosity of its users, members, and supporters.

In 2013, as I mentioned earlier, the library moved again: this time to a permanent space in Bridgeton, which the library has renovated for purpose through capital funding received from the National Lottery Heritage Fund, Creative Scotland, Clyde Gateway Urban Regeneration Company, and Museums Galleries Scotland. In recent correspondence to me, Adele Patrick described GWL's current situation this way: *Moving to a permanent home in Bridgeton into a former Carnegie Library in the historic heart of Glasgow really feels, after over two decades of being a "nomadic" resource, like finally being in the right place at the right time. The burgeoning of grassroots arts initiatives attracted by the availability of affordable warehouses, a vibrant neighbourhood minutes from the Merchant City, combined with the support of Clyde Gateway, offers us an exciting milieu in which to work. There are great opportunities for growth and development for GWL and for meaningful and much needed community engagement.*

The ongoing work of GWL is testament to the endurance and tenacity of Patrick and her colleagues in pursuing positive change in their community through a process of critical mapping undertaken "by those who live in it and who want change."[15]

The second way of thinking about engagement that I want to consider is deliberative democracy, as theorized by philosophers Jürgen Habermas and John Rawls, which describes participants engaging in a decision-making process by working collaboratively and adaptively in order to reach consensus. In this respect, a good local example is Transmission Gallery, as well as the other voluntary arts organizations run by committee that have followed in Transmission's wake, such as Market Gallery. Artist Cathy Wilkes remembers: *I understood Transmission as an art and politics group, more to do with the Free University and the anarchist movement, and the Anti-Nazi League. Most artists were making their work and not expecting to make any money out of it, and, probably, if they were involved in Transmission, they had quite strong political motivations. For example, people like Malcolm Dickson and Gordon Muir and Ann Vance.*[16]

Transmission was established in December 1983, in derelict shop premises on Trongate, next door to Terry's Tattoo Parlour. Transmission was conceived as Glasgow's first artist-run gallery and was organized by the Committee for the Visual Arts, a not-for-profit organization that described itself, in the gallery's first press release, as "a varied group of young artists dedicated to the exhibition and promotion of contemporary art and the integration of art into community life."[17] Crucially, the gallery was established not to generate sales of works but to offer opportunities for the exhibition of work and a social space for discussion. Transmission committee member Malcolm Dickson later wrote that "voluntary spaces…are fundamentally different in kind from those based on a hierarchy of paid administrators 'doing a job.' This approach is based upon trust and a sympathy to other peoples' points of view."[18] This strand of thought was decidedly unpopular with Timothy Mason, who was the conservative director of the Scottish Arts Council during the 1980s. The Transmission committee's steadfast refusal to appoint a paid administrator perplexed and irritated the Scottish Arts Council, which seemed unwilling at that time to understand the ideological framework of the gallery. This resulted in the gallery being refused sufficient public funding throughout the 1980s, instead relying on holding several fundraisers such as jumble sales and auctions of work in order to continue their program. Transmission also found significant support for its activities by reaching out to other artist-led initiatives in other cities and establishing artist exchanges with organizations such as Catalyst Arts in Belfast and City Racing in London.

Today, Transmission committee members continue to support and encourage the work of others, motivated by a belief in the importance of community. The gallery operates along the same basic model as it did from its inception in 1983: it is run by a committee of volunteers who can serve for a maximum of two years. As curator Will Bradley notes, "The uniqueness of Transmission follows through, and the reason it does is because of that two year structure, because so many people have been really committed for that period of time."[19] Importantly, the organization continues to be guided by its annual general meeting, during which the membership is invited to review the preceding year's program and finances and to discuss any arising issues (for example, in more recent years, the gallery's constitution has been under review, with members proposing Transmission should enshrine within it a gender-neutral exhibition policy). In following such a process, Transmission offers a workable model for deliberative democracy in action, which has inspired other organizations, both within Glasgow and in cities elsewhere.

Another constant in Transmission's history has been the relative paucity of funds with which its ongoing program of exhibitions and events is delivered. In 2013–14, the gallery received £70,000 from Creative Scotland. For comparison, in the same period, other arts organizations active in Glasgow received the following (considerably larger) amounts: Arika, which organizes experimental music, film, and art events, received £126,000; visual arts organization the Common Guild was given £190,000; Tramway, a visual and performance arts space, received £303,000; and the Centre for Contemporary Arts got £550,000. Transmission's slice of the local public-funding pie is one of the smallest slivers, and yet the gallery continues to make an important contribution locally and internationally.[20]

One significant change in the circumstances of Transmission has been the development of the Trongate 103 complex, which was built up around the gallery in 2009–10. This development has had multiple repercussions for Transmission as an organization. Specifically, complex negotiations around issues of access and purpose arose for Transmission, as the gallery came to fall under the umbrella of the larger Trongate 103 "arts resource." I think this ambivalence between artist-initiated groups and public funders is well summarized by the title of Transmission's 2014 annual members' show: *Vision and Values*—a phrase reminiscent of the mission statement of Creative Scotland, the main funding body for the arts in Scotland. Transmission is, by its nature, an organization that continually revises its vision and values according to the views of the incumbent committee and current membership, making the gallery both sustainable and unpredictable, but not, perhaps, consistent in the manner of other arts organizations with paid administrators.

The final concept for ways of thinking around artist-led projects that I want to touch on is agonistic pluralism, a term coined by political theorist Chantal Mouffe to describe the process of working to create an arena where differences can be confronted. This concept has resonance in relationship to the Free University, which was operated from various flats around Glasgow between 1987 and 1992 and run by local artists, writers, and curators Malcolm Dickson, Carol Rhodes, Nicola White, Billy Clark, James Kelman, Alasdair Gray, and Keith Miller. The flyer for the Free University's inaugural meeting in a flat on West End Park Street read: "Part free university, part late/cheap café, unemployed centre, artspace etc. DEMAND THE IMPOSSIBLE." The organization's was derived from Joseph Beuys's Free International University, which the German artist established in Düsseldorf in 1973. Beuys made several return journeys to Scotland following his first visit to Edinburgh in 1970, to give lectures, exhibit his work, and meet and collaborate with artists in Scotland. His death in January 1986 prompted a reexamination of his ideas, from his use of low-cost materials to his idea of "social sculpture," which he used to refer to the meaning generated between people involved in a variety of discourses. The notion of social sculpture informed many of the debates around the Free University and several other free educational organizations that have operated in Glasgow since the 1990s, such as Culture Club, Glasgow Open School, the Invisible College, and the Parallel School. I believe that tonight's event and the other International Artist Initiated exhibitions and events that David Dale Gallery has devised follow in that tradition,[21] although they have been conceived to coincide with the Glasgow 2014 Commonwealth Games and thus have been funded by Culture 2014. This International Artist Initiated event is truly public facing—being free, open to all, and simultaneously broadcast online.

International Artist Initiated provides a good example of how DIY practitioners can harness the potentially positive aspects of political conflict—for example, by campaigning for funding to support creative endeavours and through engaging with local communities and with local government. Methods of negotiating difference through empathy—as discussed by sociologist Richard Sennett in his 2012 book *Together*—will be important in outlining future possibilities for artist-initiated projects. In Sennett's view, the challenge for humans is to try to get along with people they don't like. He observes that "today, the crossed effect of desire for reassuring solidarity and economic insecurity is to render social life brutally simple: us-against-them coupled with you-are-on-your-own. But I'd insist we dwell in the condition of 'not yet.'"[22] Learning to get along with people we don't like might be the key challenge for some of today's artist-initiated projects, especially as the real cost of such unpaid initiatives has increased so dramatically in the last six years, since the 2008 financial crisis.

The UK Institute for Fiscal Studies calculates that, after inflation, the real hourly pay of workers under the age of thirty has collapsed by 11 percent since 2008, and household incomes are down 15 percent, as so many live in shared housing and shared rooms.[23] Since the financial crisis, market forces have brought an increased sense of competition to the cultural scene in the United Kingdom—competition for audiences, for attention, and for funding. The reality of the current situation is that the inequality of access to art and culture reflects wider social inequalities. The existing class divides have been increased by the introduction of university fees in 1998, and they are further reinforced following graduation by unpaid "opportunities" such as internships, which rule out the participation of anyone who cannot afford to work for free.

A 2012 survey conducted by the Scottish Artist Union (SAU) confirmed that three-quarters of visual artists in Scotland earn less than £5,000 a year, putting them in the lowest socioeconomic group of income earners, alongside pensioners, casual and lowest-grade workers, benefit claimants, and students. The social change organization the

Joseph Rowntree Foundation, which aims to solve poverty, each year releases a report on how much income is enough to pay for a basic, but socially acceptable, standard of living; in 2013, the report concluded that a single person needed to earn at least £16,850 a year before tax. How are aspirant cultural workers to make up the difference? As writer and curator Isla Leaver-Yap said at a 2012 meeting organized by the SAU to discuss nonpayment of artist's fees: "If only the people who can afford not to be paid are making art, then those who can't don't."[24] The SAU has, in recent years, begun to campaign to establish best working practices for cultural producers and the institutions that contract their labour, taking a lead from New York–based activist group Working Artists and the Greater Economy (W.A.G.E).

In the contemporary situation, the wealth generated through the shopping-and-services economy of post-Fordian cities such as Glasgow tends not to be redirected back to the local population to improve their educational and recreational possibilities. An economic survey following the 2006 edition of Glasgow International, a biennial of contemporary visual art, found that for every £1 the city invested, £9 came back, leading to a substantial increase of budget for the festival: from £70,000 in 2006 to £400,000 in 2008.[25] As Francis McKee, director of the Centre for Contemporary Arts, has noted, "It wasn't that the city didn't like contemporary art—but once they saw the economic benefit it became clear that Glasgow International was working for the economy of the city."[26] But how much of the revenue generated during the 2008, 2010, 2012, and 2014 editions of Glasgow International has come back to local independent organizations, and how much has gone to chain and franchise businesses (hotels, shops, bars, and restaurants) overseen by a centralized, tax-evading management? For instance, typically 95 percent of money spent in large supermarkets leaves the local economy for good, compared with 50 percent of that spent at local independent retailers.[27] In the UK, those companies that have benefitted from the cultural regeneration of postindustrial cities like Glasgow, Liverpool, Manchester/Salford, and Belfast do not necessarily feed money back into those cities. That is why I believe that artist-activists have an obligation to engage with larger power structures in order to highlight the relationship between the service economy and the creative economy, and ultimately to argue for changes in legislation to outlaw tax evasion by businesses—especially those that profit through exploitation of their workers—with a view to channelling those funds into public services. As market strategist Stephanie Flanders recently noted in the *Guardian*, "To ensure growth in the economy…you have to give the 'wealth creators' the incentive to increase both the pie and their slice of it." She continues: "We also have evidence—from the [International Monetary Fund], of all places—that in unequal economies, more redistributive taxes might promote faster growth."[28]

So—how do artist-activists increase the pie? I believe the answer is to maintain our predilection toward social cooperation, collectivism, and conviviality while at the same time working to convince others that this is not only the most commendable but indeed the only feasible approach. In his 1962 essay "The Creative Process," novelist and activist James Baldwin writes: "The precise role of the artist…is, after all, to make the world a more human dwelling place." For artists, this does not necessarily entail professionalizing. But one approach that does open itself up to us is bringing the qualities that distinguish artist-led organizations to bear on business practices—to enact a convergence of ideology and business practices orientated toward safeguarding the community in which we all participate.

1. This text is a lightly edited version of a talk presented as part of International Artist Initiated, at David Dale Gallery, Glasgow, on July 29, 2014, which coincided with the 2014 Commonwealth Games in Glasgow.

2. Kenneth Clark, *Civilisation* (1969; London: John Murray, 2005), 1–14.

3. Kevin Wehr, *DIY: The Search for Control and Self-Reliance in the 21st Century* (London and New York: Routledge, 2012), book description, https://fillip.ca/ft0w.

4. See Bob Black, *The Abolition of Work and Other Essays* (Port Townsend, WA: Loompanics Unlimited, 1992).

5. Chris Barker, *The SAGE Dictionary of Cultural Studies* (London: Sage, 2004).

6. Brent Luvaas, *DIY Style, Fashion, Music and Global Digital Cultures* (London: Berg, 2012), 6.

7. Stine Hebert and Anne Szefer Karlsen, eds., foreword to *Self-Organised* (Bergen: Open Editions, 2012), 11.

8. "History," Dischord Records' website, n.d., https://fillip.ca/hwau.

9. Merlin James, "Artist-Run Glasgow," *Art in America*, April 13, 2013.

10. Adele Patrick, "Making Space for Women: A Review of the Work of Women in Profile and Glasgow Women's Library, 1988–2009" (paper, Subject in Process symposium, Centre for Contemporary Art, Glasgow, September 5, 2009). This symposium was co-organized by myself along with Kathryn Elkin and Louise Shelley.

11. The main funders of Trongate 103 are: Culture and Sport Glasgow, Scottish Arts Council, National Lottery Heritage Fund, Scottish Enterprise, and Glasgow City Council. At the time this talk was delivered in 2014, the building housed the following organizations: Street Level Photoworks, Project Ability, Glasgow Print Studio, Transmission Gallery, Sharmanka Kinetic Theatre, Glasgow Independent Studio and Project Room, and Glasgow Media Access Centre. For further information, see Trongate 103's Facebook page.

12. Patrick, "Making Space for Women."

13. Project-specific funding comes from funders such as Glasgow City Council and Glasgow Life, which support the GWL's Lifelong Learning Programme, Black and Minority Ethnic Women's Project, and Adult Literacy and Numeracy Project.

14. The funding of the Glasgow Women's Library has improved since this text was written in 2014. In 2018, GWL was a finalist for Art Fund Museum of the Year, and the library has been recognized in recent years as a Nationally Significant Collection. As of 2020, GWL is a registered charity and receives funding from National Lottery Heritage Fund, Glasgow City Council, Creative Scotland, and the Scottish Government.

15. Patrick, "Making Space for Women."

16. Cathy Wilkes, in conversation with the author, August 2001, quoted in Sarah Lowndes, *Social Sculpture: The Rise of the Glasgow Art Scene* (Edinburgh: Luath, 2010), 106.

17. Transmission Gallery press release December 1983, quoted in Lowndes, *Social Sculpture*, 67.

18. Malcom Dickson, "Hit the North," unpublished essay on Transmission, 1996, quoted in Lowndes, *Social Sculpture*, 90.

19. Will Bradley, quoted in Lowndes, *Social Sculpture*, 358.

20. In 2020, Transmission continues to operate as "a registered charity, held

together by a combination of state funding, voluntary labour, and the ongoing construction of its community." "Info," Transmission Gallery's website, n.d., https://fillip.ca/0xtm.

21. International Artist Initiated, organized by David Dale Gallery, was an exhibition and events program that coincided with the Glasgow 2014 Commonwealth Games "intended to act as a catalyst for discussion and collaboration between artist initiated projects internationally. It included the participation of artist-initiated projects from Commonwealth countries: Fresh Milk (Barbados), Fillip (Canada), Cyprus Dossier (Cyprus), Clark House Initiative (India), RM (New Zealand), and Video Art Network Lagos (Nigeria). For more information, see "International Artist Initiated: Glasgow 2014 Cultural Programme," David Dale Gallery's website, 2014, https://fillip.ca/dvgq.

22. Richard Sennett, *Together: The Rituals, Pleasures and Politics of Cooperation* (2012; London: Penguin Books, 2013), 280.

23. Paul Mason, "The Young, Skint and Self-Employed Need a Radical New Labour Market," *Guardian*, July 20, 2014.

24. Isla Leaver-Yap, quoted in Chris Sharatt, "Artists' Fees: "The Cost of Labour Must Be Paid For," a-n, September 20, 2012, https://fillip.ca/sj9u.

25. Francis McKee, in conversation with the author, quoted in Lowndes, *Social Sculpture*, 397.

26. McKee, quoted in Lowndes, *Social Sculpture*, 397 .

27. Emma Simpson, "English Councils Propose 'Tesco Tax'," BBC News, July 26, 2014, https://fillip.ca/35n7.

28. Stephanie Flanders, "Capital in the Twenty-First Century by Thomas Piketty—Review," *Guardian*, July 17, 2014.

Sean Dockray

A Note on Digital Infrastructure

In the summer of 2012, I travelled to Luleå, Sweden, where Facebook was building a new data centre. So much of the physical infrastructure of computational capitalism is tucked out of sight—in generic, windowless buildings, on the periphery of cities, or, in this case, up near the Arctic Circle. When I took the fifteen-hour train ride north from Stockholm to see the data centre, it was still under construction. I thought that maybe visiting Luleå would be like seeing the parts of an unedited film, as if the pieces might explain more than the whole. I could see the centre before the last of the cladding went on, before the security cameras were hooked up and the fans started humming. At the same time, I knew perfectly well there would be nothing to see. Facebook wouldn't actually be *there*, because it is everywhere.

The facility is based on the same basic layout as the company's facility in Prineville, Oregon. Most notably, the entire top half of the structure is devoted to cooling. The idea in Luleå is that the cold Arctic air enters into this space and is mixed with the hot air produced by running thousands of servers. It is progressively filtered and humidified until it gets to a precise temperature and moisture content, whereupon it is blown through the hot servers to keep them from breaking down. The first day I visited, a large group of men emerged from a door near the top of the data centre building and descended the temporary staircase in a line. To build the site, Facebook employed 220 people through the Swedish construction company NCC. Originally, it was estimated that 300 workers would be needed—but that was based on American techniques, where more of the structure is built on site; in Sweden, components are outsourced and shipped to the site, meaning they need fewer hands. After construction was completed that March, there were likely only thirty to fifty permanent jobs created at the facility.

The internet connects (separates) these fat buildings from our thin computers. And as storage needs expand, our devices get thinner by the year. You can picture the evolution: from desktops to laptops to tablets to mobile phones. To make our computers more mobile, processing power and storage is externalized to the cloud. But this distance—this spatial expanse—is overcome by fast connection speeds and smooth interfaces. The devices are literally smooth—so smooth they seem to have been produced by magic, untouched by the human hand. The dominant aesthetics of user-interface design appeals to principles of simplicity, cleanliness, and clarity. And we also don't have to sit through thirty seconds of electronic noise while the modem connects our device to the internet. More and more, it's a question of how many Wi-Fi networks there are or how many bars we have, not whether or not we're connected.

The Facebook construction site is carved out of the forest, as if the trees have been shaved off like a beard. One day, there will be three giant buildings here, each containing four server halls, where the actual computers will do their thing. But for now, there is just this first building and a hole carved out of the forest where the rest might be someday. This data centre's servers are meant to handle traffic from Europe and the Middle East. This means that the so-called Facebook revolutions in these areas—like those protests and revolutionary movements in Iran, Egypt, and Tunisia—would happen *here*, in Luleå. At least in part. There are many reasons for building the data centre here, and one of the most important is Sweden's politically stability. Risk analysis has declared the country a safe investment. The air is cold, so to speak.

I became interested in data centres in 2011, after coming across a photograph of what their interiors hold: the server racks have a striking resemblance to library stacks. When you think about computer tablets as books, the comparison becomes even more unsettling. (The proliferation of data centres comes at just the moment library collections are being deaccessioned, hours cut, and some branches closed entirely.) On these devices, a person needs to agree to certain "terms of service," have a unique, measurable account, and provide payment information. In return, access is granted. This access is not ownership in the conventional sense of having possession of a book, or even in the digital sense of a file, but rather the granting of a licence that gives the person a "non-exclusive right to keep a permanent copy, solely for your personal and non-commercial use"—thus contradicting the first sale doctrine of copyright law, which gives the "owner" the right to sell, lease, or rent their copy to anyone they choose at any price they choose. Such contradictions are symptoms of the shift in property regimes, or what economic and social theorist Jeremy Rifkin called "the age of access." He writes that *property continues to exist but is far less likely to be exchanged in markets. Instead, suppliers hold on to property in the new economy and lease, rent, or charge an admission fee, subscription, or membership dues for its short-term use.*[1]

Of all the reasons Facebook ended up in northern Sweden, the single most important one is the Lule River and the cheap hydroelectric power that it generates through fifteen power plants scattered along its length. It used to take decades for the cost of electricity to exceed the cost of a server, and so electricity was a marginal expense. But now, it takes only a few years until the cost of running the thing costs more than the thing itself, making electricity decisive. It also used to be that buildings required a lot of power to operate. A paper mill or a factory, for example, would have to be situated near to a river in order to generate enough water power to push the machinery into motion. With motors and electrical power stations and high-voltage transmission lines, a factory can now be situated almost anywhere, as long as it's hooked up to a source of electricity. The sources of power were able to become more and more distantly situated, located in places one would rarely visit.

Microsoft (which has moved quite deliberately into data centres) released a publication in 2009 about the "fourth paradigm" in science, which observes that today's most important scientific research is engaged with observing, analyzing, and visualizing *data* and not the *material world*.[2] We discover new diseases and their cures by looking through computers. And this data—a model of the world and its phenomena—is stored and processed in data centres. But the cloud is not confined to scientific data; here *everything* is abstracted into data—business transactions, music and film, correspondences, personal photos, and so on.

The closest power plant to Facebook's Swedish data centre is about thirty kilometres north of Luleå, in Boden. The data centre will consume as much electricity as the small city of Boden does. In 2011, the year before construction on Facebook's Luleå centre began, data centres worldwide consumed as much energy as the entire country of Sweden. It seems as though the scale of data centres is so large and their activity so opaque that we need to form an understanding of them through comparison. Philosopher Martin Heidegger discusses hydroelectric plants on the Rhine in *The Question Concerning Technology*, describing how, in contrast to the windmill, which directly converts wind into energy, the hydroelectric plant stores up the energy of the river to be converted at will—and thus nature itself has become a resource, a thing for human use rather than simply a thing in itself.

It's difficult to tell if anyone is working at these power stations. In one video I saw on the internet, a woman is seen driving around Norrbotten County and checking up on the infrastructure to make sure that everything is okay. Once these stations are built, there's not much of a need for anyone to actually be there—in fact, it is probably a liability for someone to be there, because what if they get bored, or angry about the terms of their last contract? This is likely how it will be with the Facebook data centre, once it's finally done. There will be very few workers and they will be employed not to keep things running—that's something else—but rather to stop things from falling apart.

The biggest investment in Luleå, prior to the data centre, was the steel mill built in 1940. A railway connects the mill to iron ore mines in the mountains to the northwest— trains roll in several times a day, delivering product from the Malmberget and Kiruna mines. There, much of the drilling and shuttling is done with automation and remote control. Since the late 1970s, the Swedish steel industry has been restructured, which means that it has introduced more computer control, and thus eliminated many jobs. At that time, the entire industry was "in trouble"—or, in other words, it wasn't profitable.

In a video clip, one of the engineers building the Facebook data centre in Oregon says, "This is a factory, it's just a different kind of factory than you might be used to." I think that the Luleå steel mill is the kind of factory he assumes we might be used to. The steel mill almost seems proud compared to the data centre. It is visible, upright, and muscular. Something from a past era, really; or maybe a passing era. The data centre is monstrous: an absurdity in the landscape, trying to be discreet, trying to move in without drama, and then keep to itself. It doesn't give much of itself—in fact, all it really does is collect data. Its workers are spread across the globe, usually bent in front of a computer, but more often now gazing into their hands. They enter data, upload a hundred million photographs per day—and the data centre must always be on to collect it all.

The future of Luleå is not in steel—it is in data. The government rebranded the area as "the Node Pole" to attract other technology companies to bring their data to this region. They advertised one site right next to the steelworks, and another was a former sawmill. It's a paradigm shift, say the businesspeople.

When I visited, the people in the blue offices refused to give me a tour or let me visit the building. I found out later that, prior to my arrival, a Google executive had surreptitiously gone on a tour and taken some photographs, resulting in a minor scandal. Data centres are supposed to be very secure.

These buildings store an immense amount of equipment and technology, and that equipment stores an immense amount of data. Really, Facebook is constructing a mine here. There is valuable raw material in there somewhere, but no one knows quite what it is yet. One hundred million photographs are uploaded to the mine every day, and they want to know what's really in there. Algorithms try to figure out what structures exist underneath and through the ones that we can see. Or maybe it's not a mine, but a power plant for human resources. Our social energy as a resource that can be stored and used at will. This data centre would be the placid side of the dam, and the algorithms are the things that open the gates and convert all that social movement into energy, and into work, and into profit.

No one knows how many data centres there are on the planet, but estimates put it at nearly nine million. Because these centres require so much capital investment, decisions on where to locate them are not based on sentimentality, ethics, or ideology, but on risk and cost-benefit analysis. They spread across the planet according to an autonomous logic outside direct human control. They find themselves in unlikely places, occupying relics of the twentieth-century like Model T factories, limestone mines, printing plants, military bunkers, and even shopping malls.

One can't help but wonder how many data centres there will be when this is all over. But will the age of data centres ever be over? If it does meet an end, what kind of super-ruins will splatter the landscape? Will the data have been migrated to a less hostile climate? Or will bits of the infrastructure remain, left for the future archaeologists of the fourth paradigm?

What kind of culture can we produce on platforms like Facebook? Data centres are typically viewed as mere tools for organizing and publicity, no different than, say, a cell phone or a poster, and humans simply make use of whatever is available to us. But the restructuring that's been occurring is much deeper than that, in the same way that a lab culture that used to be in a petri dish is now in a data centre. It seems as though so much culture—artist-run and otherwise—has by now been platformed.

Where does one draw the lines between 1) platforms that one is willing to use, 2) alternative platforms that should be constructed in place of hegemonic or corporate ones, and 3) activities that must resolutely reside outside computation and digital networks? Even within and across these divisions, there are further subdivisions, recombinations, and movements.

1. Jeremy Rifkin, *The Age of Access: The New Culture of Hypercapitalism, Where All of Life Is a Paid-for Experience* (New York: J.P. Tarcher/Putnam, 2000), 4.

2. Anthony J. G. Hey, ed., *The Fourth Paradigm: Data-Intensive Scientific Discovery* (Redmond, WA: Microsoft Research, 2009).

Chris Fitzpatrick and Post Brothers
A Productive Irritant

Parasitical Inhabitations in
Contemporary Art

The parasite is an infectant. Far from actually transforming a system's nature, its form, elements, relations, and paths, the parasite makes the system change its condition in small steps. It introduces a tilt. It brings the system's balance or the distribution of energy into fluctuation. It irritates it. It infects it…brings us close to the subtle balances of living systems.

—Michel Serres[1]

In 1969, artist Harvey Stromberg walked into the Museum of Modern Art in New York with a notebook, measuring tape, and a camera. Posing as an eager student, he returned on a regular basis, pretending to study the museum's collection when, in fact, he was surreptitiously measuring and photographing various features inside and outside the museum in order to make an artwork. Later that year, after printing over three hundred of the photographs he had taken—of light switches, keyholes, bricks, air vents, and so on—Stromberg printed the photos out at a 1:1 scale of what they depicted and backed them with adhesive. In a series of visits to the museum, he attached his photos to the walls, floors, and other surfaces—subtly, and without authorizization from the institution. Although they were often found and destroyed by museum employees, Stromberg was never caught.

Rosalind Constable noted in a 1971 issue of *New York* magazine that Stromberg originally executed this solo exhibition anonymously, but after two years, decided to claim authorship of the work in order to make "people be aware there are conflicts between museums and art-ists"[2]—namely around who is allowed to exhibit and who is not. By humorously inserting his own work directly into the interior and exterior architecture of the museum, Stromberg confused what the institution had sanctioned and what it had not.[3] Stromberg inhabited the museum as a foreign agent, adopting tactics that offered practical and conceptual strategies of artistic production through acts of "parasitical inhabitation."

An Irritant

A parasite is defined as an organism that lives in or on another organism, extracting what it needs from its host without giving anything positive in exchange. We consider Stromberg's project parasitical because, like a parasite, he entered his target's body through a point of weakness, exploited its faculties and facilities, and thereby showed the museum's impenetrability (its curatorial selection, accessions committees, etc.) to be, like his photographic illusions, a facade. He walked in the front door. When artists are working parasitically, context (the site, its history, its claims to authority, its funding and organizational structures, and its habits) is perhaps the primary material being occupied and consumed.

When we speak of parasitical practices in art, we must first refer to the work of French polymath Michel Serres, whose book *The Parasite* (1980) discusses its namesake as a vehicle for introducing "irritants" to any given order, causing subtle changes that can be productive and cumulative.[4] Through a disciplinary promiscuity akin to the parasite's ability to trespass corporeal boundaries, Serres's text investigates the appearance of parasitical activity in literature and science, bridging the domains of biology, anthropology, and information theory to arrive at a conception of how systems operate. Serres breaks down three familiar uses for the word "parasite": the "biological" parasite, the "social" parasite, and the parasite as communicative "static" (derived from the French word for noise, *parasite*). For Serres, these linguistic significations are not distinct, but interrelated. Serres breaks away from conventional notions of parasites, arguing that parasitism is not merely antagonistic, but that its effects are productive, not solely reductive; its disruptions are indicative of complex yet fundamental relations between people and between things, whether sentient or not.

For example, in its most traditional conception, the biological parasite enters a target host's body with the aim of diverting and feeding off the host's energy. Along this line of thought, there would be no mutual exchange. With Serres's notion of the social parasite, however, which may be analogous to an uninvited guest, an exchange occurs that is uneven and complex. For instance, in this scenario, the guest takes hospitality and food from the host without giving an equivalent back. Yet there are other forms of exchange: conversation, pleasantries, and humour are on offer for food, drink, and temporary shelter in an immaterial-to-material transaction. In doing so, the social parasite redirects the surplus energies of the host, similar to the biological parasite. Finally, Serres's notion of the parasite-as-noise introduces interference into communications—disrupting, feedbacking, and dispersing information as it moves between messages and their reception.

Throughout Serres's discussion, these three conceptions of parasites operate neither as autonomous nor distinct entities. Rather, they are mutually defined in that there exists always a level of static, so to speak, in social relations. In other words, Serres argues that there are always disturbances in bodies, human or otherwise. And, there is always a loss in any act of exchange, but also something gained. The parasite is not any one of these phenomena but is actually all three (biological, social, noise) in constant play. In each instance, the parasite intercedes in exchange, but Serres shows us that the parasite is not any single conception or phenomenon, but rather operates in constant negotiation.

Stromberg's inhabitation is similarly complex. While he may have exploited both MoMA's prestige and space to create his work of art, wasn't the museum's status in turn reaffirmed, having been targeted by Stromberg as a host endowed with resources to spare? The potential and actual results that can be and have been achieved by artists working parasitically is but one interest we have in the strategy. In addition, the complexity of the relations that lead to such gestures and actions is of significance. The figure of the parasite extends to artists a means of surveying, articulating, questioning, and contaminating relations, a tool to determine loopholes, interdependencies, differences, and positions within affective relations. Through this observation and redistribution of component logics and positions within systems, the parasite becomes an expert in its host's patterns and can then subvert and redirect them. With Serres's discussion of parasites in mind, in the following essay we have chosen three forms of biological parasites as models through which contemporary artistic practice can be considered.

First, in *Candiru (Invasions Upstream)*, we will look to the candiru *(Vandellia cirrhosa)*, a freshwater fish that detects urine and then swims up this stream into its host. Its operations provide us with a model to think about the forcefulness of a parasitical intrusion, and how the detection of weaknesses in a potential host can lead to tangible access otherwise impossible to achieve. Second, in *Cymothoa Exigua (The Tongue-eating Louse)*, we follow a crustacean parasite that latches onto a fish's tongue, drains it of blood, and then effectively replaces the host's tongue with itself. Related to artists working in more discursive modes, the parasite offers a model for considering artists who mirror, redirect, or overtake the voice and authority of their hosts, and who insert "static" into communications of which they would otherwise not have access. Finally, in part three, *Toxoplasma Gondii*, we will consider a feline parasite that has infected over half of the earth's human population. Spread through contact with cat feces, this strange parasite is notable for the way in which it affects its host, changing its behaviour, but also for the manner in which it is spread (and how easily). Through relating *Toxoplasma gondii* to artistic practice, we can see that the entire field of relations is always already parasitical—a key point made in *The Parasite*.

When Serres argues that the entire field of relations is parasitic, what interests us is that what parasites actually attack are, in fact, those relationships. In other words, what is useful is not just the operational modes to be gleaned from parasites, and not just the antagonism or exploitation of the host, but how parasitism is causal; parasites offer tactics, but their tactics create legible effects. Moreover, parasites appear to turn their hosts into parasites, but the alterations caused by the parasites reveal that their hosts' statuses were already parasitical.

It is not our intention to suggest a canon of parasitical practice. Nor should this be misunderstood as a compre-hensive historical survey. Rather, we aim to proffer certain artists' parasitical operations as effective strategies for the manipulation of context, the introduction of unsuspected tactics, the identification of weakness within seemingly taut and enclosed systems, and the ability to disguise one's appearance or to take on that of one's host. To ride communication vectors and exploit the logics and surplus of their targets, these artists embed themselves within a system to reveal the system's dependency on logics of exclusion.

Our interest in candiru and *Cymothua exigua* (as parasites and as frameworks) lies less in any antagonistic position or romance of transgression and more in their strategic implications. With *Toxoplasmosis* we are especially concerned with the way in which the parasite affects the behaviour of its host. In general, our interest in parasites is in how they negotiate their surroundings and the ways in which their presence brings about responses—how certain implicated foundations can become productive for change; how certain infiltrations by those routinely excluded can interrupt the status quo; how specific hosts call for precise manoeuvers and offer discrete potentials; how an outside operator's ability to intrude and use the system's nomenclature can divulge an infrastructure's integral aspects; and how to negotiate and disrupt such naturalized or stratified relationships.

I. Candiru (Invasions Upstream)

Although their operations and specific conditions vary widely and they can, at times, be beneficial to their hosts, parasites are generally thought of as unwanted, harmful invaders. They exist through external attachments to, or physical infiltrations of, a host organism's body. Once inside, the parasite draws energy from its new environment, but generally ensures that it does not take too much, as this might run the risk of depleting the vitality both parasite and host require to live (though in many cases, the parasite's host is a vessel to be extinguished before moving on to another host).[5]

If the word "parasite" is almost always a pejorative, it is perhaps because the parasite's identity is contingent on it being a nuisance—a stranger to the host despite their intimacy. For Jean-Luc Nancy, it is crucial that the parasite-to-host relationship is contentious. Nancy, contemplating the paradoxical experience of a human hosting an alien organ after a heart transplant, suggests that such an "intruder" enters its host "by force, surprise, or cunning, in any case without any right to do so and without invitation."[6] For Nancy, that intruder's status is always bound up in issues of corporeality and proximity, for without "an element of the intruder in the stranger" or the parasite in the host, the intrusion is without the necessary "strangeness" to be perceived as such.[7] In other words, an invitation or any allowance given to an intruding force would negate that very intrusion. When individuals ingest roundworms to lose weight, for instance, does this willing introduction of the parasite negate its harmful potential? And, how does the act of voluntary bloodletting change the patient's relation to the leech, when that leech is put in service to medicine? What do the processes of regulation, invitation, and control, therefore, render? As Serres reminds us, the guest can disgrace and abuse the charity of a host. In doing so, he notes the similarities and dissonances between the invited parasite and the parasite as unwelcome intruder, which offers a nuanced sketch of how parasites and their targets renegotiate their positions when confronting one another.

For Serres, *The parasite is "next to," it is "with," it is detached from, it is not sitting on the thing itself, but on the relation. It has relations, as one says, and turns them into a system. It is always mediate and never immediate. It has a relation to the relation, it is related to the related, it sits on the channel.*[8] Of course, the host can also abuse the guest, but there can also be intermediaries who add further complexity to the field of relations. For example, Trisha Donnelly contributed a total of four projects to the 54th Carnegie International in 2004, including *Dark Wind* (2002), which periodically sent the sound of wind rustling through the galleries, and *Night Is Coming (Warning)* (2002), in which the omen "NIGHT IS COMING," appeared to pulse, as it was projected onto the wall. And, in *Letter to Tacitus* (2004), she selected a museum guard who, dressed in an elegant suit, recited a letter (written by Donnelly) to the Roman senator, consul, and historian, Cornelius Tacitus, each day. As a far subtler contribution, Donnelly circulated unannounced among the lavish opening dinner attendees inconspicuously dressed as a waitress serving water. Donnelly's presence was barely registered by the guests. Only curators Laura Hoptman and Liz Thomas were aware of the performance, and their collusion with the artist—that is, their withholding of information from the guests—furthers the complexity of Donnelly's gesture, while at the same time allowing it to occur. Unlike Stromberg, Donnelly was invited into the institution, but once inside, Donnelly infiltrated the situation's social and material relations (the class and labour dynamics of the celebratory fanfare) by embedding herself so mimetically within the opening's context— an act akin to the artist's invisibility in plain sight. Would many of the attendees Donnelly served have interacted differently with her had they known she was an invited artist and not a waitress?

An Unattended Exit, An Unintended Entrance

Donnelly's gesture shows that parasitism can be highly nuanced, but in its most traditional conception a parasite elicits an image of a forceful invader penetrating the body of the host (entering by puncturing the skin, etc.)

or sneaking in through the host's day-to-day activities (in water, waste, food, etc.). Exploiting the weakness of their targets, the parasite finds channels by which to burrow and feed, which the examples of both Stromberg and Donnelly support in an art context. Yet to best exemplify the force behind Nancy's ideas around an invader's intrusion, let us cite an overt intruder—an Amazonian freshwater parasitic catfish known as the candiru. Until recently, its disturbing behaviour has, for the most part, existed only in local legends and fiction. William S. Burroughs mentioned the invasive behavior of the candiru in his 1959 novel *Naked Lunch*, describing it as "a small eel-like fish or worm about one-quarter inch through and two inches long" that "will dart up your prick or your arsehole or a woman's cunt faute de mieux, and hold himself there by sharp spines."[9] What makes the candiru's tendency to invade and parasitize the human urethra so abject is that it exposes the vulnerability of our most intimate orifices.[10]

Ethnological reports of the candiru's attacks on human genitals date back to the late nineteenth century, but the first documented case of the candiru parasitizing humans was only in 1997. The fish penetrated the victim's urethra while he was standing in the river urinating, where it actually emerged from the water, travelled up the urine stream, and entered the man's penis, filling the entire anterior urethra.[11] The candiru's agonizing operations resonate with many artistic practices that transgress borders—strategies that are useful for entering proscribed zones of exclusion, while showing how simply and economically it can be achieved. Moreover, the candiru's manner of travelling through waste reveals how parasites operate in ecosystems more generally—their specific role in the regulation of surplus and excess. Just as the parasite itself is that which the host organism wants to expel, the candiru enters in through the organism's system of exclusion, the surplus waste products that the host wishes to dispel.

For historian William H. McNeill, however, it is a question of distribution. In *The Human Condition* (1979), he describes the history of civilization through microparasites (micro-organisms, fungi, insects, small animals like mice and rats, and other organisms that live off of humans specifically) and macroparasites (humans who feed off of the labour of others). He argues that, in the course of human development, microparasites such as pests and disease have thrived by infesting dense populations, serving as a means of population control.[12] For McNeill, the development and circulation of microparasites and macroparasites served not only to regulate and exploit surplus, but remain, in fact, the primary motivation behind clashes of civilization.[13] The parasite's actions are, thus, seen through a classic economic model of scarcity—that is, parasitism follows a predatory model where organisms vie for limited resources. Surplus appears through the unequal distribution of biomass, and parasites serve to balance ecosystems over time through homeostasis.

But to understand the parasite's behaviour, it may be more beneficial to move from the idea of a "restrictive" economy of scarcity, as McNeill proposes, to a "general economy" of surplus, as Georges Bataille attempts in *The Accursed Share* (1949). For Bataille, the infinite outpouring of solar energy and its movement through the chemical processes of organisms creates a superabundance of energy that must be expended. Unlike predators, parasites do not play into a simple food chain of carbon distribution but extract the excesses produced by these processes. For Bataille, "If the excess cannot be completely absorbed in growth, it must necessarily be lost without profit; it must be spent, willingly or not, gloriously or catastrophically."[14]

The "accursed share" is that excessive and non-recuperable part of any economy that is destined to one of two modes of economic and social waste: it is either spent through spectacle, luxury, or the arts; or in the destructive acts of war and sacrifice. A parasite and its host are always at war. Like McNeill, Bataille sees war as a parasitical act, one that is meant not to gain energy, but to expend energy and eradicate surplus. Luxury, and especially art's extraneous and ostensibly nonproductive expense, is not grounded in use but in a production of consumption. A society's nature is shaped by its use of this excess: how it expends, unloads, squanders, discharges, or defecates surplus in various ways. Bataille believed that in order to undermine the operations of restrictive economies, one must enter through a general economy of abundance, uselessness, and excess. Just as the candiru exploits its host's waste as a means of entry, parasitical artists use whatever technical systems or apparatuses they can find to enter into their targets' bodies through excesses, drawing on the hosts' output, energy supplies, and cycles. As Seth Price attests, "Production, after all, is the excretory phase in a process of appropriation."[15]

Infiltration

An intruder disrupted the neat numerical order implied by the title of the historic *9 at Leo Castelli* (1968), as well as the exhibition itself. On display at Castelli's warehouse,[16] the exhibition was organized by artist Robert Morris and was to include works by artists Giovanni Anselmo, William Bollinger, Eva Hesse, Stephen Kaltenbach, Bruce Nauman, Alan Saret, Richard Serra, Keith Sonnier, and Gilberto Zorio. Although barely documented, *9 at Leo Castelli* was an important moment in the history of exhibitions and the development of anti-form, particularly for the way the raw condition of the site influenced the arrangement and composition of the works on display. Yet while the exhibition officially included the works of only seven artists (as the works of Giovanni Anselmo and Gilberto Zorio were not delivered in time),[17] the artist Rafael Ferrer also participated, uninvited, by filling a stairwell with fallen leaves during the exhibition's opening.

Although Ferrer knew Morris, he remained an artist outside the show. Ferrer asked his students to deposit the leaves quickly and without fanfare. Arriving first at Leo Castelli Gallery, two of Ferrer's students poured four bags of leaves into a mound on the gallery floor, within an exhibition of paintings by Cy Twombly. They then proceeded uptown to the warehouse, where they filled a staircase with the remaining leaves they had brought. By inserting his own work into these spaces, Ferrer tapped not only the context of the exhibition itself and his exclusion from it, but also the spotlight exhibitions afford, simultaneously bringing more attention to his practice in return. To return to Bataille, perhaps the abundance of leaves in Ferrer's gesture serves as a sign of excessive energy accumulated, used up, and discarded by an organism, and Ferrer's delivery of the leaves, referential as they are, constitutes an addendum to the display of "anti-form" works, while perhaps implicitly mocking the phenomenon that such impoverished and base materials could be re-appropriated for economic and symbolic surplus.

Parasitical Mobility

Like Ferrer, Polish-Romanian artist Andre Cadere is also known for inserting his own work into other artists' exhibitions, often uninvited. Yet whereas Ferrer brought everyday, essentially unaltered leaves inside the white cube, Cadere brought art objects, crafted by hand inside his studio, outside and into public, or inside another artist's exhibition. With these objects, Cadere eschewed the slick fabrications and phenomenological aims of Minimalism and also, as Astrid Ihle writes, "the hegemony of the Ecole de Paris and of the avant-garde movements of Nouveau Realisme and Op Art."[18] Cadere's objects were portable and could be displayed in any conditions or context. They did not need a prescribed gallery space to exist; Cadere authorized his objects to exist as artworks regardless of context.

Cadere's public work sometimes took the form of serial colours, spray painted on walls or curbs, but he is best known for presenting *Barres de bois rond*—cylindrical, wooden rods of different lengths, circumferences, and weights. The *Barres* display varying chromatic patterns according to a system of Cadere's design, which contains an error that intentionally obscures that system.[19] But these physical objects were only part of his practice. For Cadere, galleries were not sites of display, but "systems of power" to be subverted. His exhibitions, therefore, took place wherever, whenever, and however he wanted them to occur—announced or not, indoors or out.[20] Cadere stated, "My art is the situation of my work in the art world."[21]

Mark Godfrey writes that "Cadere was one of the first artists to realize that objects were inseparable from market and institutional contexts: half of his focus was on the systems of distribution in the art world."[22] Eventually, Cadere's presence became a common and well-known occurrence, one that was not always appreciated. Daniel Birnbaum relays that during *a 1973 opening…Cadere anticipated that he would be prevented from bringing a large barre into the gallery and so [he] hid a very small second rod in his pocket. Cadere fought his host's attempts to expel his presence; after being denied entry with the larger work, he smuggled in this miniature parasite instead, and a tiny striped rod soon appeared on the gallery floor.*"[23] Birnbaum's use of the word "parasite" is fitting (a term also used by Astrid Ihle[24]), as Cadere's *Barres* not only became a symbol of his contention with the gallery systems he entered, but also one of transgression or trespass, navigating around those who would attempt to block his access.

By the mid-1970s, Cadere was increasingly invited to exhibit his objects, which changed his status within the system he occupied.[25] When Harald Szeemann invited him to participate in documenta 5,[26] however, it was under the condition that Cadere must arrive in Kassel on foot, with *Barre* in hand. Cadere instead faked the voyage through a series of postcards entitled *Marcheur de Cassel* (The Kassel Wanderer), and later announcing he would arrive by train, which led to Szeemann's irate exclusion of the artist. Cadere, of course, showed up anyway; disinvited by the curator, his presence and that of his object became all the more parasitical. The artist's uninvited self-insertion into the gallery exploited, like that of Ferrer, the fact that in order for galleries to exist, they must be both private and open to the public.

Appearances / Embodiments

An alien in an alienated world, a parasite seeks out its place by relating itself to others and immersing itself in systems. The regulated and formalized operations of exhibitions serve as both metonyms and exaggerations of political, cultural, or social arrangements as a whole, and, accordingly, subversion inside and outside of such domains unveils the tenuous ideological boundaries and functions of exhibitions. Just as Ferrer and Cadere execute both critical gestures and acts of wanting to belong and participate by invading such sites, the Italian-born Swiss artist Gianni Motti often enters into generic scenarios outside the confines of art—including public events, political proceedings, and mass media—whereas Motti's structural analysis of his hosts allows him to place himself into the world in unpredictable ways. In 1995, for example, Motti emerged on a professional soccer field alongside players, warmed up with the athletes, and took a seat on one of the team's substitute benches. Entitled *Ala Sinistra, La Maladière Stadium, Neuchâtel, National A League football match* (1995), Motti's almost unnoticed parasitical action was witnessed by several thousand spectators and recorded by television and newspaper cameras.[27] Like the contained exhibitions that Ferrer and Cadere entered, the soccer field is a delineated zone for a limited group of approved agents to act according to certain rules. By simply appearing, Motti broke both the rules of who may appear and the sovereignty of that particular domain. The soccer field is shown as an ideological space, one where the invisible actions of a subversive artist or the spectacle of a crazed fan breaks down the system. Enacting the desire of the audience to identify with the players, Motti resists the limitations of specialization and undermines the integrity of the game.

More activist than prankster, Motti infiltrates systems and seizes opportunities when they appear. In 1997, while attending the 53rd Session of the Commission on Human Rights in Geneva, Motti noticed a vacant seat reserved for Indonesia's delegate and replaced the absent representative, voting alongside the attending commission members.[28] When the time came to vote on the 48th resolution concerning ethnic minorities, Motti rose and made a speech on ethnic division, aesthetics, and human rights. Representatives of Indigenous Americans and other marginalized ethnic groups all rallied to the words of the "Indonesian delegate" and walked out of the assembly in solidarity with Motti's position.

Motti infiltrates a host and takes responsibility for actions not taking place in the social body, introducing ideas previously excluded from the conversation.[29] Unlike the gallery system Cadere railed against and Ferrer trespassed into, the primary audiences for Motti's interventions are completely unsuspecting spectators and agents, rendering the artist either invisible or hypervisible (as he both follows and undermines the given protocols of participation) by making a statement to an audience that does not expect one.[30]

In his quest for recognition and dispersal, Motti constructs his own self-identity by proxy, using events and their mediation as a network in which to place himself.[31] Over the course of a week in 2000, the more sensitive readers of the Swiss daily newspaper *Neue Luzerner Zeitung* began to notice a surreptitious and unknown figure appearing in images accompanying the articles. In one report with the headline "Eine Flugreise In Die Bunten 60er-Jahre" (A Flight Through the Colourful '60s), Motti appears entering a domicile through a door directly behind a woman posing on period furniture. In another article, headlined "Der Restaurator Im Ständeratssaal" (Restorer in the Senate Hall), two people admire and point to a wall fresco with Motti beside them, looking curiously at the images. While in most of the reports Motti barges into the scene at the exact moment the camera flashes, the image accompanying an article on a teacher's meeting features Motti sitting alongside the participants in an act of solidarity. Motti's seemingly random, though in reality highly calculated, appearance in these images was both a form of anonymous promotion and the introduction of a tangential narrative. As a witness to the events pictured rather than a maker of news, Motti's position in the newspaper constituted a tertiary position, which the artist occupied as silent corroborator, a bystander. Moreover, by irritating the readership by offering an unsubstantiated pattern of appearance for an unnecessary character, Motti was subsequently featured in other newspapers for his actions, expanding his influence further, proliferating to infect other hosts.[32]

Other Embeddings

With the *Mythic Being* series (1972–75), Adrian Piper inhabited social conventions, city streets, and, like Motti, the newspaper, as sites for disseminating the appearance and actions of her male alter ego, the "Mythic Being," into the public sphere. This histrionic caricature of a young Black or Latino male appeared mustached and afroed, smoked, wore shades, and exuded an aggressive masculine persona, interrupting and exaggerating deep-seated yet unacknowledged fears and stereotypes of young minority men. Just as we are all constantly at odds with our personal identifications and the learned, indoctrinated regimes in which we operate, Piper stages identity as a parasite, foreign to the host she occupies; she is both within and outside the culture to which she has been made to inhabit, and both within and outside herself. However, Piper's adoption of various personae affords her a parasitical means of inhabiting other perspectives, however disingenuously.[33] Like Cadere's propensity for public display, Piper's character would appear in both "culture-related locales" (galleries, openings, concerts, etc.) and on the streets or on public transportation.[34] Piper's actions were obliquely complimented by the Mythic Being's concurrent appearance within sixteen single-panel works, published as advertisements in the *Village Voice* almost monthly between 1973 and 1975.[35] Each included the same image of the Mythic Being and a thought bubble containing different, brief, dated passages culled from Piper's personal diary.[36] Publicizing her private thoughts, these phrases were treated as "mantras" by the artist by which she disassociated her voice and anxieties through an inverted double. As Piper describes it: "the experience of the Mythic Being thus becomes part of the public history and is no longer a part of my own."[37]

Though Piper herself was quite well known at the time of *Mythic Being*, her gesture spoke to the exclusion and conditional representation of minority and women artists. Working around the same time, Robyn Whitlaw used her relative invisibility as a Black woman to traverse and hide behind the noise of culture and politics through her *In-Visibility Project* (1973–78). During this time, Whitlaw exaggerated her own professional obscurity by sending simple invitations for a number of her own secret exhibitions after they had closed. Whereas in the 1970s many conceptual artists were using the exhibition invitation as a site for both their work and enhanced promotion, Whitlaw questioned the "publicness" of publicity and the self-aggrandizement of artists by distorting both temporality and the art establishment's customary use of advertising procedures. A comment on the systemic neglect of non-white and women artists, Whitlaw's project was based on her concept of the "secret artist" (an incorporation of secret agent behaviour and Watergate-era deception and secrecy). Realizing the role invisibility played in the manipulation of power, she used clandestine strategies to invade zones from which she was prohibited and revealed how such prohibitions were generated ideologically and reproduced. Using a system of authentication to certify the existence of her work and its pre-emptive dismissal, her project's power lies in its absurdity, existing outside the market system's logic and expectations.

Each of these artists use invisibility to accentuate the roles visibility and invisibility play in the proliferation and reproduction of power, entering into systems by either being too visible (hiding "behind the noise and to-do of the devout,"[38] to use Serres's words) or cloaked in incomprehensibility. Theirs is a game of penetrating and exposing the intersubjective negotiation between individual and society, interrupting the system's regime of exclusion by swimming up the stream. By forcing themselves into the host, they make their own presence known and show their targeted systems as "the location relative to which the included and the excluded will define themselves."[39]

Parasitical Implications / Complicity

A parasitical gesture sharing a certain visceral quality with the candiru is an ethically complex project called *El Préstamo (The Loan)* (2000) by Guatemalan artist Aníbal Lopez (a.k.a. A-1 53167).[40] Lopez robbed an unsuspecting passerby in Guatemala City at gunpoint and used the pillaged money to fund an exhibition at Contexto space.[41] Thus the victim was unwillingly turned into a patron, funding the invitations, installation, and costs associated with the exhibition's opening reception, implicating the spectators and exhibition space as accomplices in the crime.

Lopez communicated the robbery, as event, to viewers by means of a poster that summarized what transpired and his motivations for committing the act. It also notified the audience that the liquor and food they were enjoying was courtesy of that crime. With only the poster as evidence, one can only speculate about whether or not the heist actually occurred, and those in attendance were forced either to disregard or to acknowledge and accept the professed offense responsible for the exhibition's manifestation.[42] Anyone who has been mugged will surely attest that there is a profound ethical and experiential difference between an actual and fictional robbery. Regardless, as viewers cannot independently verify it, the affect of the robbery is palpable whether the action happened or not.[43]

With *El Préstamo*, an unequal relation between each party involved in the work (artist, victim, witness, audience) exists, and Lopez traverses this chain of asymmetrical exchanges and induces a volte-face in regards to the funding of the artist—taking a system in which the artist seems to be vulnerable to the whims of foundations, collectors, and governments and making society itself vulnerable to the artist.[44] Each subject position in the act is taking without giving, complicit in the field of relations.[45] In taking money from a victim, who the artist rendered a patron, Lopez demonstrates the degree to which Serres's assertion that "exchange is always dangerous" can be true, and that the "gift is always a forfeit."[46] In this conceptualization, all exchange is predicated on abusive relations, exploitation, and unequal balances. Serres explains this idea by replacing Marx's concepts of "use value" and "exchange value" with the term "abuse value," which he defines as "complete, irrevocable consummation" that only works in "one direction."[47] Abuse value "precedes use- and exchange-value," according to Serres, because "exchange is always weighed, measured, calculated, taking into account a relation without exchange, an abusive relation."[48]

II. *Cymothoa Exigua*
(The Tongue-Eating Louse)

Consider the crustacean parasite known as *Cymothoa exigua*, the tongue-eating louse. Entering through a fish's gills, this parasite attaches itself at the base of the fish's tongue. Extracting blood, the parasite causes the fish's tongue to atrophy from lack of blood, allowing the parasite to attach its own body to the muscles of the fish's tongue stub and effectively replace its host's tongue. While the inhabited fish continues to use its tongue as before, the fish tongue—now embodied by the parasite—is no longer a tongue exactly, but a functional prosthesis and a hybrid organism. That the tongue specifically is the site of this struggle—and is also a key muscle of human speech—has symbolic significance when considering the many discursive and informational modes of parasitical practice, as does the verb form of the word "louse," which tellingly means to ruin or spoil.

A tongue-eating louse presents a model for the possibilities and problems raised when an artist appropriates the figurative "tongue," or voice, of a targeted institution. It also introduces heightened potential for parasitical artists to be instrumentalized by the institution—used, in reverse, as the mouthpiece of its target, and thus reduced to yet another vehicle for the language and operations of the host (whether a big fish or a small fish). Fish cannot speak as humans do, of course, but by anthropomorphizing the fish's tongue, the operations of *Cymothoa exigua* yields questions concerning the codes and formats of institutional address, the role of parasitical noise in communication, and the interconnected relationship between the host and parasite.

For theorists like Jacques Lacan and Louis Althusser,[49] the voice is an object of interpellation by which the subject is entered into the signifying order and positioned according to the determinations of ideologies. The tongue can therefore be seen as a vehicle for authoritative hailing. The voice of the institution beckons its public and, in doing so, simultaneously brings that public's existence into being—reproducing the ideological network of policies, tastes, positions, and actions to which one must subscribe as a constituent. These claims are circulated by an institution's internal agents through a variety of structures; in art such forms range from press releases, publications, wall texts, and other didactic materials to events and educational activities, as well as the normative curatorial processes of including, excluding, and arranging objects within exhibitions.

Reversed Lip-synching

Just before Stromberg began his illusionistic inhabitation of MoMA, there was a clear appropriation of the institution's voice in Whitlaw's *Monument to the Unknown Artist* (1968). Through this work, a subversive gallery tour through MoMA, Whitlaw drew connections between the struggle for recognition in the artistic canon and the violence of the Vietnam War, "cleverly recontexualiz[ing] culture itself as a battleground strewn with casualties."[50] By covertly replacing the customary audio guide tapes available for MoMA visitors with a revisionist rereading of MoMA's galleries, she accentuated the absence of work by "unknown artists," primarily African Americans and women.[51] By verbally deconstructing the established meaning of the works on display and asserting that the works played to elitist ideological desires, Whitlaw's substitution articulated a message counter to the voice of the institution, parasitically appropriating her host's mode of address to both expose and derail the function of that one-way system of communication from art institution to audience.

Like Stromberg's photographs, Whitlaw's tapes were uninvited irritations to the gallery. Security officers eventually found and destroyed the tapes, presumably because ventriloquizing the institution compromised the authority of the museum, effectively overriding the official code such that "one tongue invades another."[52] Just as Lacan and Althusser describe the subject's anxiety that the voice coming from one's mouth is not one's own (but rather that of the ideological state apparatus), such gestures of inhabiting the tongue frustrates power positions and exposes the tenuous authority of the institution's language. Inhabiting the tongue makes clear to the host not only that its own voice can be appropriated, but also that its authoritative communication is not objective nor indifferent, but rather constituted by ideological decisions by specific actors.

Critical Echolocation

While Stromberg and Whitlaw each entered their voices into an institutional frame, the institution's voice can also be replaced when it exits the space of the museum or gallery. For example, rather than locate its intervention at the source of institutional communication, the British artist collective BANK intercepted and redirected outgoing messages within the communicative channels of several hosts, specifically press releases from commercial galleries. Formed in 1991, BANK spent nearly a decade presenting similar, critical parodies of the art market through a variety of means, including the adoption of pseudo-corporate identities.[53] In BANK's *FAX BAK* project (started in 1998) and the related *Press Release* exhibitions (first shown in 1999 at Gallerie Poo Poo, London), BANK collected and edited publicity materials issued by galleries, commenting on the grammar, content, tone, form, and style of the texts directly onto the press releases in circulation at a given time. BANK then faxed the documents its members altered back to the galleries that issued them, and later exhibited these documents as works.[54] The attention paid to these generally one-way streams of information was redirected in almost real-time, away from the abstracted subjects to which they referred and back in on their points of origin, stimulating reflections on not only the significance of the press releases, but of the artists, institutions, and discourses involved. BANK's parasitical methodology sabotaged the institution's rhetoric by mirroring its voice and occupying its physical circuits of transmission. Ultimately, BANK's interventions showed press releases to be inflated advertisements masquerading as critical commentary and contextualization. Strategically, BANK's position as a collective limited any individual's liability for the group's actions, thereby diluting any potential for recourse.[55] This echoes corporate structure, suggesting another parasitical inhabitation—that of the shielding properties of incorporation.

BANK's *détournement* of press releases was effective, forcing galleries to rethink the language they employed and the curatorial and programmatic choices they made, as well as the images they projected, their graphic identities, and so on. BANK challenged the authority of the institutions, as well as the larger system in which they operate, by seizing the tongue from which they speak to change the conversation. BANK's parasitic inhabitation affirms Barthes's rhetorical question: "Does the best of subversions consist in disfiguring codes, not in destroying them?"[56] By locating its work within its hosts' press releases, BANK detaches the format from its parasitical dependence on another and shows the mechanism of dissemination as the primary material, site, and receptacle for events and ideas. The parasitic press release becomes a host for another order of parasites that enters through and appropriates the domain for counter messaging.

A Slower, Parallel Stream

Today, discursive and promotional channels are often confused as equivalent means of mediation. Some forty years after the introduction of conceptual art strategies, press releases do sometimes operate as the primary site for the work's dissemination in a globalized arena where it is possible to find out about almost everything but impossible to know and see everything in its entirety.[57] Nearly ten years after *FAX BAK*, the American duo Dexter Sinister engaged in a similar form of parasitical practice when they were invited to participate in the 2008 Whitney Biennial. Whereas BANK used the press release as material and site, for Dexter Sinister the press release offered more of a "frame of reference" and a specific institutional mode of circulation as opposed to a specific generic structure.

Collaboratively, Dexter Sinister produced and released a rich cache of documents from the Commander's Room at the 7th Regiment Armory (the offsite mirror of the museum where most of the biennial's programming took place). In this context, Dexter Sinister's "press releases" took the form of general press releases, logos, re-typeset versions of texts, essays, archival documents and memos, email exchanges, a loose chapter of a novel, re-released magazine articles, book releases, and much more.[58] They also created an alternative audio guide for navigating the Whitney Biennial, much like Whitlaw did at MoMA. Whereas BANK intercepted official communications, altered them, and then rerouted them back to their sources, Dexter Sinister joined the publicity office for the biennial, releasing information in parallel with and in the same channels as their host, yet distributing a very different stream of information designed to expand and slow, rather than contract and expedite, the superficial conclusions the biennial usually disperses through these channels for reasons of accessibility, brevity, and time.

Unlike BANK's *FAX BAK*, Dexter Sinister did not launch "a direct critique against the institution, or anyone else—at least not primarily or directly,"[59] but instead introduced "forms of communication and noise" in order to examine "the ways in which information is released and distributed."[60] Looking back to artist Hans Haacke's well-known *Shapolsky et al. Manhattan Real Estate Holdings, A Real Time Social System, as of May 1, 1971* (1971), we see an artist invited to exhibit his work at the Guggenheim Museum in New York, only to have that invitation terminated because of the implications of that work. Haacke, in examining the real-estate business of Harry Shapolsky over a twenty-year period, revealed ties between Shapolsky and the museum's trustees. Whereas Haacke was invited into the museum but soon became an overtly critical irritant in that space—in other words, a guest turned intruder—Dexter Sinister's response to their host was far less intentionally antagonistic. They forced a slowness of reception and a plurality of information, which are, of course, antithetical to what marketing channels generally achieve. Turning again to Serres: "his parasites are eating him up, and their noise covers his voice."[61]

Serres has observed that the French word *parasite* translates to "static," and the parasite-as-static is in fact a paramount model for the parasite's intercession into the exchange of information. Both Dexter Sinister's and

BANK's projects introduce a certain level of noise into the transmissions they hijack, but their productive ends show noise to be a necessary artifact to any form of communication. There is a direct correlation between the intensity of activity on the channel and the communication of the message, between noise and information, between parasitism and functionality.

Resembling the Tongue

The American artist group the Yes Men parasite specific forms of address and assume the semblances of other entities, which grants them access to sites or contexts that are otherwise inaccessible, such as television programs, closed-door conventions, and other speaking engagements. Yet while they are officially invited to speak, they do so in disguise as their confused hosts are not aware of *who* it is they are actually inviting. Whereas BANK intervened in the communications of others, the Yes Men actually communicate *as* others: they pose as particular people or invent representatives of existing companies. Whereas Dexter Sinister introduced a parallel stream of information into and beside an authoritative institutional stream, the Yes Men, camouflaged, become an institution's mouthpiece.

In fact, the Yes Men's Andy Bichlbaum posed as a spokesman of Dow Chemical named Jude Finisterra on BBC World TV in 2004, on the twentieth anniversary of the 1984 Union Carbide chemical spill in Bhopal, India. As Finisterra, Bichlbaum announced that Dow Chemical, the company that took over Union Carbide in 2001, was finally taking full responsibility for the disaster, in which at least twenty thousand people died and thousands more were made sick. Putting this landmark announcement into perspective, Bichlbaum explained this was "the first time in history that a publicly owned company of anything near the size of Dow has performed an action which is significantly against its bottom line simply because it is the right thing to do." Dow Chemical stock lost value temporarily, and surely many victims were disheartened after BBC World TV later notified viewers of the hoax, but, as Carrie Lambert-Beatty writes: "For those two hours, the world believed that there would be something like justice in Bhopal; for that time, there existed a different model for corporate decision-making, an ethical as well as financial bottom line."[62]

Just as Motti, through the spectacle of the media apparatus, took responsibility for horrible disasters and inhabited the voice of the absent Indonesian delegate to claim responsibility when it was not being taken, the Yes Men stand in for their hosts, making them accountable, speaking for them, as them, because the hosts refuse to do so. The Yes Men's uncanny ability to transform—with the aid of a business suit—into the semblance of their host, ostensibly becoming the host's representative, is a type of ventriloquism that forces the host to enunciate against its will, or even without its knowledge.

A Silent Tongue

To parasite a channel of authoritative communication is not only to make visible the falseness of an institution's voice, but also to show that these contrived pathways have real-world effects. As arbitrary as an institution's voice may seem, the symbolic pronouncements articulated in bureaucratic documents regulate the movements, behaviour, and self-identification of subjects. The power granted in law to certain actors makes their decisions inviolable, and therefore the approval of the state is necessary for a subject's self-constitution (let us not forget the experience of people "without papers," who, in their exclusion from the system, are therefore illegal and thus rendered invisible and silent, though this invisibility can also be a form of agency).[63]

In the flow of detached bureaucratic exchange there are often hiccups or mistakes that defer the normal passage of information through the appropriate channels to open up a space for artists to enter, where proclaimed impartiality can force the state to unknowingly accept false claims. For instance, the Vietnamese Danish artist Danh Vo has a curious ongoing project through which he constructs the life story of a fictional son by way of bureaucratic recognition.[64] In this work, a fictitious birth certificate begets a chain of events and procedures that constitute the experience of the absent son, presumably terminating with an official death certificate. In relation to Vo, the documents he collects and appropriates express, through an official tongue, the determination of people's movements and actions and are codifications and traces of such transactions. Thus, a child exists because the documents say so.[65] By using the language and formats of official documents, Vo is subversively playing with what John Searle refers to as the institution's "status indicators"—"policeman's uniforms, wedding rings, marriage certificates, driver's licenses, passports, etc."[66]— that serve as markers of power, permission, obligation, and authorization.

Ana Teixeira Pinto observes in Vo's work that "in the staged clash between bureaucracy and biography, the dismaying outcome is not that bureaucracy might impair biography but that biography is an effect of bureaucracy."[67] Vo himself has conjectured that his strategies and creative negotiation of social apparatuses may be an outgrowth of his experience as an immigrant, perhaps similar to the way in which Cadere viewed himself as a marginalized outsider for being part Romanian.[68] Nevertheless, Vo's work shows that constraining systems can be and are often under-mined, but also that these codes are social and historical constructions.

There's a similar sentiment in Kristin Lucas's *Refresh* (2007). On October 5, 2007, the artist officially changed her name from Kristin Sue Lucas to Kristin Sue Lucas in the Superior Court of California in Oakland. Trading in her name for the exact same name, the artist asserted that she wanted to "refresh" her identity as though she were a web page.[69] Divorcing the particularity of the name from the body, even temporarily, questions the construction of subjectivity in relationship to formal measures and there-fore demonstrates the contingency and artificiality of iden-tity. Lucas petitioned the court for a name change in the standard procedure, and after some deliberation, it was eventually granted.

Lucas put statutory procedure into a feedback loop, forcing administrators into a double take of the system they invest in and maintain.[70] Her deference to the legal system "is both crediting the government with more power than it actually has, and tacitly raising the question of whether, in fact, the judge has the authority to grant a new lease on life."[71] Lucas entered, irritated, and provoked the mouth-piece of the institution to question its own regimes philo-sophically and, in doing so, forced the court's voice, the judge, to not only acknowledge her, but to accept her exis-tential change. In its noisy obstruction, the parasite rein-vents the host, becoming an integral part in the system by forcing it to reorient whatever message the host transmits.

III. *Toxoplasma Gondii*

It is perhaps that we, like everything else, are parasites. On parasitism John Brown writes: "Nature is not without a parallel strongly suggestive of our social perversions of justice, and the comparison is not without its lessons."[72] Indeed, parasites operate with a brutality on par with humans, a brutality well beyond the violence of Lopez's previously mentioned robbery. On a certain level, separating ourselves from parasites is as futile as distinguishing the "built environment" from "the natural world."

For instance, Brown notes that *the ichneumon fly is parasitic in the living bodies of caterpillars and the larvae of other insects. With cruel cunning and ingenuity surpassed only by man, this depraved and unprincipled insect perforates the struggling caterpillar, and deposits her eggs in the living, writhing body of her victim.*[73] Of course, Brown is using hyperbole, but if we read him literally, his statements unfairly anthropomorphize and moralize the behaviour of parasites, citing the "innate cruelty" with which they "eat their way into the living substance of their unwilling but helpless host, avoiding all the vital parts to prolong the agony of a lingering death."[74] Every living thing takes, at some point, without giving back. And every living thing is infested with parasites, which further contain their own unique species of parasites; as each parasite has its own parasites, parasites make up the majority of life on earth.[75] Parasites are catalysts in evolution, their adaptability to the conditions of their hosts forces the hosts to transform. The same can be said for artists working parasitically.

Deconstructing the notion of the parasite by reversing and breaking down the fictitious opposition of "host/parasite," Jacques Derrida and J. Hillis Miller each unmasks the paradoxical etymology of "guest" and "host" (where parasite implies a host, and guest, host, hospitality, and hostility, all derive from the same root, the French *hôte*).[76] For both writers, parasites undermine the integrity of social, symbolic, and linguistic systems by elaborating endless chains of dependence, citation, and influence—the various ways ideas, ideologies, and institutions host contradictory concepts they'd prefer to exclude. The host's hospitality toward the guest is contingent upon the host being, first, a guest in its own domain, with each position dependent on one's acknowledgment or exclusion of the other's right to be there. Their mutual determination illustrates the impossibility of sustaining the host position as a controlling subject on which the principle of hospitality is based. When brought to bear upon the formations of social systems and particularly art institutions, theories that stress the interrelation and interchange between parasite and host offer a nuanced way of thinking through interventionist strategies.

Let's return again to Whitlaw. Curiously enough, she makes an appearance in Bob Dylan's memoir *Chronicles* (2004), where he tells the story of meeting the "outlaw artist" at a dinner party. After describing her as walking "in a motion like a slow dance," the singer/songwriter recounts asking Whitlaw, "What's happening?" Her response, in true parasitical fashion: "I'm here to eat the big dinner."[77] An unwelcome guest that gobbles the surplus of her host, Whitlaw positions herself as a social parasite. As Serres reminds us: "To be a parasite means: to eat at somebody else's table."[78] The host and the parasite share the food at the table, but the host is also the food, "his substance consumed without recompense, as when one says, 'He is eating me out of house and home.'"[79] The intruder arrives as an affront to the host's home (hostility); the gracious host welcomes the parasite in (hospitality). She takes from the table and gives nothing in return. In this way, hospitality begets hostility and vice versa.[80] Extracting surplus from the host and exploiting the hospitality on offer, Whitaw was at the dinner not only to procure sustenance parasitically, but also to interrupt the structure of affairs where manners govern behaviour, reversing the hierarchy of inviter/invited by making visible an unsaid and corrupt social contract.

Tag

If everything is always already parasitical, then why is it that when artists work parasitically they are able to achieve perceptible results? What is it about the conditions of art practice and institutions today that compel artists turn to such a strategy? Let's look once more to biological parasites for guidance. After all, it could be that, for all of their creative and industrious trespass and transgressions, the most gifted and effective parasites are those that possess the ability to make their hosts come to them. Where the candiru locates an opening and enters through its potential host's waste, other parasites operate with an even more complex mode of infection. One such parasite is the single-celled parasitic protozoan *Toxoplasma gondii*. While *Cymothua exigua*'s manner of replacing its host's tongue with itself demonstrates an impressive mimetic corporality, *Toxoplasma* actually manipulates the functions, even the minds, of its host, forcing it to act counter to its own self-interest. *Toxoplasma* replaces the mind from within and, in a way, remotely. Like parasites that inhabit intermediate organisms in order to enter another, more desirable host down the line, *Toxoplasma* rides a chain of mammalian and avian interactions in order to enter its preferred host: the cat.

Sexually reproducing in the belly of felines, *Toxoplasma* spreads through processes of digestion and defecation. When prey, such as a rat, comes into contact with the predator's feces (or contaminated soil, water, or meat), it picks up the parasite, which alters the behaviour of the infected, reducing its ingrained cautionary fear of cat waste, and causes it to become more likely to be captured by its predators. When the cat eats the rat, the cat ingests the parasite as well—*Toxoplasma* has thus completed one cycle, and the process may begin again. The cat becomes a machine for the production of parasites, as well as a channel for their dissemination (defecating them on one end, re-ingesting them at the other).

Some parasites can only survive in specific hosts, but *Toxoplasma* is astonishingly versatile; it is able to live in thousands of species—including humans, with over half of the global population playing host. In most humans, the parasite remains dormant, forming a silent pact with its intermediate host by symbiotically sharing space with the body's defenses.[81] Recent studies have found, however, that even the quiescent *Toxoplasma* may affect human behaviour, connecting its prevalence to everything from schizophrenia, to increased risk-taking and aggression, to cultural differences.[82] In terms of cultural production, *Toxoplasma* can be related to artist Joe Scanlan's statement that "success is not a matter of status, but of circulation."[83] Its distribution is almost incomprehensibly widespread.

Appropriating Appropriation

In its host's house, a parasite must be humble and quiet, for being too visible can be fatal. Consider once more Whitlaw's stealthy chicanery. In 1984, while the "Pictures Generation" of artists was reaching a pinnacle of success, Whitlaw was apprehended while breaking into the house of a New York dealer who represented many well-regarded artists who use the strategy of appropriation in their own production. Ralph Rugoff explains that "during a pre-trial hearing, Whitlaw maintained that if theft could be art—at least in the hands of appropriation artists—then her action, and those of thousands of other thieves, should likewise be judged by aesthetic, rather than penal, codes."[84]

Whitlaw's gesture charts a chain of exploitive relations, calling each actor involved a parasite. Attempting to appropriate from the proprietor of artists who appropriate, Whitlaw's project can be seen as appropriately illustrating Serres's assertion that "the parasite parasitizes the parasites."[85] If other artists could benefit from the theft of cultural signs, objects, and images, then surely Whitlaw could continue this chain of colonization, extending the logic of exploitation back to the things themselves. As the French anarchist Pierre-Joseph Proudhon famously wrote in 1840: "Property is theft!"[86] The individual expropriation of goods replicates the general appropriation of labour and resources in capitalism. If artists, dealers, and collectors could benefit from the theft of cultural signs, objects, and images, then surely Whitlaw could continue this chain of colonization, extending the logic of exploitation back to the things themselves.[87]

For Serres, humans are the parasites of parasites, the grand parasites of all nature. He asks, "What does man give to the cow, to the tree, to the steer, who give him milk, warmth, shelter, work, and food? What does he give? Death."[88] As Marcel Mauss, Bataille, Miller, and many others have attested, the gift always comes with a reciprocal obligation, an unequal exchange that never finds a balance and serves the interests of the giver as much as the receiver.[89] But traditionally an artist becomes an unwelcome guest when they abuse the hospitality of his or her host, turning malicious or critical intentions onto the institution itself. The artist remains at an impasse located between the false distinctions of opposition and complicity, still adhering to a dependency on the very institutions that critical practitioners have sought to circumvent since the '60s.

The mutualistic parasitism that emerges from Serres's idea of dinner guests suggests another, more homeopathic possibility. Perhaps the host itself needs the parasite, just as our bodies need bacteria and other organisms to maintain homeostasis. The host uses the parasite to regenerate and invigorate, inviting criticism in order to question, develop, and reify its status.[90] This "impulse [for an institution] to criticize itself from within, to question its institutionalization," is not a defensive strategy, but is, as Benjamin Buchloh describes, one of the "essential features of modernism."[91] One can see the evolution of "institutional critique" in the recent curatorial trend towards "New Institutionalism," which instrumentalizes certain forms of critical practice by inviting it in placidly. Still, there are cases in which artists, aware of the shared benefits for both the artist and the institution, inhabit that mutualism, subverting the exchange to disrupt and expose it for what it is, but in doing so, also show that such mutualism does not entirely sap the potential it generates.

A Parasitical Precipice

In the spring of 2000, the Viennese artist collective GELITIN and fourteen other artists were invited to share an official studio residency on the ninety-first floor of one of the World Trade Center towers in New York. GELITIN's contribution was a "club house" made of cardboard, which concealed the group's activities from their hosts and the other residents.[92] Using this privacy productively, the four members of the collective realized a project entitled *B-Thing* (2000). Undetected, the group removed a window and replaced it with a cantilevered balcony of their own construction. A group member stood upon the platform for almost ten minutes and was photographed from an orbiting helicopter flying a small clique of in-the-know collectors and dealers as observing participants in the project.

GELITIN immediately dismantled its contraption and the project thus unfolded without incident.[93] Still, while the group's intervention shares some resemblance to those discussed in the *Candiru* section for the way in which access is gained through subversively exploiting a weakness in the autonomy of the host's system, *B-Thing* is slightly different. Without the building, the balcony would fall. However, it also seems to suggest that in order for the institution to remain a unified body, it must have a parasite, an internal difference, which forces the host to reorient and defend its boundaries. Such intersubjective negotiation shows that the parasite is never simply external to its host, but rather engaged in a reciprocal exchange where not only does the parasite "come to live off the life of the body in which it resides," but "the host incorporates the parasite to an extent, willy-nilly offering it hospitality: providing it with a place."[94] The parasite then "takes place"; it ruptures the sovereignty of the host's domain, turning the host's hospitality to hostility by confusing and occupying the space between outside and inside. Previously whole constructions are shown to be heterogeneous, operating less as a destructive move, and more as a supplementary displacement, a shift in the site's regularized operations.

This dilemma between complicity and critique is even more pronounced in art institutions. Since at least the '60s, practices variously described as "political art," "interventionism," or "institutional critique" have reproduced the figure of the artist as an antagonistic, parasitic force that attacks the stable object of "the institution," either divulging the institution's latent and manifest ideological and political intentions, or seeking to eradicate the space entirely. As the tongue-eating louse's predicament attests, co-optation may be inevitable for such attempts and might therefore be seen as superficial gestures lacking critical potential. For Andrea Fraser, such gestures are "victim[s] of [their own] success or failure, swallowed up by the institution [they] stood against."[95] While some may believe parasites risk reifying their host systems, treating ideology and institutions as static things, parasitical practices involve defamiliarizing the host, disrupting normative procedures, and making clear that systems of relations are exactly that: contingent social models enacted by the acceptance and accordance to certain rules that are not only artificial but made up of actors and asymmetrical relationships that are performed in specific ways.

The Intestine or the Tapeworm?

A constructivist reading of Serres's work, where the parasite's interruption rejuvenates and forces evolution in the host, frustrates numerous critiques in that such "interventionist" gestures lack critical potential. To return to Burroughs, a useful question might be: "Which came first, the intestine or the tapeworm?" Did the parasite evolve to exploit the habits of the host, or did the host develop according to the terms set out by the parasite? In what ways does the parasite violate the integrity of the host's homogeneous and defended domain, making clear to the host that its sovereign body was never its own? Perhaps the tapeworm and the intestine codeveloped, providing the perfect conditions for both to extract surplus from nourishment. The vast majority of our bodies are populated not by our own genetic material but by parasites.[96] Like the fish and the tongue-eating louse, where the parasite is effectively the same as an organ, the host's home is actually already populated by functional divergent organisms.[97]

The parasite is as much "you" as you are yourself, and what constitutes "you" is the collectivity of these internal and external interactions.

The host's defenses are what Donna Haraway refers to as "biopolitical maps,"[98] responsible for negotiating challenges to the sovereignty of the self, identifying what belongs and what doesn't. As Ed Cohen suggests, "What the parasite reveals is that the 'life of the body' also belongs to life in general, which is why the para-site can eat both with us (as guest, as commensal) and from us (the literal meaning of parasite). In so doing, the parasite confronts us with the fact that life does not properly 'take place' within a proper body."[99] "We" are no more autonomous than "they," and our parasites are on as intimate terms with our organs as our organs are to themselves.[100] Of course, the affective workings and effective dispersion of *Toxoplasma* suggests an intimacy of another sort—the collapse of any lingering semblance of distance between "us" and "them." In more clearly institutional terms, Andrea Fraser states: *It's not a question of inside or outside, or the number and scale of various organized sites for the production, presentation, and distribution of art. It's not a question of being against the institution: We are the institution.* [101]

The parasite is entrenched in the system in more than one sense: it is lodged in its host and it is a trespasser. Intimacy and enmity are not antithetical but rather mutually defined—a strategy of continuous association and dissociation that allows critical positions to be established and shifted. Marisa Jahn, writing about "embedded practices" that infuse into certain cultural, economic, and social systems, suggests that, due to their proximity and dependence on the host system, such practices "therefore signify not from a position of pure oppositionality (antagonism), but one in which the oppositionality is irreconcilably bound up with an empathic relationship to the larger whole (agonism)."[102] She raises the point that antagonism depends upon an essential and static system to attack face to face and destroy, while agonism (a political doctrine taken up by such thinkers as Michel Foucault, Ernesto Laclau, and Chantal Mouffe) emphasizes the positive aspects of dissent as a "permanent provocation,"[103] one that both recognizes dependencies and differences without the delusions of consensus. The host is shown not as a stable, closed, or homogenous entity, but rather a body politic that is at constant contestation with itself.

What makes a project parasitical is not only that it enters and feeds off a system, but that through its interruption, the project lays bare the parasitical interrelations within the system itself. These component relationships are what parasites feed on; parasites exploit systems of exploitation, interfering with perceived balances by deferring the normal route. Unencumbered by boundaries, such cunning acts of infringement enter into the unacknowledged economies of the host, the excesses and waste that it wants to deny. When parasites permeate paths of interaction and communication, they not only profit from modes of circulation but also by manipulating and deconstructing crucial codes. These efforts impart the role noise and interference plays in the transmission of information. While parasites are dependent on the context in which they operate,[104] theirs is a game of asserting their presence in the host while deferring and distracting the system's mechanisms. Even when invited into the dominant field of discourse, the parasite asserts itself as a stranger, one who recognizes not only the hidden pacts of hospitality and property, but also how the host is only a position that can be displaced.

Through many examples we've shown what parasites can offer artists in terms of models. And parasites tell us much about their hosts and the systems in which those hosts operate. But what is parasitism exactly? Is it a strategy of convenience, an operational channel for riding the waves of already established communication in order to exploit its scale and power? Does the parasite identify with its host? Is its embeddedness an empathetic gesture—towards identification or belonging? If host and parasite are constantly reversing relations, then what can be offered by identifying and naming these positions? What is at stake in a parasitic action? What happens when roles are inverted and dependencies revealed? Does the parasite reflect an impasse in transgression where there is no longer an oppositional position from outside, but where change is only conceivable from the inside? What can the parasite tell us about the interdependencies necessary for social and communication systems? The intimate yet poisonous interaction between parasite and host surely provides a more nuanced way of charting exploitation between parties, but does interrupting essentialist binary models of abuse allow for identification between others, or does it wipe away the problems between them? Does the parasite offer a model for the host, a way of institutional arrangement that recognizes and evolves through intrusion? Can an institution be built that reveres and learns from the parasite without making it one of its own? Is the parasite contagious? Can subtle interruptions in specific spaces effect broader structural and ideological shifts? When some projects bring external or marginalized voices into the institution, what is their dependence on the institution's contradictions? Is their inclusion just a simple use of a middleman so that the institution does not have to confront its own exclusions? In every case of parasitical practice, the first question is, who is parasiting whom? Though this is not the last question.

Perhaps to think through parasites is to use the parasite

as an optical device with which to see relations break down; perhaps to work parasitically is to make those relations more visible. And yet perhaps it is less about why than what for. Both questions (why and what) are, of course, inextricably bound to how, but what we've sought to show is that parasitical inhabitations are not simply a mode of operation, a tactic, or a medium for cultural production. Surely, the most advantageous factor in using parasites as a framework is the way in which parasites reveal the complexity of all given relations between things (sentient or otherwise), as well as how parasites render binaries worthless. What emerges from this clarity of vision is the ability to study and disrupt those relations. How parasites shift according to certain rules and how their hosts must shift according to their parasites is the very point of parasitic gestures—it is how parasitic gestures become more than gestures. It is how they effect change.

1. Michel Serres, *The Parasite*, trans. Lawrence R. Schehr (Baltimore: Johns Hopkins University Press, 1982), 293–94.

2. Rosalind Constable, "The Longest Running One-man Show in Town," *New York*, June 28, 1971, 56–57.

3. For Brian O'Doherty, even a fire hose presents "an esthetic conundrum" within the white cube, which operates parasitically, subsuming anything that enters its space—symbolically divorcing it from the exterior world its architecture serves to hide. Brian O'Doherty, "Notes on the Gallery Space," in *Inside the White Cube: The Ideology of the Gallery Space* (Berkeley: University of California Press 1986), 15.

4. Serres, *The Parasite*, 293–94.

5. Some parasites draw so ravenously from their hosts that they can debilitate them to the point at which they cannot protect or feed themselves adequately (e.g., mites causing mange in dogs).

6. Jean-Luc Nancy, "The Intruder," in *Corpus: Perspectives in Continental Philosophy*, trans. Richard A. Rand (New York: Fordham University Press, 2008), 161–62.

7. Ibid., 163.

8. Serres, *The Parasite*, 64–65.

9. William S. Burroughs, *Naked Lunch: The Restored Text Edition*, eds. James Grauerholtz and Barry Miles (New York: Grove/Atlantic Inc, 2001), 38.

10. The small, almost translucent fish normally hides in mud and attacks the open cavities of larger fish (most often the gills), eating its flesh and blood.

11. The urogenital surgeon Anoar

Samad attended to a man from Itacoatiara on the Amazon River who sought medical attention for obstruction of his urethra. "Trichomycteridae candiru," *Oregon Piranha Exotic Fish Exhibit*, last modified July 7, 2009, https://fillip.ca/i1ue.

12. The development of surplus goods left humans open to macroparasites—to thieves, then warlords who levied taxes in exchange for protection, shaving off the surplus while leaving enough behind for producers to continue. This process of parasitism evolved into vast divisions of labour and value.

13. *If microparasitism may be likened to a nether millstone, grinding away at human populations through time, human-to-human macroparasitism has been almost as universal—an upper millstone, pressing heavily upon the majority of the human race. Between them, the two forms of parasitism usually tended to keep the peasant majority of civilized populations close to bare subsistence by systematically withdrawing resources from their control.* Just as microparasites have circulated throughout the globe via trade, macroparasites have likewise evolved in the form of war, agents of theft who steal the resources and identities of whole nations. W. H. McNeill, *The Human Condition: An Ecological and Historical View* (Princeton, NJ: Princeton University Press, 1979), 8.

14. Georges Bataille, *The Accursed Share*, vol. 1, *Consumption*, trans. Robert Hurley (New York: Zone Books, 1991), 21.

15. Seth Price, "Dispersion," *Distributed History*, 2002, http://distributedhistory.com/Dispersion2008.pdf (PDF), 14.

16. *9 at Leo Castelli* was on display from December 4–28, 1968, at the gallerist's warehouse, then located at 103 West 108th Street, New York, New York.

17. Annie Cohen-Solal, *Leo and His Circle: The Life of Leo Castelli* (New York: Alfred A. Knopf, 2010), 507.

18. Astrid Ilhe, "Andre Cadere: Interventions in the Public Domain," in *André Cadere: Peinture sans fin*, eds. Karola Grasslin, Fabrice Hergott, and Alexander van Grevenstein (Koln: Verlag der Buchhandlung Walther Konig, 2007), 43.

19. In a sense, the intentional error ensured that each *Barres de Bois Rond* arrived with its own parasite, a thing both in and out of place.

20. Cadere presented his rods throughout Europe and in New York, bringing them to opening receptions for artists such as Robert Ryman, Daniel Buren, and Barnett Newman, or to biennials. However, he also took them on the subway and to cafes, parks, and other public spaces.

21. Karola Grasslin, Fabrice Hergott, and Alexander van Grevenstein, eds., "Interview with Linda Morris," in *André Cadere: Peinture sans fin* (Koln: Verlag der Buchhandlung Walther Konig), 17.

22. Mark Godfrey, "Andre Cadere: Staatliche Kunsthalle Baden-Baden, Germany," *Frieze*, March 2008, 181.

23. Birnbaum is referring to Cadere's intervention into an exhibition of Valerio Adami's paintings at Galerie Maeght in Paris, which he cites in "Andre Cadere: Staatliche Kunsthalle Baden-Baden, Germany," *Artforum*, January 2008, 271.

24. Ihle, "Andre Cadere: Interventions in the Public Domain," 55.

25. Cadere was keen to keep his contrived outsider position, a position that is echoed by Nancy: *Once [an intruder] is in, if he remains a stranger,*

and for all the time he remains, instead of "naturalizing himself," his arrival does not cease: he continues to come and never stops being an intrusion; he continues to be without right and familiarity and habits, but he remains a disturbance, a turbulence amidst the intimacy. Otherwise the extraneousness of the stranger is eliminated before he walks over the threshold. Jean-Luc Nancy, "The Intruder," 166.

26. The inclusion of an artist's work in documenta could be seen as the ultimate symbol of acceptance and appreciation of that work, but such an invitation would present a negation of that artist's parasitical status.

27. The artist was asked to produce a new work for an exhibition at the Centre d'Art Neuchâtel. Motti went to a Swiss first division soccer match between the Neuchâtel / Xamax and Young Boys football clubs at the La Maladière stadium instead, targeting a significantly broader public than an art show could provide.

28. *ONU,* intervention at the 53rd session of the Commission on Human Rights, UN, Geneva (1997).

29. Perhaps the most overt example was in 2004 at the semifinal of the French Open tennis championship during a visit by the American president George W. Bush. Gianni Motti, sitting in the VIP stand opposite live television cameras, wore a hood on his head and kept his hands behind his back, alluding to the controversial images taken of prisoners by soldiers at Abu Ghraib. While this event injected politics into sports, such a gesture also brought excluded views into a site already for protest. Robyn Whitlaw had an "appearance" in a 1972 *Life* magazine photograph by Arthur Schatz, which shows the artist holding up a blank white sign above a packed street of umbrella-toting SDS anti-war protesters. Her gesture was an act of protest and a forfeit, an elaboration of the impasse of dissent and the invisibility and silence of numerous voices within the movement. Whitlaw's action protests the site of protest itself, intervening into the protest's field of relations rather than the content of the demonstration.

30. Additionally, since 1985, Motti has claimed responsibility for numerous eclipses of the moon or sun, falling meteorites, earthquakes in California and the Alps, and even the 1986 explosion of the Challenger shuttle (*Eclipses,* 1986; *Revendications, Terremoto, revendication,* 1996; *AFP,* 1986). An autocratic proclamation, Motti's claiming of catastrophe and change renders the world readymade, parasitically inserting himself into global causation.

31. One can say that Motti resembles Woody Allen's character Zelig (from his 1983 movie of the same name). The faux documentary concerns Leonard Zelig, a Jewish New Yorker who comes to fame in the 1920s when it is discovered that he compulsively imitates whatever social milieu he finds himself in, transforming himself both physically and mentally into a reflection of the people who surround him.

32. Similarly, the artist David Horvitz has been inserting himself anonymously into photographs appearing in Wikipedia entries, on an ongoing basis. See Jeff Khonsary, "The Encyclopedia That Anyone Can Edit," *Fillip* 14, Summer 2011, 98–103.

33. Can a parasite and a host be one and the same at the same time, and in the same body?

34. Whereas Piper's previous public actions in the 1970–71 *Catalysis* works

played out the relationship between abject difference and public indifference or disgust, the *Mythic Being* series is noticeably more ambiguous.

35. *To distribute the fictional persona, Piper devised a complex mathematical structure, like those she employed in earlier works, through which she would "isolate" and mine 144 passages from her diary, mount the same number of performances, then "publicize" and circulate the same number of two-dimensional works through a "widely distributed newspaper." The artist did not follow through with the strict numerical component of the project.* Cherise Smith, "Remember the Audience: Adrian Piper's Mythic Being Advertisements," *Art Journal* 66.1 (2007), 46.

36. The first advertisement appeared in the "Theatre" section of the *Voice*; the remainder was published in the "Gallery" section roughly once a month from October 25, 1973, until February 2, 1975. There is one significant exception: the ad work for June 27, 1974, was censored by the *Voice* because it contains the phrase: "DON'T FEEL PARTICULARLY HORNY, BUT FEEL I SHOULD MASTURBATE ANYWAY JUST BECAUSE I FEEL SO GOOD ABOUT IT. 6-6-70." A small, rectangular text advertisement appeared in its place and announced that the original advertisement could be seen at the Jaap Rietman Bookstore on 157 Spring St.

37. Adrian Piper, "The Mythic Being: Getting Back," in *Out of Order, Out of Sight*, Vol. I, *Selected Writings in Meta-Art 1968-1992* (Cambridge, MA: MIT Press, 1999), 117

38. Serres, *The Parasite*, 218.

39. Ibid.

40. Since 1997, Lopez has worked under the name A-1 53167, his Guatemalan ID card number, as a gesture of both erasing assumptions about his cultural identity and immersing himself within a bureaucratic system.

41. Like a parasite, Lopez terrified and threatened his host by hijacking his victim's reserves and diverting those resources into other uses.

42. Erin Starr White, "Lifting: Theft in Art, Fort Worth Contemporary Arts," *Art Lies*, Winter 2008, 96–97.

43. Lopez's work is in some ways a literalization of an action Adrian Piper performed as part of *Mythic Being. Getting Back*, a performance in collaboration with David Auerbach, Piper described as involving *my loitering on the sidewalk reading a newspaper, while David, a stranger, reads over my shoulder and tries to strike up a conversation containing many of the features just described. I react with violent and barely suppressed anger, asking him to please get out of my face. Shocked, he withdraws, having appropriated the newspaper I've finished reading. But my hostility hasn't been fully expressed, so I decide to mug him and steal his money. I follow him to the nearest park, jumping him from behind, throwing him to the ground, and making off with the newspaper (he has no money).* Adrian Piper, *Out of Order, Out of Sight*, 147. Whereas Piper's performance was staged and included a knowing victim—and thus an accomplice in reality—Lopez recasts his audience as unknowing accomplices in what is a true crime, or so we are led to believe. In both projects, the inter-subjective game of parasitical power becomes apparent by making visible the ways in which one position in an antagonistic relation is contingent on its opposing force.

44. Implicitly elaborating the dependence of the artist on the charity of patrons, foundations, and

governmental bodies, Lopez intensifies this subjection, exaggerating the servile relationship between producers and funders into one where the artist violently demands support rather than waits for "grants."

45. Since we are not party to the exchange, we are left to assume that the victim is either a wealthy beneficiary of capitalist exploitation, a victim of such a system, or, more realistically, one who is abused by both inequitable economic relations and an active, interpellated agent within those structures. Perhaps this is why the work is titled "the loan" and not "the theft" or "the payment": though the money has been taken from the patron, it will be returned in symbolic capital.

46. Serres, *The Parasite*, 80.

47. Ibid.

48. Ibid.

49. See Louis Althusser, "Ideology and Ideological State Apparatuses (Notes Towards an Investigation)," in *"Lenin and Philosophy" and Other Essays* (London: New Left Books, 1971), 121–73.

50. Ralph Rugoff, *Circus Americanus* (London: Verso [Haymarket Series], 1995), 77.

51. If the museum is a monument for "the unknown artist," then its existence is as a trace marking the absence of those excluded, unknown, or refused. A tool for critique and iconoclasm, Whitlaw also advocated for an alternative mode of interaction with masterpieces, even encouraging visitors to appreciate the tactile quality of a Jackson Pollock painting by feeling the surface.

52. Doris Somner, *Bilingual Aesthetics: A New Sentimental Education* (Durham, NC: Duke University Press, 2004), 60.

53. BANK took its name from the site of its first exhibition, which was on display within a disused bank in London. BANK attempted to reclaim control over every aspect of its work by inhabiting all of the roles of presentation, such as marketing and funding as well as artistic and curatorial practice.

54. It is a common complaint that interpretive materials drain a work of its "blood," its "life," which would then cast critics, curators, historians, and other cultural workers as vampiric. The standardized proofreading marks BANK employs are a means of imposing upon and reforming the text, borrowing from standardized institutional codes and personal regiments, reopening whatever closure these documents may imply or cause. Moreover, BANK's coded and graphological inscriptions are themselves a parasitical language, semantic and asemic alike.

55. Grading the press releases issued by galleries on a scale of 1 to 10 and inscribing them with critiques ranging from coy to scathing, BANK in turn received letters and answering machine messages from the galleries, which ranged from calculated thanks to unmitigated anger.

56. Roland Barthes, *Sade/Fourier/Loyola* (Baltimore, MD: Johns Hopkins University Press, 1997), 123.

57. The role of advertising in art's distribution and constitution has become increasingly expansive throughout history, but the inflated use of promotional channels as the primary site for art's appearance or existence may be an inheritance of tactics and aspirations from the conceptual art of the '60s. Conceptual artists and entities such as Robert Barry, Bulletin, On Kawara, and Stephen Kaltenbach, among others, used these channels (press releases, postcards, subscription

lists, mail art networks) as sites for the materialization and movement of ideas, but also depended upon such formats to justify, commercialize, and announce the very existence of their ideas. Such gestures dialectically emphasized the correlation of "primary information" ("'the essence of the piece,' its ideational part") and "secondary information" ("the material information by which one becomes aware of the piece, the raw matter, the fabricated part, the form of presentation").

58. Other activities included two days of curator Raimundas Malasauskas randomly calling a payphone in the Armory from the Commander's Room and reading Tom Marioni's *Predictions '78* (1978) to whoever answered.

59. Adam Kleinman, "Dexter Sinister," *Bomb Magazine*, March 2008, http://bombsite.com/issues/999/articles/3117.

60. Kleinman, "Dexter Sinister."

61. Serres, *The Parasite*, 216.

62. Carrie Lambert-Beatty, "Make Believe: Parafiction and Plausibility," *October* 129 (Summer 2009), 51–84.

63. This gesture of modifying the body through bureaucratic procedures resonates with an earlier but also continuing project, *Vo Rocasco Rasmussen* (2003–), where the artist marries and immediately divorces several people (who have been in some way influential in Vo's life) in order to accumulate a succession of last names. A response to debates in Denmark regarding homosexual marriage (Denmark was the first to legalize same-sex marriage, but, until recently, did not allow same-sex partners to apply for adoption), Vo's gesture redefines the structure of marriage by parodying its formal protocols.

64. If bodies are ruled by documents, the artist asserts, then "performance art" today is not dependent on the presence of a body, but rather on the relationship between social rites and their certification. Vo mentioned this line of thinking in a conversation with Post Brothers.

65. John Searle, "What Is an Institution?" *Journal of Institutional Economics* vol. 1:1 (2005), 15.

66. Ibid.

67. Ana Teixeira Pinto, "Danh Vo's 'All your deeds shall in water be writ, but this in marble' at Isabella Bortolozzi Galerie, Berlin," exhibition review in *Art Agenda*, October 27, 2010.

68. Carr, "Artists at Work: Danh Vo."

69. *When you look at a web page, you are seeing the data that is assigned to it by a server. If you hit the 'refresh' button on your keyboard but nothing on the server has changed, then what is seen on the screen appears to be the same, but in fact, this is a whole new set of data retrieved from the server.* Marisa Jahn, "'Refresh': Versionhood and the Multiplicity of the Self, An Interview with Kristin Lucas," in *Byproducts: On the Excess of Embedded Artistic Practices* (Toronto: YYZ Books & REV-, 2010), 113.

70. Because the judge ordered a court recess for two weeks while he determined the case's legitimacy, the judge was forced into a philosophical and methodological paradox.

71. Jahn, "'Refresh': Versionhood and the Multiplicity of the Self," 114.

72. John Brown, *Parasitic Wealth or Money Reform: A Manifesto to the People of the United States and to the Workers of the World* (Chicago: C. H. Kerr & Company, 1898), 162.

73. Ibid.

74. Ibid.

75. *Every living thing has at least one*

parasite that lives inside it or on it. Many, like leopard frogs and humans, have many more. There's a parrot in Mexico with thirty different species of mites on its feathers alone. And the parasites themselves have parasites, and some of those parasites have parasites of their own.... Scientists have no idea just how many species of parasites there are, but they do know one dazzling thing: parasites make up the majority of species on Earth. According to one estimate, parasites may outnumber free-living species four to one. In other words, the study of life is, for the most part, parasitology. Carl Zimmer, *Parasite Rex: Inside the Bizarre World of Nature's Most Dangerous Creatures* (New York: Free Press, 2000), xxi.

76. *If the host is both eater and eaten, he also contains in himself the double antithetical relation of host and guest, guest in the two-fold sense of friendly presence and alien invader. The words "host" and "guest" go back in fact to the same etymological root: ghos-ti, stranger, guest, host, properly "someone with whom one has reciprocal duties of hospitality." The modern English word "host" in this alternative sense comes from the Middle English (h)oste, from Old French, host, guest, from Latin hospes (stem hospit-), guest, host, stranger. The "pes" or "pit" in the Latin words and in such modern English words as "hospital" and "hospitality" is from another root, pot, meaning "master." The compound or bifurcated root ghos-pot meant "master of guests," "one who symbolizes the relationship of reciprocal hospitality," as in the Slavic gospodi, Lord, sir, master. "Guest," on the other hand, is from Middle English gest, from Old Norse gestr, from ghos-ti, the same root as for "host." A host is a guest, and a guest is a host. A host is a host. The relation of household master offering hospitality to a guest and the guest receiving it, of host and parasite in the original sense of "fellow guest," is inclosed within the word "host" itself.* J. Hillis Miller, "The Critic as Host," *Critical Inquiry* III, no. 3 (Spring 1977), 440.

77. Bob Dylan, *Chronicles*, vol. 1 (New York: Simon and Schuster, 2004), 66.

78. Serres, *The Parasite*, 17.

79. Miller, "The Critic as Host," 442.

80. Jacques Derrida offers the term "ipseity" to describe the twin poles of hospitality and hostility, which he sees as a kind of choreography of complicity and intersubjective negotiation between multiple entities. Jacques Derrida, *Monolingualism of the Other; or, the Prosthesis of Origin*, trans. Patrick Mensah (Stanford: Stanford University Press, 1996), 24.

81. *Toxoplasma* can be deadly, however, for those with depleted immune defenses, particularly afflicting fetuses that haven't developed defense mechanisms and people with AIDS. In this sense, *Toxoplasma* becomes also an illustration for how a parasite can be benign in some circumstances (in carriers with adequate immune defense), but deadly in others. The same strategy can yield different effects depending on the host and how the parasite positions itself along the chain.

82. See Carl Zimmer, *Parasite Rex*, 92–94; E. Fuller Torrey and Robert H. Yolken, "*Toxoplasma gondii* and schizophrenia," *Emerging Infectious Diseases* 9, no. 11 (November 2003), http://cdc.gov/ncidod/EID/vol9no11/03-0143.htm; Jaroslav Flegr, "Effects of Toxoplasma on Human Behaviour," *Schizophrenia Bulletin* 33, no. 3 (January 2007), 757–60; Kevin D. Lafferty, "Can the Common Brain Parasite, *Toxoplasma gondii*, Influence Human Culture?" *Proceedings of the Royal Society B* 273 (2006), 2749–55,

https://fillip.ca/blog.

83. Elisabeth Wetterwald, "Consumption and the Self: Elisabeth Wetterwald Interviews Joe Scanlan," in *Rue Sauvage* (Dijon: Les press du réel, 2003), http://thingsthatfall.com/interviews/dispersion.php.

84. Ralph Rugoff, *Circus Americanus* (London: Verso [Haymarket Series], 1995), 77.

85. Serres, *The Parasite*, 55.

86. Pierre-Joseph Proudhon, *No Gods, No Masters: An Anthology of Anarchism*, ed. Daniel Guerin, trans. Paul Sharkey (San Francisco: AK Press, 2005), 55–56.

87. Whitlaw's meta-appropriation calls into question the authorship and ownership of the imagery those artists used to call into question the authorship of others, while also appropriating the imagery from the dealer who would claim to have owned those objects, and thus the stolen imagery they contain. In the end, the dealer opted not to press charges in order to save himself from further embarrassment.

88. Serres, *The Parasite*, 5.

89. To be a parasite means to divert food, money, energy—anything material—from its destined path. Once at the host's table, the parasite *in return…must regale the other diners with his stories and his mirth. To be exact, [the parasite] exchanges good talk for good food; he buys his dinner, paying for it in words. It is the oldest profession in the world* (Serres, *The Parasite*, 34). In other words, when an artist is invited into the home of the art institution, the unspoken pact is that the artist must be thankful and exchange the benefits of financing and resources for the symbolic capital of their works.

90. Vaccination, Serres reminds us, is based upon this principle: the parasite that enters the body as contaminant then protects it against further contamination: *These logics shifting around minimal angles are at work in other systems as well. Parasitology, as we shall soon realize, uses the vocabulary of the host: hostility or hospitality. First of all, the parasite is always small; it never exceeds the size of insects or arthropods. In fact, the most numerous are protozoa or bacteria or viruses. Their small effects are usually well-tolerated by the organisms, which quickly rediscover their health, that is to say, their silence (at least relatively). This equilibrium that is well taken care of, thanks to the defense systems, is more solid than the preceding one. With the expulsion of Tartuffe, Orgon's fly is vaccinated against the next devout man. In vaccination, poison can be a cure, and this logic with two entry points becomes a strategy, a care, a cure. The parasite gives the host the means to be safe from the parasite. The organism reinforces its resistance and increases its adaptability. It is moved a bit away from its equilibrium and it is then even more strongly at equilibrium. The generous hosts are therefore stronger than the bodies without visits; generation increases resistance right in the middle of endemic diseases. Thus parasitism contributes to the formation of adapted species from the point of view of evolution.* Michel Serres, *The Parasite*, 34.

91. Benjamin Buchloh, "Allegorical Procedures: Appropriation and Montage in Contemporary Art," in *Art after Conceptual Art*, eds. Alexander Alberro and Sabeth Buchmann (Cambridge, MA: MIT Press, 2006), 29.

92. One can hardly consider GELITIN's clubhouse parasitic, as they were invited to create it, and context does not really provide GELITIN's primary material. However, if one considers the balcony the group created behind the clubhouse, a more complex

set of relations emerges: between inside/outside, guest/host, guests/other guests, visible/invisible, support/risk, etc.

93. In fact, the group's gesture would have gone entirely unnoticed had it not published an account of the action in an artist's book containing detailed sketches and documentation. Some have suggested that *B-Thing* was just an elaborate hoax, a fantasy produced through documentation. Accordingly, witnesses and accomplices have wavered from admitting to its fabrication to producing evidence of this truth, suggesting that the work is either a fake event made to look real or a real event cloaked in speculation in order to defer responsibility.

94. Jacques Derrida, *Limited Inc.*, trans. Samuel Weber and Jeffrey Mehlman (Evanston, IL: Northwestern University Press, 1988), 90.

95. Andrea Fraser, "From the Critique of Institutions to an Institution of Critique," *Artforum*, September 2005, 278.

96. *Consequently, the parasite reveals that 'the body' itself does not exist as a proper and proprietary given—that is, as a natural fact—but rather incorporates a scalar narrative, a fiction, that emplots us within what we call 'a life' by emplotting us within ?it.' What we name as the body situates us within a life story that binds up space and time, suturing us to our 'selves' as the jealous proprietors of our much coveted vital property. The parasite therefore addresses us as 'an enemy' only insofar as we identify the body and identify with the body as the essential psychological/political/biological metonym for our life. By perturbing this putatively natural metonymy, parasites reveal the underlying paradox of modern political ontology—which perhaps explains in part why viral epidemics seem to trouble us biologically, politically, economically, and psychologically.* Ed Cohen, "The Paradoxical Politics of Viral Containment; or, How Scale Undoes Us One and All," *Social Text* 106 (Spring 2011), 23.

97. *I love the fact that human genomes can be found in only about 10 percent of all the cells that occupy the mundane space I call my body; the other 90 percent of the cells are filled with the genomes of bacteria, fungi, protists, and such, some of which play in a symphony necessary to my being alive at all, and some of which are hitching a ride and doing the rest of me, of us, no harm. I am vastly outnumbered by my tiny companions; better put, I become an adult human being in company with these tiny messmates. To be one is always to become with many. Some of these personal microscopic biota are dangerous to the me who is writing this sentence; they are held in check for now by the measures of the coordinated symphony of all the others, human cells and not, that make the conscious me possible. I love that when "I" die, all these benign and dangerous symbionts will take over and use whatever is left of "my" body, if only for a while, since "we" are necessary to one another in real time.* Donna J. Haraway, *When Species Meet* (Minneapolis: University of Minnesota Press, 2008), 4.

98. Donna Haraway, "The Biopolitics of Postmodern Bodies: Determinations of Self in Immune System Discourse," in *American Feminist Thought at Century's End: A Reader*, ed. Linda Kauffman (Cambridge, MA: Blackwell Publishers, 1993), 199–233.

99. Cohen, "The Paradoxical Politics of Viral Containment," 23.

100. As Steven Shaviro reminds us: *My intestines are on as intimate terms with their tapeworms as they are with my mouth, my asshole, and my other organs; the relationship is as "intrinsic"*

and "organic" in the one case as it is in the other. Just like the tapeworm, I live off the surplus-value extracted from what passes through my stomach and intestines. Who's the parasite, then, and who's the host? The internal organs are parasitic upon one another; the organism as a whole is parasitic upon the world. My "innards" are really a hole going straight through my body; their contents—shit and tapeworm—remain forever outside of and apart from me, even as they exist at my very center. Steven Shaviro, "William Burroughs," in *Doom Patrols: A Theoretical Fiction about Postmodernism* (London: Serpent's Tail, 1997), 101.

101. Fraser, *From the Critique of Institutions to an Institution of Critique*, 278.

102. Marissa Jahn, "Byproducts and Parasites" in *Byproducts: On the Excess of Embedded Artistic Practices* (Toronto: YYZ Books & Rev-, 2010), 12.

103. Michel Foucault, "The Subject and Power," in *Critical Inquiry* 8, no. 4 (Summer, 1982), 790.

104. In Arthur Danto and others' "institutional theory of art," artworks themselves can be seen as parasitic on the ideological, symbolic, and economic mechanisms of the institution, which has the authority to recognize an object as art. Conversely, the institution itself is parasitic on its artifacts to make an empty room into a zone of discourse. Equally, site-specific artworks often are regarded as parasitic on the context of the site of display, where not only is the work embedded on or in the host, but also the project extracts meaning and materials from its host's reserves.

Plate 1
Kate Craig, 1987. Photo by
Hank Bull.

Plate 2
Film still from *The Hart of
London*, 1970. Directed by
Jack Chambers.

Plate 3
Miranda July and Julia
Bryan-Wilson, *Big Miss
Moviola*, no. 2, *Underwater
Chainletter*, 1997, detail.

Plate 4
Cover of *Strike* 2, no. 2
(May 1978).

Plate 5
Installation view of David
Rabinowitch, *The Wide
Field Piece*, 1967, in the
exhibition *Heart of London*,
National Gallery of Canada,
Ottawa, 1969.

Plate 6
BANK, document from
FAX BAK, 1999.

Plate 7
Dexter Sinister, press
releases sent as part of
True Mirror, 2008.

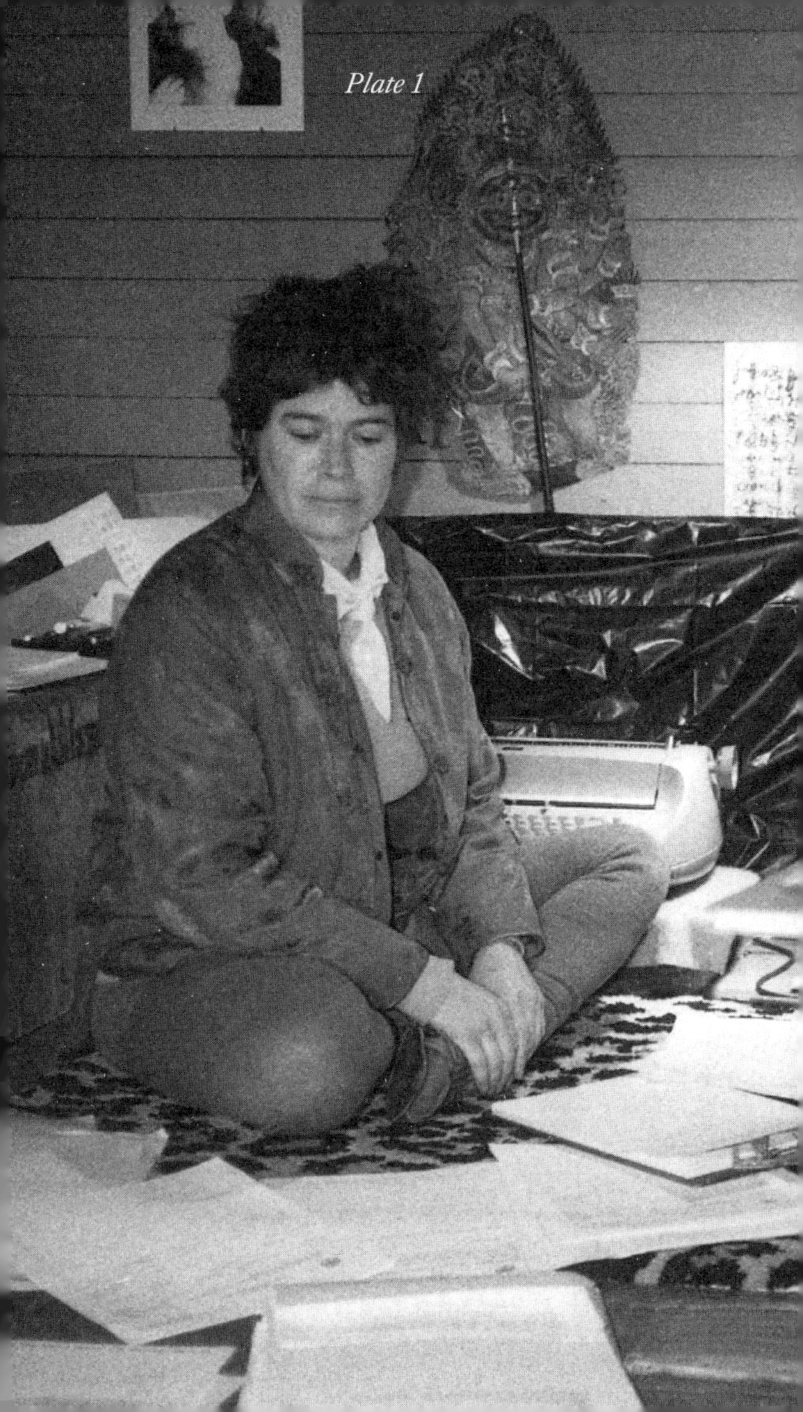

Plate 1

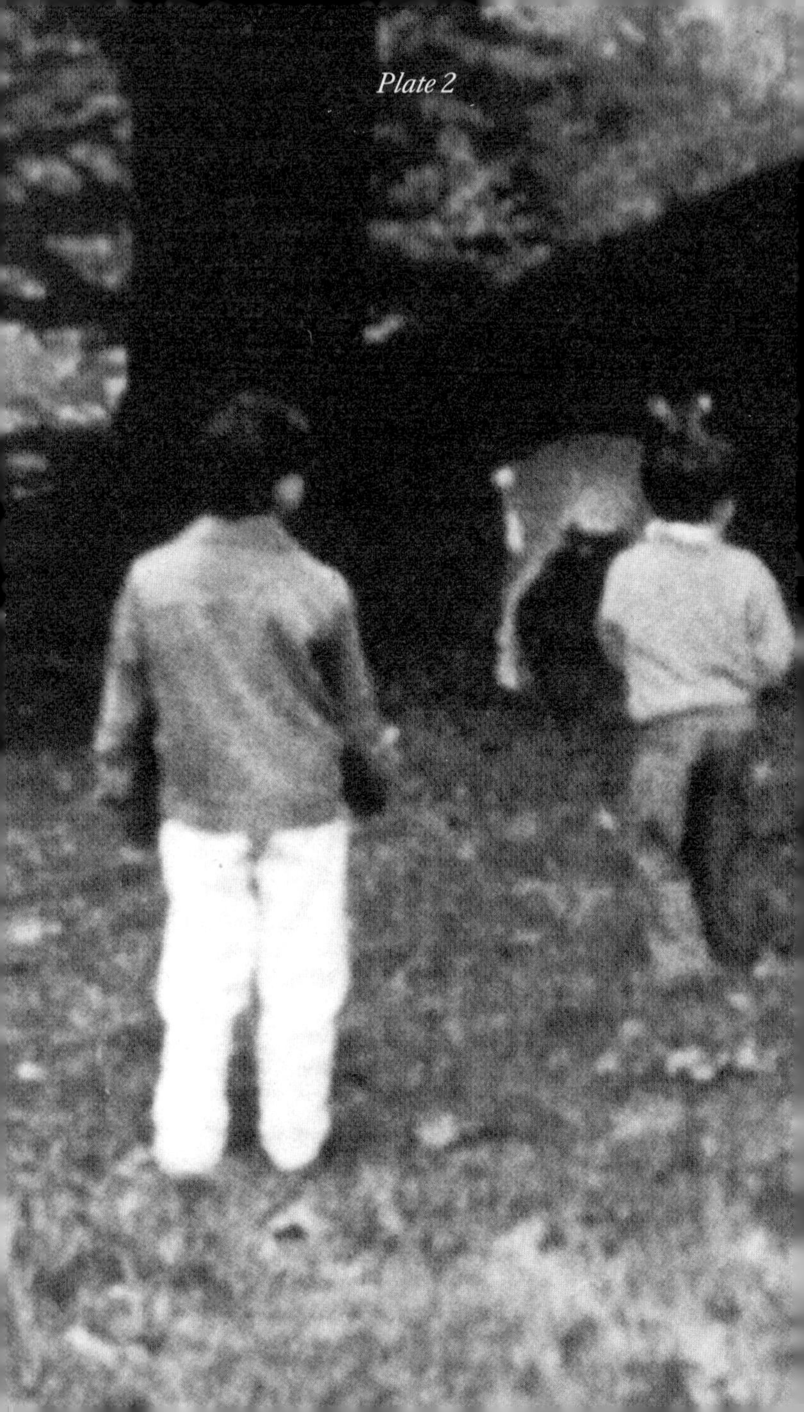

Plate 2

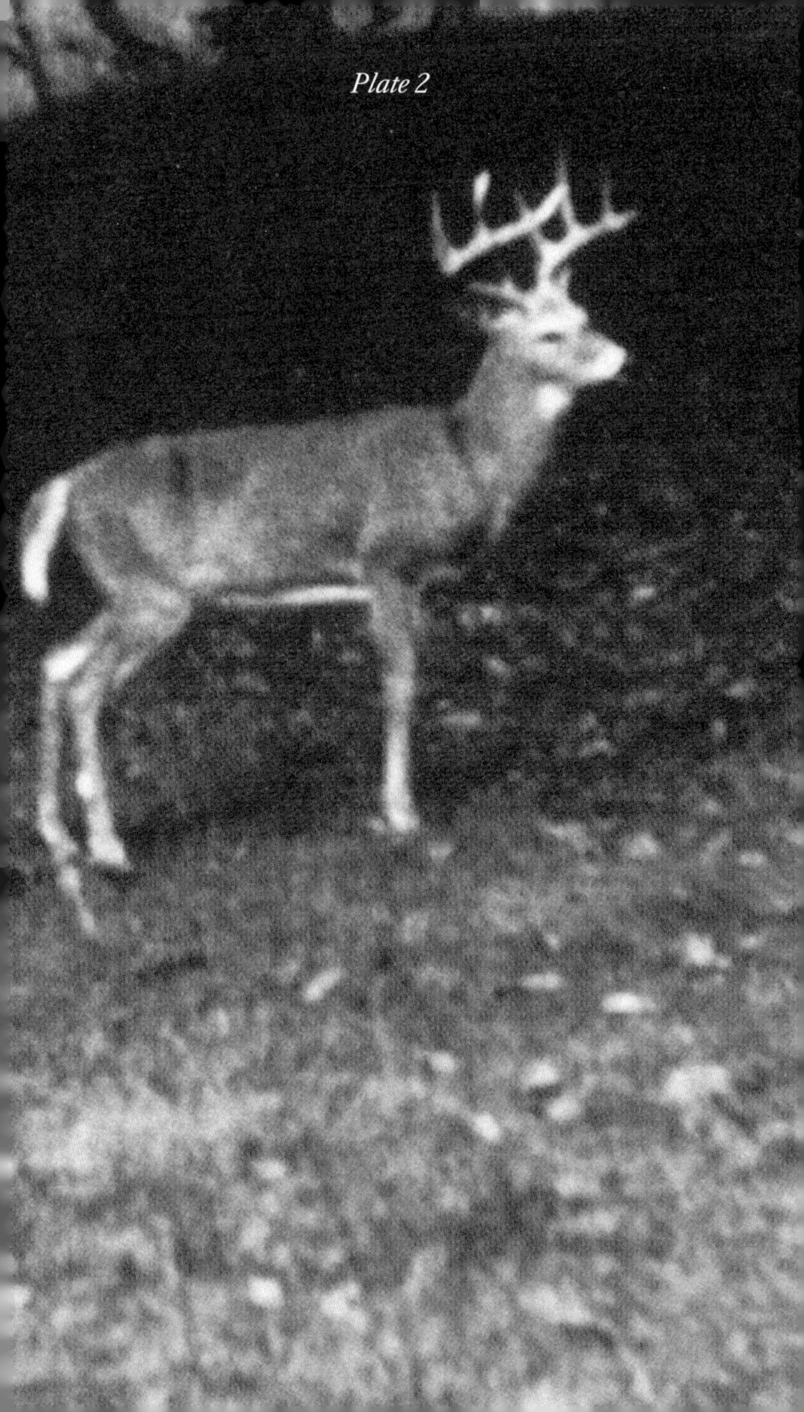

Plate 2

JULIA BW:

So for a long time I was doing Big MM alone and that was fine because there wasn't that much to do. In the last few months though, everything has gotten crazy-in-a-good-way. Now there are two of us working at the Big Miss Moviola Headquarters. I would like to introduce Julia BW:

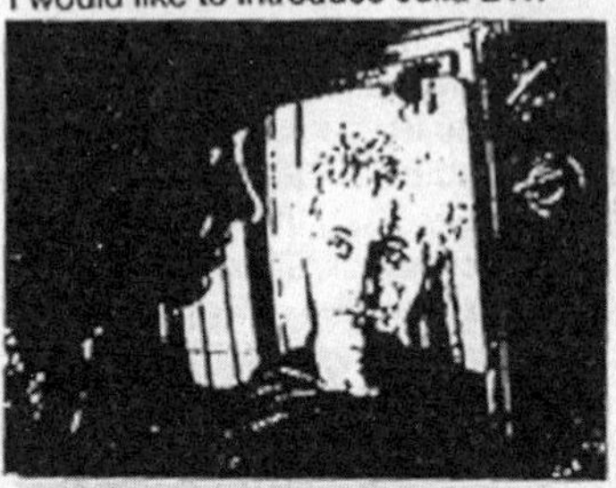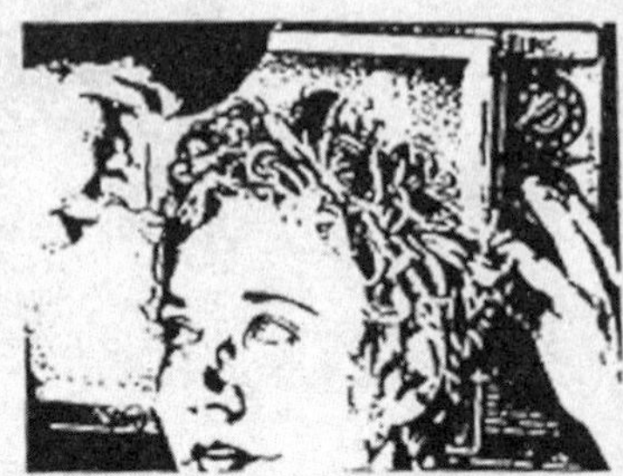

"Miranda and I met at a video show I was curating. We had one of those coy party conversations where we were talking to each other even when we were talking to other people. Afterwards, we got drinks at the Pump Room. It works out well: I put together publicity, set up screenings, act as a body double, plot and scheme. We have different kinds of skills so we can cover more ground together. Basically, we help each other dream the impossible dream."

JULIA ON JOANIE 4 JACKIE:

Joanie 4 Jackie = girl 4 girl = women helping each other do it. The Portland version of Joanie 4 Jackie is specifically for teenage girls, since dismissing teenagers is part of the conspiracy that wants to keep women silent. Our first thought was to have a Gala Affair showing all kinds of movies made by junior- and high-school girls. It would have all the hype of Prom only it would celebrate the complex Reality, not this one exclusive fantasy. But of course for girls to make the movies in the first

SHE IS:
A CHALLENGE AND A PROMISE

YOU SEND HER:

YOUR SCI-FI, SOAP, AUTO-BIOGRAPHICAL, PORNO, WESTERN, STOP-ACTION, CONFESSIONAL, PRE-COLONIAL, DOCU-DRAMA, ACTION-ADVENTURE, HOW-TO, KUNG-FU, TRUE CRIME, ROMANCE FLICKS

SHE SENDS YOU:

THE INTERNATIONAL VELVET VIDEO CHAINLETTER THAT CAN'T BE BROKEN. IT'S BEEN U.P.S.ED AROUND THE USA AND NOW IT'S FORCED TO MAKE A CRASH LANDING. THE RADAR-READER SAYS IT'S FALLING FAST: 10 MILLION MILES AN HOUR. IT'S HEADED FOR: YOUR MAILBOX. IT IS: HEAVY. CATCH IT WITH YOUR TONGUE OUT.

YOU ARE:
THE LADY GLITTERATI OF THE UNSEEN-UNDERWATER MOVIE REVOLUTION.

Plate 4

STRIKE

ART COMMUNICATION EDITION, VOL. 2, No. 2, MAY,

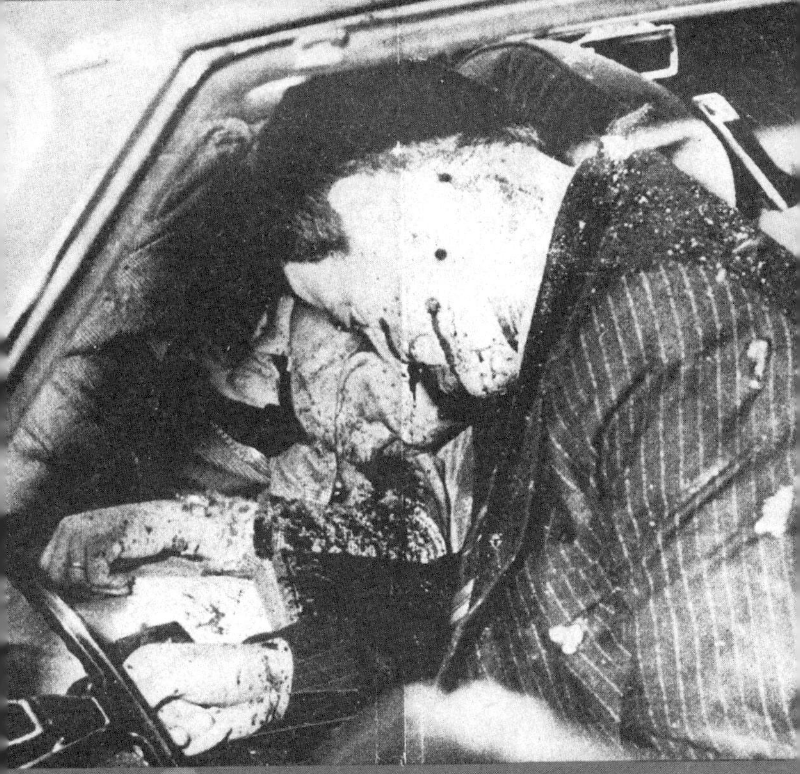

TORTURE
POST-MARXISM
RED BRIGADES

.DA & U.S....$.50
.CE F3
.ANY DM2
.Y LIT500
.D.KINGDOM 30p

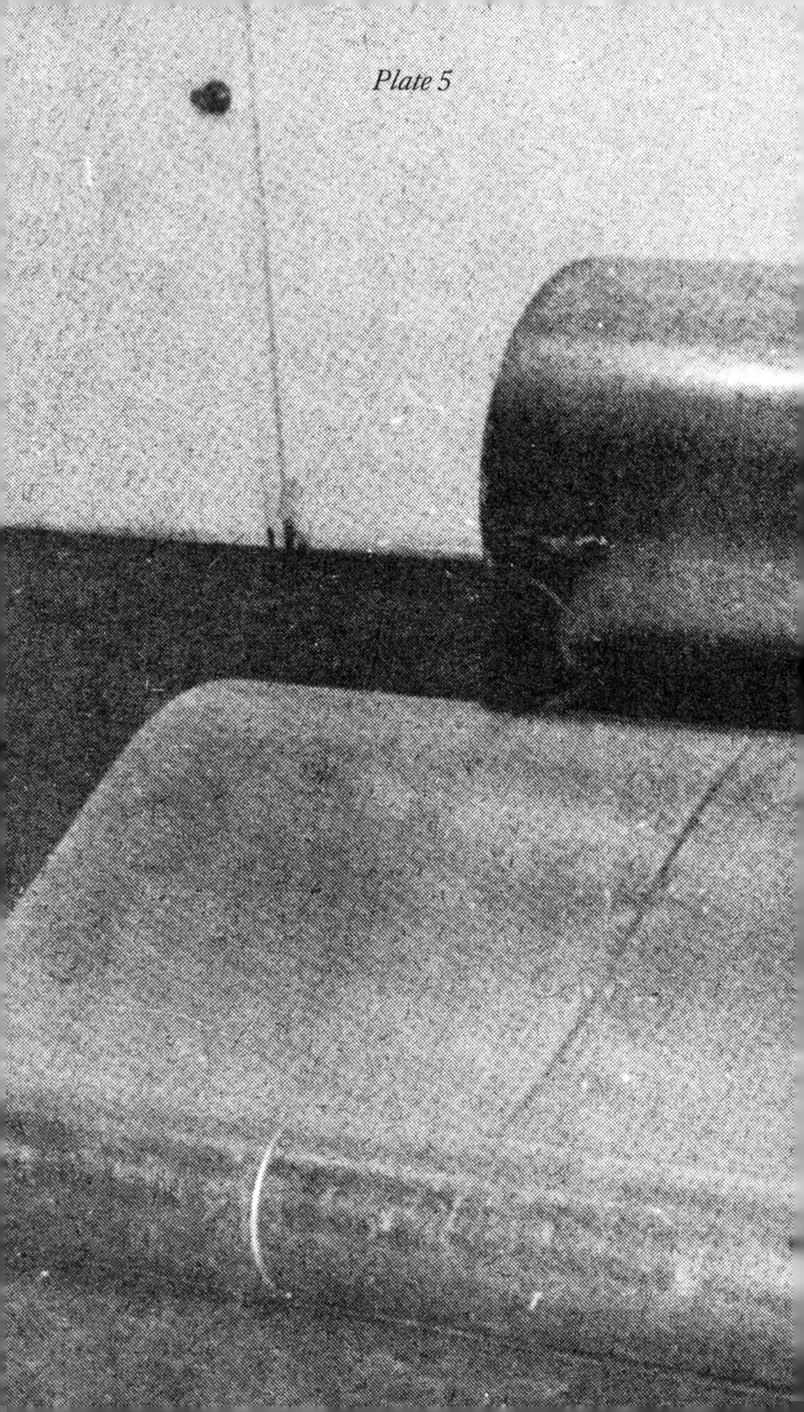

Plate 5

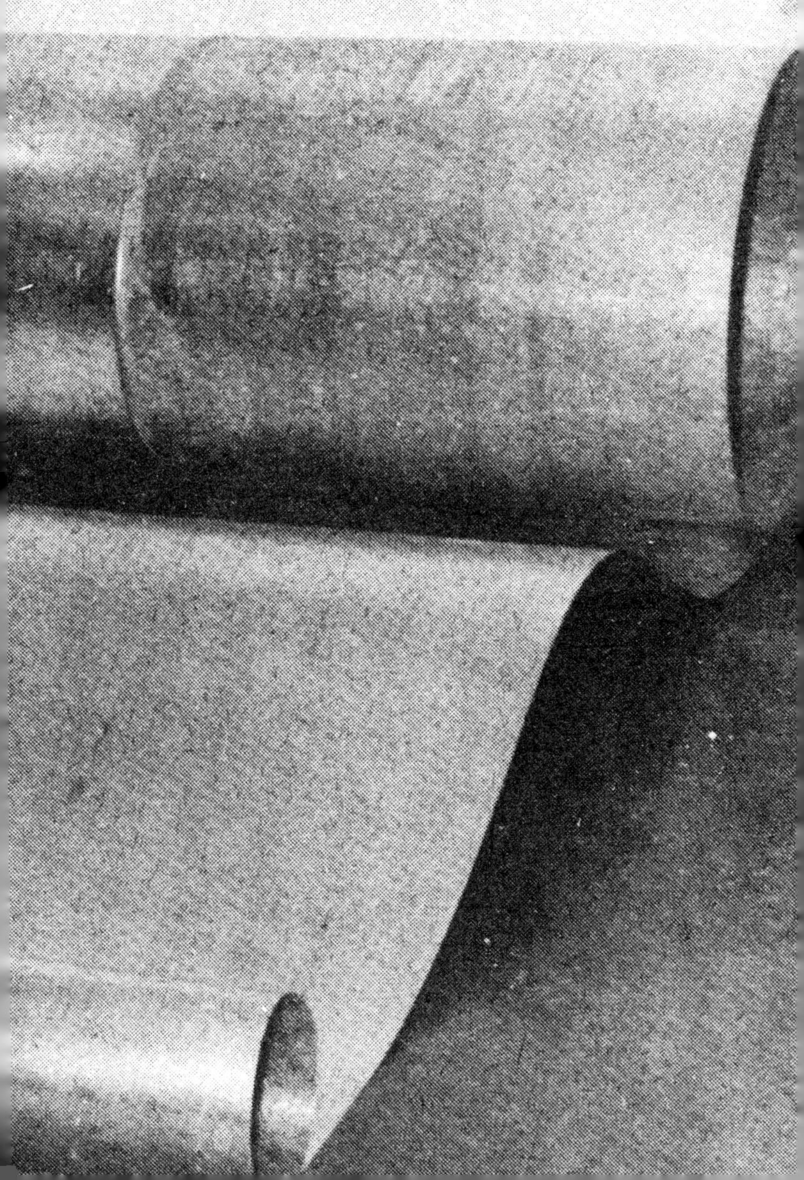

Plate 5

THE BANK
FAX-BAK SERVICE
Helping You Help Yourself!

This would seem to cover the whole of human experience – BE MORE SPECIFIC!

BAD LOGO .. — What about S.F.G or S. Friedman Gallery ↓ (sounds more corporate)

Stephen Friedman Gallery

25 – 28
Old Burlington Street
London W1X 1LB

Tel +44 171 494 1434
Fax +44 171 494 1431
e-mail frie@dircon.co.uk

press release

Kerry Stewart
3 December 1998 – 23 January 1999
Preview Wednesday 2 December 1998 6–8pm

Stephen Friedman Gallery is pleased to present an exhibition of new works by British artist Kerry Stewart.

Known for her offbeat portrayals of characters from the realms of everyday life and of fantasy, Stewart's life-size figures evoke connections with childhood, which are at once appealing and disconcerting. However damaged and defenceless her figures may be, they are always stiffened by a curious spirit of obstinacy.

Stewart's work shows a consistent preoccupation with human isolation which is often suffused with humour. Whether exuberant or forlorn, phantoms or outcasts, her figures stir buried memories in a naive yet complex way implying that the legacy of childhood impinges on adult life at every turn.

Alien or familiar, Stewart's figures are disturbing and oddly funny. Eyes meet us with blank stares in *Ghost* and *Manager*, whilst *This Girl Bends* suggests a terrible eagerness to comply. In this show a snowbound car with its headlights shining references moments of acute entrapment. Inspired by footage of the followers of cult murderer Charles Manson, a girl/follower crouches, listening, on a driveway at night.

Born near Glasgow, Kerry Stewart lives and works in London. She has taken part in numerous group and one-person exhibitions in this country and abroad, such as *Material Culture* at the Hayward Gallery, *Belladonna* at the ICA and the British Council touring exhibition *Pictura Britannica* last year. From 9 January until 20 April 1999 Stewart will participate in a group show at the San Francisco Museum of Modern Art entitled *Looking at Ourselves: Works by Women artists from the Logan Collection.*

Forthcoming exhibition: Lucky DeBellevue and Alexander Ross, 28 January – 27 February 1999.

Gallery hours are: Tuesday to Friday 10am – 6pm and Saturday 11am – 5pm

For further details please contact Patricia Kohl on: +44 171 494 1434

Handwritten annotations:

'at once appealing and disconcerting' – your press releases always use these opposites eg: "This work is black and white" or "This work is both serious and frivolous" This technique just means you have nothing to say about the work.

bit archaic and uncool – but NICE – GOOD! 'realm' is a bit pompous for everyday

This last sentence is completely meaningless – CONGRATULATIONS!

WHAT IS? "Stewarts work", "stewarts preoccupation" or "human isolation". – be more specific

"I don't you mean "ramming it down your throat?"

AND AGAIN "What exactly IS 'acute entrapment' when its at home? ethically problematic

I haven't seen this piece of work but this sounds ridiculous.

is this a female – follower) or a follower-of- Manson who is female? Anyway, sculptures don't listen.

Here we go again – "naïve yet complex" – black BUT white. Overuse of opposites as a method of description. Meaningless and clichéd. Well done! 4/10

Yeah, right – we've all read "The Beginners Guide to Freud" – try and sound more brainy

WHITNEY MUSEUM OF AMERICAN ART

945 Madison Avenue at Seventy-Fifth Street   New York, New York 10021   (212) 249-4100

For Release
On receipt
11/9/70

WHITNEY SCULPTURE ANNUAL TO BE 50% WOMEN

John I.H. Baur, Director of the Whitney Museum, with curators Robert Doty, James Monte and Marcia Tucker, announced today that the 1970 Annual Exhibition of Contemporary American Sculpture has been selected on the basis of fifty percent representation by women and 50% by men, equally divided between whites and non-whites. The Annual opens December 12 and continues to February 7, 1971.

For many years the policy of the Whitney Museum has been directed towards advancing the interests of women artists. Founded by a women artist, its board headed by a women, it has organized more one-man shows by women artists than any other New York museum, and a substantial part of its permenent collection is comprised of work by women. It is, therefore, only natural that the Whitney be the first museum in the United States to acknowledge the justice of equal representation for women as a means of responding most fully to the needs and aspirations of a major portion of the art world's. The Whitney Annual, New York's only regular survey of the current scene, presents the ideal opportunity to offer women artists a greater role in directing the nature of American art today.

In a statement issued jointly with the Museum's Board of Trustees and the curators who selected the exhibition, Mr. Baur stressed that fact that "while percentages are not to become a museum policy for all exhibitions, increasing awareness of the achievements of special interest groups has led us to feel that an equal male/female representation at this time is a salutary and necessary step."

The Whitney Museum's schedule for the next six months also includes two shows by women artists (LOUISE NEVELSON and LEE LOZANO, opening November 10 and December 2, respectively), a selection of women's art from the permenent collection (Dec. 7 - Jan. 19), and BLACK ARTISTS IN AMERICA (April 6 - May 16).

For further information: Stephen Weil
                         Leon Levine
                         Ronni Roland

Is There Space for Art Outside the Market and the State?

Artist-run culture has emerged in part as an alternative to the market and the limitations market-driven priorities have placed on the artist in terms of creative autonomy. Highly dependent on state sources of funding in many contexts, artist-run culture has, to some degree, forfeited autonomy to the state in order to meet bureaucratic funding requirements or to avoid censorship and ideological conflict.

In this light, "the state vs. the market" dichotomy significantly moulds contemporary artist-run activity, including the means of production and distribution for contemporary art. This Oxford-style debate, held on October 12, 2012, examined this dimension of artist-run culture by focusing on the grey zone, if there is one, between reliance on state programs and policies and the vicissitudes of the market.

For
Jaleh Mansoor
Deirdre Logue
Matei Bejenaru

Against
Dirk Fleischmann
Gregory Sholette
Payam Sharifi, representing
Slavs and Tatars

Moderator
John O'Brian

October 12, 2012
Simon Fraser University
Vancouver, Canada

John O'Brian: I would like to welcome you to the first of two evening debates at this convention. The second will also be in this hall, at the same time tomorrow. Disagreement is generally in strong supply within artist-run culture, as we have seen from the sessions that occurred earlier today, but the opportunity to air differences of opinion rarely takes place within the format of an Oxford-style debate. This evening is an experiment, an attempt to find out how a debate with rules and restrictions might shift (or not) the discussion. We cannot do any worse than the second US presidential debate last week in Denver, Colorado. At least, I hope not.

W.G. Sebald remarked in his book *Rings of Saturn* that there was a sticky relationship between the market for art and the state in industrial Europe—or, as he also put it, there was a relationship between the history of sugar and empire and the history of art. Many collectors were sugar barons with important positions in government. "It seems to me," he writes, "as if all works of art were coated with a sugar glaze or indeed made completely out of sugar." To what extent does Sebald's metaphor persist today? We should soon find out.

(John O'Brian explains the rules of the debate, introduces the members of each team, and leads the audience in an initial vote. The crowd votes, raising primarily using yellow cards, indicating "Yes.")

Matei Bejenaru: When I received the invitation to participate in this discussion, I was thinking that this is a question for a Canadian audience because you have had such a dense network of artist-run centres for more than forty years. So for today's debate, I would like to focus on the situation [in Romania] where I'm from. There, the answer is "yes": there is art, but we don't have a state; we don't have a market.

But we have other states. We have other states that are investing in different institutions that make young elites spin around these institutions. So here we can open a very complex discussion about what artistic freedom is in times of self-colonization and cultural hegemony. I would say that there is a certain freedom but also every penny that comes into an institution might somehow have an agenda.

We have some examples of people who are supporting art institutions—*le mécénat* (in English it is "philanthropists," or "patronage"). And in some cases, there is freedom—at least from the outside.

And, we have banks. But of course, you would laugh if I said "banks." But even the PR of the banks is somehow unprofessional and they don't follow precisely what is happening with the institution that they are supporting. I think that sometimes they pay money and they don't understand what they are paying for. So for them, just to show them copies from the newspapers or media coverage is enough for them to be successful. Even when we know that the [art] institution is digging at the basis of the foundation of the funding institution.

So, [in the context of Romania,] there are these three possibilities: other states, philanthropists, and banks.

That's it.

Gregory Sholette: I take this debate to be a provocation more than a precise argument because we haven't defined what we mean by space here. But from a traditional Marxist or Marxian position, there would not and could not be a space outside of capitalist markets given that capitalism is hegemonic, even with regard to socialist countries, few as they may be. Therefore the reproduction and circulation of capital gives rise to markets for goods but it also determines the way governments operate. So if art is a form of production and consumption then it logically takes place within this administered space of capital. Now much has been written about these kind of assertions and, to be honest, it sounds like a debate that is from a bygone era: a time when our lives were buffered from the needs and desires of the capitalist economy. These filtering mechanisms that used to exist, particularly the ones that have disappeared in the United States and other extremely neoliberal situations, these filtering mechanisms are not really outside of capitalism and culture would be included in it. One might even say they afford it as a false sense of protection from the marketplace, which so many states today have basically ripped away.

At the same time, we can thank the rise of neoliberalism and extreme free-market economy for helping us lay bare our predicament. By stripping away government protections they've forced us to come face to face with what? A face to face encounter with the limits of capital. Between the inside and the outside. So is there an outside after all? Does it exist? For example, our opponents might argue that the Occupy movement emerged from a place outside the system, and then forcefully took back space, quite literally and symbolically, that had been appropriated by capital—privatized by capital. We—on our side—perhaps would say that Occupy already existed, that it was already inscribed within the system as a force that emerged along with a collapsing economy. A force with nowhere else to go except to pile up inside, like so much creative class productivity made excessive by the system's failure.

I would say that both of these positions are somewhat true and therefore, maybe the question we've raised needs to be adjusted. Regarding art: something that Simon Sheikh observed was that institutions actually require the omission of certain subjects in order to institutionalize, and these willful acts of exodus and rebellion are not so much artists themselves taking charge of a situation and radically leaving—they are actually the way the institution itself begins to ground its discourse in its existence. And if he's correct—and I think he's actually saying something quite similar to the Dark Matter thesis that John [O'Brian] mentioned before—then what is inscribed inside the space of the institution is outside.

How can this be? I'm going to give you a quick example and sorry I'm speaking quickly but we don't have a lot of time here. The example I'll default to is the PAD/D [Political Art Documentation/Distribution] Archive. It was an archive of social and political art. We organized it in the 1980s. Today that archive is inside the Museum of Modern Art in New York, one of the pillars of the institutional-cultural regime. It's actually housed in Queens, so technically it's outside the museum, but not really.

It's an archive of cultural excess containing examples of collectives and projects and social experiments that are now largely forgotten. And it represents, in a sense, the tip of the iceberg of a larger shadowy space of over-production that is at times also in opposition to mainstream artistic and capitalist institutions, which is to say this supplementary, even redundant archive does not belong to some fantastic alien cosmos, it is instead fully inscribed within the institution's ideological architecture. It's a necessary absence-presence, or presence-absence, and it's filled with micro-histories, resistant practices, and partially submerged outlaw memories. At the same time its very existence attests to the fact that opposition to cultural hierarchies is not uncommon, it is in fact present everyday—it's even commonplace. It's an outside that we encounter all the time, much like the invisible labour that constructs exhibition walls, fabricates artworks, teaches younger artists, and even administrates events like this. So this PAD/D archive is sometimes raided for research by the museum, and sometimes we even see some of the work in it—posters and documents—put in the gallery for temporary exhibitions. But there's never been the archive presented in its totality, because to do that, the museum would then have to acknowledge what it has to oppose: it's Dark Matter.

Deirdre Logue: I was a late addition to tonight's debate and I feel in some ways I have the advantage of being completely unprepared for tonight's discussion. So I'm fresh, it's just going to come out. I do have some notes because I wanted to mention a few things—as you know, I work for an organization called Vtape which I think has very effectively worked the market and the state over the years to benefit artists quite directly. This is a space that we should perhaps consider: a space of subversion, a space where organizations can find themselves on the perimeter of market and state. Flying as close to the sun as possible without getting completely burnt to a crisp.

I would also like to argue that, in this subversion or idea, we can't ever fully pull ourselves out of these complicated spaces of implication. Knowing that most of us either work, as I do, for the market: educational museum markets, festival markets, video art distribution markets. We are always knocking on those doors. But yet I think it is even *harder* to fully extract ourselves from our implications with the state.

I essentially work for the Canada Council for the Arts: a "launderette" of government funds through organizations and into the hands of artists. So maybe there are spaces that most of us occupy whether we like it or not. But maybe there can also be freedoms found in these spaces, outside this market and the state as we know it.

I think the position I'd like to offer—very much on the fly—is that [this] space is actually an *embodied* space. This space for art, outside the market and the state, resides in the body of the artist. The body of the artist resides in our optimism, in our fighting against the pessimistic tendencies that the market and the state force us to experience everyday. To argue for an optimism, we need to create possibilities for spaces. We might not see them right now, we might not see the space that art can find outside the market and the state. I think it is our obligation to be optimistic that those spaces can be created—that there is a possibility for those spaces—and that in a last-ditch effort, if you don't see them around you, that there is the possibility that they actually reside within us.

The idea of space certainly needs to be defined in this discussion. I think that this space can be conceptual, that these spaces can be a ready-made, they can be a garage, they can be a person [or] people, they can be a thought.

Dirk Fleischmann: Let's talk about the market first. Speaking about my own position as an artist I can say: I am not in the art market and the art market does not need me. And that's OK.

Actually, I never believed in the art market. Since the day when I became an art student, I was sure that I would never succeed in the art market. The average income in Germany is 3,200 euros. That is 40,000 euros a year. If I have to share with a commercial gallery I would have to sell artworks worth 80,000 euros to achieve that. I knew that would not happen to me.

And I know well enough that I don't have the mindset to produce for a market. Actually I am very bad at fulfilling the expectations of others. That's actually one of the reasons why I became an artist; I would not be able to fulfill the demands of the art market. And when I visit art fairs I feel depressed.

So if the question of the day was: Is there a space for art outside of the market I would certainly insist: YES, there is space outside of the art market and I would sit on the other side of the podium with you.

I would argue that I found a way to sustain my art from my own income. And the story goes like this:

As a student I had big ideas and I wanted to make big paintings. I was into abstract expressionism and my teacher was Hermann Nitsch, the bloody Vienna Actionist. I was fascinated and amused by his megalomania and I also wanted to do big projects but my budget for art was fifty euros per month. With this budget I could afford to do only one painting and it would be finished within a few hours. That was frustrating.

So I searched for a way that my work could produce money rather than consume [it]. Actually I got some inspiration from artist-run spaces in Frankfurt, where I come from, where I studied. Do you know how they tried to cover their expenses to run exhibitions? By selling beer at the openings. And every opening was a party. And drinking was not only fun, but it also served a good cause.

So, in 1998, my second year at art school, I did an experiment: Instead of wasting fifty euros on another messy painting I invested the money in chocolate bars that I purchased from a wholesale shop. For one Snickers I paid twenty-five cents. I put the chocolates on the table in my studio in the art school and I put a price tag of fifty cents on it. After one week it was sold out and I had one hundred euros in the cash box. Much better.

I made one rule for this experiment, and this is still valid for me today: I would re-invest all income on new products or to start other economic projects. After two months I was able to offer the complete range of goods that a regular kiosk would carry, including beer, like the artist-run spaces. So, during the day the chocolate sold. In the night it was time for the beer.

When I graduated in 2002, I invested all profits in a photovoltaic power plant that I built on the roof of my art school. Since then, I have been selling the electricity, which financed the production of a shirt collection in the Cavite Economic Zone in the Philippines—a project that Naomi Klein described in her book *No Logo*. The shirt that I am wearing now is from that collection that I designed. And currently I am paying a farmer in the Philippines from the income of the shirts and the electricity to take care of *myforestfarm*, which is a project about carbon emissions trading. Actually this project is financially breaking my neck at the moment.

I can tell you: It is really much easier to sell a bottle of beer than a carbon credit, and at the moment my economic strategy is in danger. I am not going to lament about this now, but I will talk about that project tomorrow morning in Session 6.

As you know, I was born in Germany. I attended a public art school in Germany. My first group exhibition was Manifesta which was funded by the European Union. My first solo show was in an artist-run space, which was in its seventh year and was funded by the city of Frankfurt (that was after the initial beer period). I use the funds from my art projects only to sustain the projects themselves, but for my living I have to do jobs. I got 3,200 euros for my assistant job at that public art school in Frankfurt where I graduated. Remember, that is the average income in Germany. And in 2006 I got a travel grant from the Hessian Cultural Foundation and the Kunstfonds Germany. So from 2006 to 2008, I was nomadic.

I was also able to get into several residency programs in Asia and those were publicly funded by other governments. And since 2009, I have been teaching at a University in Korea.

So my art is definitely not outside of the state. I can only speculate what my art would be like without state support. I leave it up to you to draw conclusions from my case about the general question if there is space outside the market and the state. And I am looking forward to discuss this matter further with the other panellists and audience in the Q&A part of the debate.

Thank you, and thanks to the Goethe Institute for paying my air ticket to attend this conference.

Jahleh Mansoor: Within the parameters of this format—which requires pretty schematic thinking—I just have three main points. Can art exist outside the state and the market? The first, speaking as an art historian: Yes. The state, as it is now—functioning as a vehicle for art production—is a fairly new system, as is the market. They haven't existed forever; they are not natural; they can easily end.

Now, in the interest of answering the question more fully, I wanted to re-circumscribe the state as "the state apparatus." We can locate the museum to the middle of the eighteenth century in its current iteration. Now it's more or less dis- solved by the market. We can't tell ourselves that a museum—as a state apparatus and as itself indepen- dent from a market system—ex- ists any longer. So, as Greg points out, that has indeed collapsed and that is symptomatic of the kinds of movements and convolutions we might see to come. We can locate the market [in the way that it functions now, as an enabler, as an artistic practice] to the middle of the nineteenth century, say, with Courbet's Pavilion in 1855, or we could go back to the middle of the seventeenth century with Vermeer and Rembrandt.

The first gallerists were selling beer. And then they started to sell pictures, and that had a lot to do with technological changes that in turn had to do with ideological changes. So again, Greg brought up this issue of changing hegemony; it's precisely these reasons, which justify his position. I think there will inevitably be nothing but a position outside the state or the market (if there is a position at all) because both are young entities, and both are failing.

We find ourselves in 2012—all of us sort of "puppets" in the art world—having to make the annual round of the biennials and the triennials, and this and that. That phenomenon begins in the middle of the nineteenth century, where the state and the market intersect. Where the two axes of evil intersect.

The Great Exposition of 1851 and the Exposition Universelles of the 1870s are the paradigm for what we are suffering now. I'm subscribing to a base and superstructure model, which I am guilty of, and admit to.

We may very well be on the other end of an arc that is only about a hundred and fifty or sixty years old. It came into being to facilitate artistic practice, again: Courbet, then Manet, then the Impressionists. It is no longer facilitating artistic practice. It is time that these tensions are volatilized and dynamized if we are going to have interesting art again. I would argue that there has to be a position outside the state and the market if we are going to have art at all. Or, the other solution is to dissolve what we are calling "art," which is also a possibility.

I want to make a second point, from the position of an art critic: The most interesting practices of the last fifteen years are coming from autonomous and semi-autonomous artistic spaces: artist-run centres. The last three Whitney Biennials have been extracting value as though from a straw through independent spaces. I could rattle off a few in the Lower East Side of Manhattan (e.g., Scorched Earth, Orchard)—and there are many here in Vancouver, which is pretty special.

My third point! As an armchair activist of sorts, who spends a lot of time on the internet, [I've seen] the state and the market failing anyway. Artists will forge a space outside because they *must* forge a space outside, or they won't...

Payam Sharifi: After arguing for a case study of the Dia Art Foundation, and Masjid al-Farah, the Sufi mosque with the Dan Flavin installation, which arguably comes from outside of the market (or the state, depending on how you look at it), it seems a bit disingenuous to be on the other side of the fence today. Maybe there is an answer to that: You could say, "Yes, there is a space, but..." The Russians have a great word, which is *da-niet* [yes-no].

But I wanted to talk a little bit about what, we—as Slavs and Tatars—started about six years ago. We had been working for about ten years doing things other than art, and I continue to do so. And I think it gives us a certain faith in institutions, even though it is not very fashionable.

We existed almost exclusively,

thanks to institutions, until this month. We never exhibited in a commercial gallery. I think that it would be only thanks to institutions and the state (primarily state-funded institutions in Europe) that we were able to grow from a small publishing concern that printed six-to-ten page pamphlets five or six years ago to working with other media. I think that taking that leap of faith wouldn't normally happen in the market itself, but it happened thanks to the state.

But one thing I'd like to focus on is the idea of re-investing energy—or asking some very simple, stupid questions on smart subject matter (like Molla Nasreddin, our mascot). To that end, maybe actually correcting what we feel are certain excesses, or blind spots, in the market and the state as opposed to trying to reinvent the wheel. And this generally flows with our belief that we'd prefer to be in the rearguard rather than the avant-garde, because we don't believe that the avant-garde is so avant-garde. You can look at leftist politics, for example: and leftists seem to be some of the most closeted Islamophobes across the political spectrum.

A lot of our practice is about creating a space of hospitality or generosity within state-run, state-funded, or even privately funded institutions. There is so much discourse about participation but it's all a very theoretical discussion, and there's nowhere to sit within a museum.

Another example—a kind of correction for us—is rethinking the notion of artist books. Artist books, for us, are an equivalent of insider trading of the financial industry, except in art. What happens is that an artist is invited to do a catalogue for a show at an institution, and what he or she does is invite a critic to write about him or her. The critic makes the artist look good, the artist makes the critic look good, and it's a bunch of backslapping. It's a complete waste of money, time, effort, paper, what have you.

We never allow anybody to write about us in our own books because, for us, a book is a platform for exploring and investigating areas of knowledge that have not been explored. It's not about us, it's not about us as artists or about us as individuals. And if somebody wants to write about us then they should write about us in the normal channels or platforms which are reviews and criticisms in art publications. I understand that those channels are a problematic area, because there is not much in terms of reviews nowadays, but that is something that we believe should be re-invested in, rethought, and re-engaged.

Another thing is this notion of imperceptibility. I think it's very important to have a foot in both sectors—the art market and the state—especially in an increasingly transparent world, or a world where things are more and more predictable. The most important thing that you can do is be in that place where you wouldn't expect it. Our first exhibition ever was simultaneously at the Moscow Biennale and at a boutique in Paris called the Colette, which had nothing to do with one another. In fact, one is a retail fashion shop and the other is a not-very-exciting biennial. So we would argue for that kind of maximalism.

Fleischmann: Jaleh, I found your thoughts very interesting and I wanted to extend your speculation with a quote from Andy Warhol. He said that in the future, there will be no more art; there will only be design. And this is also maybe a reason, for me, why I started to design shirts and other projects.

(Laughter)

Just since last year when *myforestfarm* came into crisis I started to work more with design-related ideas.

O'Brian: Jaleh, do you want to respond?

Mansoor: Sure. What is precisely the question?

(Laughter)

No, it's interesting—I suspect that one of the reasons we have, with each passing year, a greater number of not only MFAs, but also PhDs and graduate degrees, and the whole "edu-factory" situation, is that there are very few other places to go in the interest of exercising one's creative faculties. When you are younger, you think, "Oh, I like to make things. I'll go to art school" because where else does one make things? It's the last bastion, or reprieve, of some utterly obsolete notion of skill, craft, artisanalness, sensuality. And so these corners in "culture" become repositories for energies that have absolutely no other place to go.

So why would it not be possible to not re-instrumentalize those energies by having art school degrees, and then just roving around in circulation from biennial to biennial, and, what are these things we all apply for? Residency to residency? We don't just admit that we are interested in writing poetry, or weaving, or playing the piano. And finding a place, carving out a place, where

that would be, in and of itself, legitimate, instead of needing to instrumentalize our practices by singing for our supper when the whole point of going into these practices was to not sing for one's supper in a cubicle thereby making utterly redundant and frankly quite boring art?

Adorno makes a good point when he says that the kind of work that is so transparent—first of all, let me lay the foundation and say that I agree with Greg that there is no such thing as a work that isn't absolutely bound up to its historical horizon, its means of production, and so on and so forth. But to simply acquiesce to that, and to collapse all of the tensions: It's not simply that it reproduces the main hegemonic logic as though that were problematic ethically, it's: what is its point? I think that designing shirts is fabulous! I'm endorsing designing shirts.

Sholette: Jahleh, I think one comment I want to make about your presentation is that the people who fail are not failing outside the system; they are failing because they *have* to fail within the system. They are *made* to fail inside the system. The system always overproduces, and failure is inscribed fully within its architecture. That was my point.

The other thing I wanted to quickly say, which is actually a comment to the audience, who held up an abundance of yellow cards. My sympathies are very much with the kind of work that I think that you are thinking of and has been presented here earlier today [during the seminar]. I was really impressed, or surprised, that a lot of the work that was presented under the rubric of "anti-hegemonic" was then given extensive biographies and resumes. What do we want from the system, if we want to be outside the system? If we keep banging on its door, saying, "Recognize what I'm doing"?

Mansoor: And that is why we must stop!

Sholette: I'm waiting for tenure myself.

(Laughter)

Mansoor: [We must] stop banging on the door of the system to [have it] recognize what we are doing. We are reproducing [that system]! It's boring!

Bejenaru: My question is for Dirk. Why did you say that you couldn't produce art with fifty euros per month?

(Laughter)

Fleischmann: I did not say that. I said that my budget was only fifty euros, and it allowed me to do only one expressionist, large-scale painting, and actually I used this investment to make more art, and to make bigger projects. I hope what I'm doing is still art. Out of these fifty euros it became a multiplication of art actually and it was my way to overcome times when I had no exhibitions and nobody paid attention to me.

Bejenaru: What kind of logic is this, "to multiply"?

Mansoor: Yeah, why to just produce to produce to produce to...why?

Fleischmann: I'm interested in visiting places in the world that otherwise would not be accessible to me, like a free-trade zone in the Philippines. Or North Korea—it is only accessible for business people. So, if I have my own budget and I can invest it into making a shirt, I can enter into these kinds of structures that other people—like Naomi Klein, for example—only could describe from the outside. They didn't let her in; she had to wait at the fence. And I, as a businessman, can go inside. And I want to go to the places that hurt me, you know?

Sharifi: I think that our colleagues on the other side of the table suffer from a very dated and slightly problematic fetishization of art and creativity: this romantic idea that the artist is a last recourse of optimism. It is exactly the sort of thing that led us to where we were a couple years ago with the financial crisis because it is an emphasis on the individual.

And to take a leap, why is Apple computers so big right now? Because it is selling this idea of creativity and everybody is a creator, everybody. Yet the ultimate creator is the artist somehow? In this kind of mythos of art being this last repository outside of the market, outside of the state—when in fact, we are in the service industry, and there is nothing wrong with that. That's not a qualitative statement; that's not a negative statement. In fact, why is being in the service industry something—like being in an office job, or being in a restaurant—why is that something that is somehow less worthy than being an artist?

Mansoor: May I respond to that?

Bejenaru: Can I respond too?

Logue: And I'm next, so it works out well. Go ahead.

Mansoor: OK. Two things. Obviously

there is nothing "wrong" with working in any industry. The problem is laundering it by calling it art and thereby positing some sort of superiority to everybody else in that same "service industry." That's a real problem. And again, please come to tomorrow's session where exactly that will be worked out through the work of Santiago Sierra.

Second issue: I don't think that the three of us on this side are investing in the individual whatsoever. The individual is a completely obsolete entity. This (points to the title of the debate) doesn't say anything about whether it is an individual or a group outside the state or the market. I think your charge of a romantic idea of creativity is fair enough, hence the question: Do we even need the category of art at this particular moment?

Sharifi: Do you think it is a coincidence that art somehow occupies the zeitgeist today, like cinema did in the '70s or fashion did in the '90s? It's accompanied by a rise in individualism—do you think that's a coincidence?

Mansoor: I think the rise of art, all of a sudden, has to do with the collapse of a lot of disciplinary boundaries and parameters, so art becomes the grab-all bag for whatever you want to do. You want to DJ, you want to be a graffiti artist, you want to do this, you want to do that—it's art. You know, the so-called post-medium condition, post-this-or-that condition…

Yes, art is bound up with the individual in the nineteenth century, but I think as we move through, it needn't solely be about the individual now. I have collectives in mind. My examples are all collectives;

none of them have to do with the individual, but that's a separate topic.

Logue: I think I could follow up because I wanted to address this idea of credentials, and the list of people's bios, as well as return to this notion of embodiment. The space for artists is equal to the space for art; we are talking, in many ways, about the cultural producers as well as the cultural production. But also it's this idea that we do this collectively. The argument that I'm making for this space and the argument that I'd like to make for optimism is really an argument for working against our pessimism, which I think drives a lot of theory and drives a lot of the intellectualization around cultural production.

I think that we also know it would be a very complex and difficult to work our way all the way back to some kind of market-free and state-free notion of cultural practice.

I think it is very important that we see the future spaces for art and for artists not disempowered by tucking away what has become some of our credentials and some of the things that have brought us to some of these ideas. We can work with those. And they do bring us together. The Feminist Art Gallery is a good example, and many of the institutions by artists that we are talking about over the last day and for the two days to come are precisely the living proof that artists, academics, and activists can collectively create space, whether it be an embodied space within them through their own actions, through their own resistance, or the space between them that they create by standing collectively and in solidarity.

Bejenaru: Am I allowed to answer anecdotally?

O'Brian: You can.

Bejenaru: When I was a student in the arts in the early '90s, my best colleague left us, he went to a monastery and he became a monk. He left the school. He came back, one year after, dressed in black. He was sent back by the church to finish school; he had to have a position in the church hierarchy. I was really very emotional seeing him close to me. I was studying painting—we were always dirty—and he was so clean and his hands were clean and white, very nice. I wanted to talk to him, and I didn't know how to address him because he lived in a different world than mine. I had to talk with him, and we spoke for one day and one night.

I think we have to be romantic; we have to be optimists. We have to share some values that you don't read in the newspapers.

And I asked him this question: "What's the difference from one year ago?" And he said: "You see, I'm not wearing this (points to were a wristwatch would be), because I'm not late anymore." I think that artists have to be romantic. Artists have to dream for a better world. Why do we have to be so pragmatic?

Sharifi: Why is this only the domain of artists? Why shouldn't everybody dream?

Bejenaru: You speak too technically about these vague things for me.

Sharifi: I just think it is important not to have an inflated sense of one's own practice, that's all. And I think that too often we think that art is some kind of precious "alchemic" thing that other people don't have access to. I think that is nonsense. I think it's bullshit.

O'Brian: Anybody else on the "No" side, because you've been short-changed on time? Because I know the "Yes" side is going to say more.

(Laughter)

Somebody over there (points to "Yes" side), ask them a tough question! Or make a statement.

(Laughter)

Logue: I don't think we need to; I think it's pretty clear what's happening.

(Applause)

O'Brian: What I want to know is, why is the "No" side lying down? It seems to me that there are responses. I mean: "romantic"? You gave a brief point Payam, but I think…

Fleischmann: I don't feel like lying down. I agree with many points coming from the "Yes" side.

(Laughter)

Sharifi: We knew we were being set against a tough crowd and a tough question. We agree with a lot of their points. I think the question is, "Yes, but…" It's not "yes"; it's not us versus them. It's this kind of demonization of the market and this kind of dismissal of the market and the state, which I object to entirely. I think it's characteristic of a division of people into camps.

I think the state and the market are incredible, at times—absolutely incredible. It's so easy to critique. Why not say, "You know what? Look at all the good examples." It's not cool to big-up something; it's not cool to actually commemorate something. It's very cool and easy to critique. The question is, how can we do both: commemorate and critique at the same time?

Sholette: Can I give an anecdote too? There's a financier—no, he's not really a financier; he runs a finance company outside of Philadelphia. He also has a daughter who has an art gallery in New York City, and it is also an art consultancy. So she collects contemporary work and it's hung around this finance establishment—it's like a hedge fund—and the people in the hedge fund often find it uncomfortable. In an interview, the [financial CEO] said, "Well, actually that's what art is supposed to do. It's supposed to turn the institution upside-down. It's supposed to make people think like an artist—outside the box."

I think there is a real problematic situation that we are faced with now. As artists break out to do work in social spheres, as they exit the "art world" as we think of it [as a studio practice], they are becoming soaked up by the capitalist entrepreneurial system. So we are really in a new kind of conundrum. *Harvard Economic Review* said that the MFA is the new MBA, right? This is a problematic. I don't know how you could tell us that there are spaces, as you said, Deirdre, where [an artist] can embody a space that outside this sort of romanticism, or, on the other hand, get soaked up by an entrepreneurial paradigm.

Logue: Well, my argument is that we don't really have a choice but to pick the better one of those two paradigms.

Sholette: I'm voting for Obama; don't worry.

Mansoor: Deirdre made a wonderful point, that one way of trying to forge or carve out a space outside the state or market would be to surf the tension between the state and the market. You know, banks rob Peter to pay Paul and Paul to pay Peter, and so on and so forth. There's something very interesting about the suggestion that one could somehow mimic that logic against itself. There are a number of galleries, collectives, that have tried to mobilize this [logic]—among them, Reena Spaulings. Right? The model of the banker flâneur turned against itself and so on and so forth.

Sholette: But the banks have done a really good job mimicking actual banks, and we discovered they weren't really mimicking anymore.... They know these techniques as well as we do.

Mansoor: Exactly. That kind of mimetic inscription is old hat and will no longer work. It's been happening since Dada and so on. But that possibility of working the tension within the market and state is something that we saw happen with the free school in Copenhagen, which is an interesting model.

I'm very wary about the term "optimism," but I'll just borrow it for a moment. There are glimmers and flickers of those practices that tell us that there is an outside if we could just push it a little bit further. But I really object to the by-now cliché that criticism is somehow easy or facile, and one can just bash and smash everything.

It's a very difficult position to forge, to say that one, incrementally—through practice, through process, embodied, not in some theoretical or idealist way, but in one's own day-to-day process—would try to find an outside precisely because there is no outside. That is not a horizon to be scoffed at. It's quite hard to try and find the interstices that Deirdre mentioned. Let me say this: It's not a snarky, cynical position. It's not attacking for attacking's sake. It's attacking in the interest of survival. Mostly in the interest of a survival of a practice that isn't utterly transparent in mimicking the entrepreneurial system.

Logue: I think that's what we now call "innovation" though, right? It's really the working of those spaces, the working through these complications.

Sharifi: Based on our own experience, if somebody comes up to you and invites you to a collaboration, an exhibition, a project, and you tell them, "I want to make work that is somehow joyful," they are going to think you're stupid. It's a fact that generally in our milieu, it is much, much easier to create work which is somehow bringing things down. And, I agree, criticism is essential, but why does criticism have to be destructive? Why can't it be productive? Why not criticism with a smile?

I object to phrases like the "axis of evil"—even if it is [used as] a joke. [Criticism] is not always an attack. The word "compromise" is an idea of strength for many areas of the world.

Mansoor: OK. If you want to make a truly difficult, rigorous, wonderful painting of a pink flower, for example, one that is really going to explore the phenomenology of vision or some such, if you are really interested in painting—happy painting, joyous painting, energetic and dynamic painting—is it likely that the state or the market will assist you?

Sharifi: No. I mean, I can tell you that if…

Mansoor: The state and the market are both cynical, and they both want a cynical kind of art production that is going to mirror them to themselves.

Sharifi: Again, if we are all agents of the state and the market, then the fact is that all of us were conditioned intellectually to be suspicious of words like "mirth" or "cheer." Somehow it is not critical if it is mirthful.

Mansoor: How do you explain Jeff Koons?

Sharifi: Jeff Koons? Is he critical?

Mansoor: That's my…. You're mixing all these…

Sharifi: No, I'm saying that you have to be both. I'm saying that criticism, the holy grail, is to be both critical *and* commemorative. To be critical and somehow mirthful at the same time.

Sholette: Just to come at this from a different side but in the same discussion, I'm wondering how many people in here are art critics, and I wonder how many of them have really worked deeply and hard to talk about the kind of social practices that take place in a nursing home, or somewhere off with a native culture in the Northwest Territories, or, in a prison. I think what you are saying, Payam, is that the system that we have in place now, in the art world, doesn't really reward that kind of work. And so these kinds of "joyous works" if you will, that try to step outside the system, are pretty much ignored by the system. And unless [the work] is a self-conscious critique—a reproduction of some '60s activist statement, for example—it wont get much critical attention.

So we have to put some of the blame on ourselves for not stepping up to the plate if we really believe in this optimistic space. Not simply saying it exists, but actually beginning to articulate and support it in a critical way with a critical discourse. I don't see it, maybe it's there, but I don't see it.

Mansoor: Yes, we do need to support it.

O'Brian: Another five minutes maximum, before the final round of final statements. One to two minutes each.

Logue: We have to really rev it up here. Keep people entertained a little bit more.

I'm sort of confused as to how we—perhaps it is indicative of our pessimism—got to focusing on this idea that optimism is somehow counterproductive. And how that has a parallel conversation around paintings that are joyful or artworks that have any kind of happiness attached.

But I will try to take those two things and run them side by side for a moment, and suggest that art about ecstasy has been a cornerstone of [many types] of cultural production.

I know we can't strip the state or the market from what brought us all here in this room—this particular combination of individuals, or artists, academics, theorists, historians.

I mean it's in the carpets—there's nothing we can do. But to try and tear us from each other is, I think, the ultimate pessimism. If we have to call it "optimism"—I mean, give it another word, right? I think it can be called many things. We can call it "survival," we can call it.... I don't even know if I have very many words that would work here. I wrote down some stick marks.

(Laughter)

But it's not without criticality and it's not without eyes that see all the questions we might have about productive structures and infrastructures and subversion and public funding and banks.... I'm generally not optimistic. I was much better suited for the other side of this debate.

Sholette: We felt the same way over here. Do you want to switch sides now?

Logue: Well, only if there is a green card, which is a very queer colour indeed.

(A chime indicates time)

Logue: I hear music. Did I hear music? I hear music! And it sounds happy now! Before it sounded sad.

(Applause)

O'Brian: So the music has intervened, and we will now come to the third round in which somebody designated by the "Yes" side will go first, somebody designated by the "No" side will go second, and through until the final "No" has answered. I'm giving the "No" the final say.

And after a very brief pause, we will then take a final vote on the proposition.

Bejenaru: I discovered Belgrade a few months after the bombing. I had been walking in the streets of Belgrade in the beginning of the 2000s, together with my Serbian friends. And it was very painful to see what had happened there. A lot of buildings were destroyed, and the child of my very good friend—a distinguished curator and theorist from Belgrade—was born on the same day as when the city was bombed.

And in those difficult times in Serbia, just after the country was blamed for a lot of problems, I discovered something special: solidarity. When people are suffering, they need to be together. This is not happening today because the Serbians now don't need visas to travel to Western Europe. Romanians haven't needed visas to travel to Western Europe since 2005. But in that specific moment, when the society was suffering, the artists were united. Nobody was talking about money. The inflation rate was four hundred percent per month. This meant that the price of bread changed from the morning to the evening. That was a specific time when artists were together. Art was a tool for intellectual solidarity and survival.

I was fed with that spirit in the mid-1980s when I was a student of the communist Romania of [Nicolae] Ceaușescu. I was meeting East German art students in the Romanian Carpathian Mountains. We were talking about glasnost and perestroika. I have a desire to try and preserve that specific moment somehow. I think it could give us the energy, the positive energy to be creative without thinking about

gaining visibility, success, resources.

Sholette: I'll also offer a personal anecdote, though nothing quite as dramatic. When I started college, I worked as a janitor in a local factory. There were still factories in the northeast in those days, and I would basically clean the factory floor at night, and I would take scraps out of the trashcans to make my art projects. It was a computer factory—reel-to-reel computers and stuff like that. But I noticed on the workbenches of the various workers that they had built little sculptures out of scrap and put them on the desks, like little figures, animals, and tropical scenes.

And, one day, I took a piece of paper and I wrote what I thought was a very sophisticated critical comment about one of these works. I was trying to say how interesting it was, and I realized these things were really intriguing to me because I couldn't figure out how I would place them within the art-school context I was getting at that particular moment. My professors had mostly been Greenbergian students themselves.

What was this work? What was it about? There was obviously joy in the making these things, but also they were a way to kill time. And a way to steal time.

When I wrote that note [about this work], and I think in some ways I wrote it because I felt very uncomfortable with this stuff. And I wanted to mark that distance between me, who was trying to become a professional artist, and these people, who probably today aren't even working since those kinds of jobs don't exist anymore.

Logue: I feel like I've said as much as I can say, in the ways that I know how to say these things. And for someone who wasn't supposed to be here, I feel like I've done a pretty good job.

(Laughter and applause)

Fleischmann: I was asked earlier why do the projects [I work on], and actually it started before this investment of the fifty euros. I also started in a garage, and I have sympathy for this kind of format. I occupied it when I was sixteen or seventeen. I collected paint from a place that had old paints. It became my first studio. The garage was the escape from the living room of my parents. It was the first form of emancipation for me that I can actively recall. And it was like all the other projects that always have to do with escape, or trying to get outside of something.

But on the other hand, it turned out that what I became more and more interested in were ways to infiltrate, to get inside, into something else. I think this is why I do not have such a difficulty with defending the idea that there is no space outside. It is important to be aware of these other fields as other [spaces] that need to be inhabited and criticized from the inside and escaped from again.

Mansoor: I just want to emphasize what Matei said. I really don't wish to add to it. It stands.

O'Brian: And the last word goes to Payam.

Sharifi: I think that the question of optimism is an important one. I think that "optimism with criticality" is a very good way of putting it. To find a consensus as opposed to distinguishing ourselves more and more on one side of the table and the other. But I also think it's what we call a "Slavic sense of defeatism": meaning that we know that we are going to fail, but we get up every morning trying nonetheless.

O'Brian: I'll thank the speakers in a moment, but first I want you to look at the proposition that is up on the screen—"Is there space for art outside the market and the state?"—to reconsider your positions, and to have your papers ready.

All those who are "Yes" and for the motion, please raise yellow. It's a forest of yellow. But I see blue and yellow as well.

And now the "Nays," against the proposition, blues. There are more blues than when we started. But the "Yeas" have it.

(Applause)

O'Brian: I want to thank all six of the speakers. It does seem that, in an hour and a half, they have said a great deal. So a very vigorous round of applause for an excellent debate!

Should Artists Professionalize?

As artists have taken on the creation of artist-run organizations or have turned themselves or their practices into institutions, their roles have expanded, taking on the work of curator, administrator, critic, educator, publicist, and so forth. While the polyvalence of contemporary artists has enriched institutions with resources and support, any reciprocity remains subject to debate.

The professionalization of the artist, arising as a consequence of artist-run institution building and the blurring of professional roles inherent in such activity, may limit artistic potential in that artists take on increased administrative and curatorial responsibilities, among others, at the opportunity cost of artistic production. In the second debate of the convention, presenters will deliberate on the many roles of the contemporary artist, making the case for and against his or her professionalization.

For
Julia Bryan-Wilson
Jeff Derksen
Candice Hopkins

Against
Tania Bruguera
Sam Gould
Claire Tancons

Moderator
John O'Brian

October 13, 2012
Simon Fraser University
Vancouver, Canada

John O'Brian: Good evening everyone, for the second debate of two
debates of this convention. The
proposition, the question that is
being put forward this evening is:
Should artists professionalize?

Just to repeat a couple of the
things I said last night, but also
to say some new things: this is an
Oxford-style debate; that's what
we're engaging in. It is an experimental forum in the exchange of
ideas at a convention like this that
deals with artist-run culture. As I
mentioned again last night, most
of us—that is, the six speakers and
myself—have not previously participated in a debate and its formal
protocols. That sometimes leads to
surprising moments, not excluding
Freudian parapraxis.

(Laughter)

So to repeat the question again:
Should artists professionalize? This
is a deeply significant question for
artist-run culture. In the strict sense
of the word, to "professionalize" is
to impose structures. So here, the
weight of the sentence falls on the
verb. What is imposed upon necessarily is subject to controls and
regulations. There are alternatives to
professionalization and I expect we
will hear about some of them from
the three debaters, the three speakers, arguing against the question.

In a session yesterday, Jakob
Jakobsen discussed the anti-
professional and anti-pedagogical
stance of the Free University in Copenhagen as a way of taking power
in dangerous times, by which he
meant *our* times. The three debaters

arguing in favour of professionalization may be making counter-
arguments to Jakobsen, or not, as
the case may be. This is an organic
process.

Again, for those of you who were
not here last night, I want to once
again lay out what the protocols
are. There will be three rounds of
remarks by participants.

Round One: Statements of position. Total: thirty minutes. Each
debater will have four to five minutes to speak and make their case
for or against the question posed.
They will speak from alternating
positions: for/against, for/against,
for/against. The speakers will not
address one another in this round,
but they will be taking notes for the
second round. If they go over their
time, they will be subject to James
Maxwell and Kathleen Ritter, and
called to order with music.

Round Two: Here the speakers will
address one another directly. This
will be for about twenty to thirty
minutes.

Round Three: Closing statements,
very brief: six to twelve minutes
total. In this round each debater has
one to two minutes to make a closing statement and then the audience
will vote again and a photograph will
be taken. Part of what we are looking for is the degree to which yellow
turns to blue or blue to yellow.

We will now begin with the "No"
side. Claire, you're first. Please go
ahead.

Claire Tancons: I will begin by saying
that if professionalization is to be
measured by whether or not speakers on a panel have written papers
to be read, then, clearly, our panel
has already made a statement, if
you compare what's happening at
the table to my right, and what's

happening at our table. To the right we have clearly prepared papers, while to the left we have Moleskine notebooks and (looks to Tania Bruguera's materials)…Ramada Inn notepads and a pen.

Sam Gould: I have [written] two questions and a reminder to buy Jeff [Derksen]'s book.

Tancons: In any event, we really did not prepare any of this. We just sat down and I realized how the tables were being set. And I thought that it really did speak for itself already, maybe. But I think that from the get-go we should try and make a distinction between "professionalism" and what being professional might mean and be, and "professionalization," and what professionalizing might also mean and be.

And as this distinction might be what we labour on throughout this entire panel. I will obviously not try and give definitions right from the outset. I think that my contribution to the panel, by way of an introductory remark, will be sharing an anecdote with you. It's a recent anecdote, and it's based on an experience I had in Venice, last summer, teaching a curatorial class at IUAV [Iuav University of Venice] while being hosted by the Fondazione Bevilacqua La Masa, directed by the formidable Angela Vettese. Their purpose is clearly to professionalize artists. To give them a one-year span of time to do work, present work, host events, prepare for studio visits, apply for the next residency, etc., etc. However, when doing studio visits with each and every one of the maybe fifteen artists—those residing in Venice and the others residing on the Giudecca—I was delighted as to the nature of the discussion and the level of the discourse that occurred between these artists and myself, often speaking for much longer than the fifteen-minute time that they are apparently used to for studio visits with outside curators. And it was very refreshing for me because, unlike my experience as a curator doing studio visits or engaging with artists in the US and, unlike my experiences with recent MFA graduates taught in an American environment, these Italian artists were not intent on parroting curatorial speak, which is oftentimes what I find with already professionalized, but not yet professional, recent art graduates. And so, these Venetian artists, in my view—striving to get the hell out of Venice, go to Milan at worst, go to New York at best—were definitely very professional, but hadn't yet been professionalized. Some didn't have a portfolio ready, even though the work might be very good, right?

I think it's important to highlight this distinction between a *professional* artist—who might be doing his work—and a *professionalized* artist who might be going a step further and already somewhat mimicking the structure of the world in which he or she knows he or she could be active in.

O'Brian: Thank you. The next speaker is Jeff Derksen.

Jeff Derksen: Since we've already been overly performing our professionalism and we did have Skype meetings before…

Tania Bruguera: Oh my god.

(Laughter)

Derksen: I would like to unsettle some sense of professionalism and unsettle a sense of ownership in a sense, by acknowledging that we are on unceded Coast Salish Land, of course. It is important to point out in this neoliberal era.

Because we have this sort of NPR, American debate–feeling system going on here, I'll start with an anecdote.

On the campaign stump in Iowa, Mitt Romney—filled with a bright-eyed, capitalist glee—countered a heckler with the assertion that, "Corporations are people, my friend." Within the intensive mode of capitalism today and within the collapsing of contradiction that Romney reflects, let me propose that artists are people too, my friends.

What shape does [artist's] professionalization take? And what can we make of it? A deep, managerial strain runs through artists institutions, particularly Canadian artists formations, from the constructed and managed national culture down to artist-run centres. A teasing managerialism also runs through conceptual art from David Lamelas's telex machines in the 1968 Venice Biennale to the corporate modelling of N.E. Thing Co. to Maria Eichhorn's project that followed the bureaucratic steps required to obtain a plot of land.

Being optimistic and critical—which is what Lefebvre lovingly called "critique"—we can say that artists were appropriating and mutating managerial models and syntaxes before the managerial model began to appropriate and mutate the relationship of life and labour. Management then moved in to incorporate creativity. If the 1960s management project aimed at the relaxation of bureaucracy to counter the growing integration of ever larger firms, as Boltanski and Chiapello argue, then by the time artists effectively used modes and models of self-management against art institutions, as Julia's work shows us, management had begun moving into lovely notions of decentralization, meritocracy, and management by objectives.

By the nineties management promoted lean firms, linked in networks coming together for projects. A quick look at the artist-run centres and our art magazines in Canada today gives us a plethora of structures rather than a parody of structures. Directors, executive directors, associate directors, program managers, editors, publishers, assistant editors, associate editors not only run the show but they also guide the vision, the mission, and the values. Even the Secession in Vienna, the site of an original rupture, has a president, a vice president, a secretary and has an attached affective Facebook option where you can be a "friend." The first pull-down menu on e-flux's website is "clients," trumping that older artists' favourite, "archive." And for those who love corporate structures, are not gallery-organized after-opening dinners more hierarchical, more complexly and uncomfortably structured than an Enbridge board meeting?

But why do artists professionalize in a way that reflects or even builds a culture of verticality, a vertical representation, a delegation of duties and positions? Rarely are we asked to get in contact with the collective or rarely is there no one designated as a contact. Why is a culture of verticality so evident in these structures, in these institutions?

The Russian Formalists proposed parody as a model of renewal, breaking stale literary forms open to the new, which is why *Tristram*

Shandy is their favourite typical novel. But let me argue for a shift, a rupture, a moment that exceeds expectations. If parody contains a formal dialectic where synthesis is replaced with renewal, then we artists can professionalize in a way that is not an appropriation, a static parody nor a vertical calling card of cultural capital and managerial skills.

Instead I'll propose Horizontalidad or horizontalism. It's not a new idea but it's perhaps a necessary notion. It promotes the emergence of difference, the rejection of hierarchy, and insistence on process. Horizontalism rejects verticality. In Argentina, since 2001 notably, horizontalism is the mode of popular power that sees itself as a means and not an end. It is used in recuperated factories, medical clinics, and in neighbourhood assemblies. This model of horizontalism aims at consensus but it is not post-political. It assumes there will always be antagonisms. But for artists, horizontalism challenges us to rethink our parodies of professional models, our seeming love of verticality that makes us visible to other vertical structures. We must see horizontalism not as a decentred mode of organizing, for what could be more flexible and loved by the lords of neoliberalism? It is a rejection of verticality. It asks us instead, in the global north at this moment, to look to the south for philosophies of living—rather than for cheap labour.

Yes, this can sound like a parody of a [19]68 lament or an endorsement of dot com material capitalism, but what is absolutely crucial is that horizontalism is the process, the making of social subjects rather than the management, the arrangement, of social subjects.

As a process rather than a structure, horizontalism also aims at the injection of new social relationships between these subjects. Rather than the tyranny of art into life, it is life into art.

O'Brian: Thank you, Jeff. Sam Gould is next.

Gould: Thanks, Jeff. In many ways, I agree with Jeff's points. But with a few crucial differences.

To quote Gertrude Stein, as a response to how [Jeff] talked about horizontality: "We have to act as if there is no use in a centre"—constantly reconfiguring and creating a fluid relationship to the structures that we build.

That notion of parody is something that I'm really interested in. If professionalization is a mask that never comes off, it becomes your real face. It becomes fully embodied.

As an art worker, it's very important to me that we work through a certain sort of…not necessarily *anti*-structure, but a *pro*-fluidity: a consistent reconsideration of where we are within a particular critical landscape.

Again, anecdotally, one of my very good friends and collaborators was an undergraduate student of the late Minnesota senator Paul Wellstone, whom I'm a great admirer of. My collaborator, Dan Wong, mentioned that Wellstone would never use the word "radical" in class, even though it really could have been the easy way out—to call something radical. But, therefore, you don't actually have to go into what it is. The professionalization of art, or at least "culture," within this sphere that we call "art," increasingly has these words that allow us to not actually talk about what we mean. And by "meaning," I think that means what we care about, what we desire, what our values are. And we need to talk about what our values are more.

I'm not saying we need to agree on them at all, but by using this coded language, this professionalization of speech, we're constantly agreeing to not talk about messy shit. And we need to do that, because what we can do can be very powerful. I think what we can provide is a space for questioning and I think that is what being an art worker for me is all about.

As a parallel to Lefebvre or David Harvey's ideas of the "right to the city," I think we need, especially now, to start considering ideas of the "right to the imagination." We seemingly can create anything: you can put your videos up on You-Tube, you can send MP3s anywhere around the world instantly to those who have good IT connections, which increasingly is more and more people. But the way that our so-called imagination is distributed is through rigid structures, on and on. As Julia mentioned earlier today, through corporate ogres such as Google, wherein they may provide an extremely good service, but it is through very strict paradigms.

I think as art workers what we need to do is constantly reconfigure social space and encourage this right to the imagination. This right to questioning. The space in-between people. And that is something that can't be built on a hierarchy, on a structure, on something that isn't fluid. It needs to change from person to person, relationship to relationship. Thanks.

O'Brian: Thank you, Sam. Candice Hopkins.

Candice Hopkins: Should artists professionalize? They already have and they've done it on their own terms. And this isn't something that's new, professional art schools have been around now for more than three hundred and fifty years, the first being in France. And with this, we have alternative models of artistic education as well as a development of professional arts associations, both formal and informal. Systems of value and recognition for professional art are found nearly everywhere. A profession is something that's quite simple. It's a pursuit that has a sense of solidarity, it indicates specialized training in a body of abstract knowledge, it embodies collectivity or an element of service, it develops ethics. And, unlike a hobby, it's a full-time pursuit. The roots of a profession are in fact in a public declaration, a kind of performative speech act. Art is an occupation that one professes to be skilled in. On a personal level, it might imply accountability and also an ethics of practice.

As we know, Canada in the 1960s and the 1970s—a time widely recognized for its experimentation—was also remarkable for its parallel movement of professionalization [in the arts]. This marked the emergence of CARFAC, the Canadian Artists' Representation, and Le Front des artistes canadiens, an organization that was started by artists in 1968 that outlined artists' rights. The establishment of systems of governments and ethics is one of the characteristics of professionalization. This was also the time of the birth of many of the country's venerable artist-run centres—and here, as Jeff pointed to, artists are responsible for developing mandates, boards, programming, fundraising, development, outreach, governments, strategic plans, and unprecedented collaborations with [for-profit] companies—an example is the I.P. Sharp company, who developed an early model of the internet and who worked with artists as creative consultants. Through these activities, artists created new systems of knowledge.

But why *should* artists professionalize? By doing so, they in fact change institutions. Their professionalization pressures these spaces to, in turn, become more professional, accountable, and ethical. Think of the impetus for the Art Workers' Coalition and note that the term aligns art with skilled labour, work being the opposite of leisure; The Guerilla Art Action Group; and, closer to home, SCANA [The Society of Canadian Artists of Native Ancestry]. SCANA successfully fought for museums and galleries to be more representative, to exhibit and acquire the work of the great number of Indigenous artists that were practicing in Canada through the 1970s and 1980s. Their members included the first wave of professionally trained artists and this institutional knowledge, I would argue, assisted them in lobbying some of the largest museums and galleries in the nation and also creating a sense of awareness. They ultimately produced institutions, I think, that were more self-reflective and this tradition continues. So professionalization has a transformative potential.

I think it's not so much about the business of art but the art of business. Just consider the innumerable artists and collectives who take the business model as a site of art itself. In Vancouver there was N.E. Thing Co. which incorporated business just like any company and viewed the art world as a kind of parallel consumer culture. It offered goods and services, it promoted itself at trade fairs, it produced aesthetic systems divided into two things: acts, which were aesthetically claimed things, and art, which were aesthetically rejected things. And later, opened a photo imaging company and a food store.

On April 19, 1971—this is just another example—the trustees of the Boston ICA announced that they had acquired a new work by Christopher Cook. It was entitled *Information Compression Series*. The work of art was a declaration and he noted, "I will become the director of the ICA for one year. During that period I will have the same responsibilities and opportunities as a regular director. I will energize the Institute in all possible ways, carry out a varied program and attempt to establish workable, real communication between Boston cultural institutions." So professionalization is a creative pursuit in and of itself.

And, my third point, it's also a way of making space. In the mid-1800s, women artists, when excluded from male-dominated clubs and societies, formed parallel networks—salons—to encourage the sharing of knowledge and skills, founded on the ideas of the domestic. Their organizing enabled their own legitimacy as professional artists. This was what they wanted. Their network became a means to call attention to exclusionary practices and the mis-representation of their art in media.

In the early 1970s, 1973 I believe, Daphne Odjig formed the Warehouse Gallery in Winnipeg, Manitoba. It was both an education space and a place to exhibit the work of Aboriginal artists who, at the time, were not being shown in galleries and museums. It further expanded their visibility and they also initiated a print shop where they released unlimited editions of work that were sold for reasonable prices, thereby making formerly unknown artists household names.

So professionalization almost seems a natural impulse in response to marginal situations.

O'Brian: Thank you, Candice. The next speaker is Tania Bruguera, who is just consulting, collaborating with her other speakers and debaters.

Bruguera: The first point is that variety is very important. We do need some artists to be professionalized and [others] to not be professionalized, so we can make the conversation richer and to have paradigms to [respond to].

But what worries me about the idea of professionalization, having been a professor for a long time in the United States, is how the conversation about the production of cultural value is determined by questions like: "How can I get a gallery when I get out of school?" This places the question in the wrong place.

For me, the most important part is: by professionalizing, *who* is determining what is right and what is wrong, what is ethical, and what is the right way to produce, and who is deciding the value of value? We already have professionalized artists—but are they the best artists?

Audience Member: Yes.

Bruguera: Are they the best artists? Why?

Audience Member: If they have

more work discipline then they will do better work.

Bruguera: No, I think it's a big mistake—this idea that having a work ethic…. The way we are seeing professionalization is [through] a capitalist, corporative model, instead of [through a model of] self-discipline. The idea of [self-discipline] has nothing to do with "professionalization," it has to do with [being] "professional."

And the other thing that we are seeing right now is a lot of artists who are behaving as if they are part of a corporation. And these exactly are the artists who go to all the right parties, who talk to the right people, who if you are at a table with them at a dinner, they stand up and leave you with your word to talk to the right curator because you're not so important. And then these are the people who end up in all these big shows that we criticize because the art is no good. So I think this is already something that we're seeing, but again no argument can be black and white.

And again, it is a capitalistic model which is a problem. Right now it seems like there is a hegemony—only one type of society, and any other…

Audience Member (shouts): Stolen art! Stolen land!

Bruguera: Cómo? What did they say?

Gould: Stolen art, stolen land.

Bruguera: What is that?

Gould: We are on stolen land right now.

Bruguera: OK. Let's talk about that.

Tancons: I just wanted to interject, if you agree. Really what we are thinking, Tania, is that, in response to Candice, professional artists might make good art institutions and I think this speaks to a Canadian model. And I think here we might be more representative of an American model. I don't know that…

Bruguera: I'm not American.

Tancons: Professional artists necessarily make good…

Gould: I'm an anarchist. Anybody else?

Tancons: …good art. So I think we must make a distinction between professional artists building good art institutions, which I think is what Candice was predominantly talking about, versus [the idea that] a professionalization of artists enhances artistic abilities.

Gould: This notion of ethics and professionalization that was brought up is a core element. If we have rigidity to our ethics…

Bruguera: And who determines what is ethical?

Gould: Exactly, you know, ethics change with the times…

(The timer chimes)

…for next time.

O'Brian: The final speaker in the first round is Julia Bryan-Wilson.

Julia Bryan-Wilson: Before I get to the many meanings of the word professionalize, let me also emphasise that there is no such thing as a stable, single category of artist. Who are these artists that we're talking about? Are they the practicioners barely scraping by, with adjunct teaching jobs on the side to pay the rent in a nation with no state support for the arts? Are they newly graduated art students burdened by debt and a country with robust national funding? Are they village artisans struggling for survival by organizing collectives to protect their local handicrafts?

There are so many kinds of activity and so many different identities and so many divergent contexts that one could corral under the rubric of artists that it begins to fray at the seams.

Instead of asking a sweeping question like, "Should artists professionalize?," let's pay attention to local circumstances and specific histories in which this issue might ramify quite unevenly. When we speak from a space of empire in the twenty-first century, the question has long ago been answered. Starting in the Renaissance—when art began to define itself as a vocation rather than as a calling—artists have been increasingly professionalized, most notably and precipitously in the 1960s with the rise of the MFA as the terminal degree, grants earmarked only for professional artists, and art school classes routinely taught on professional practices. Which is not to say that artists shouldn't buck against the trend of packaging themselves for easier consumption—of course they should.

Still, I want to acknowledge that there is a lot of diversity in this room and many conflicting understandings of how it might be possible to make a living doing your work. If there is a space for art outside the state and the market, following last night's panel, it is—as Deirdre put it—the space of embodiment that is separate from the total administration of everyday life. It is within this space that it also makes sense to redefine professionalism. It does not [have to] denote walking lockstep to the beat of the neoliberal entrepreneurial drum, but rather [professionalism can represent] managing yourself, practicing an ethics of care when you engage with others. We might call this "minding your business." And I don't mean "business" in the white-collar sense, but the interrelational ways in which we move through the world.

"Professionalization" has become an overly simplistic, catch-all [dirty] word. But no one on our panel is saying that artists should scheme to functionalize art to make a quick buck. As we understood it, the question was not, "Should artists sell out?"—because who's going to agree with that? Nobody. But rather, [the question is], "How do you want to acknowledge the circumstances of your own production within a highly compromised economy?" Let's be strategic about how we contribute to those structures and be tactical about how we might interrupt or stall its ruthless logic. None of us think by saying yes to this question that artists should head for the galleries or put on business suits and take their marching orders from corporations. Or if we do, as both Jeff and Candice have pointed out, we take our cues from Canadian conceptualists who professionalized as a kind of drag: humorous, parodic, and incisive ways to reimagine the affiliations between collaborations and ideas of incorporation with all its interestingly absorptive and bodily overtones.

Instead of "Should artists professionalize?" we should ask, "How should artists profess?"

"Profess," of course, has many meanings. One of them is to declare oneself skilled or expert to assert knowledge, but it also means to lay claim to something falsely, insincerely, or deceptively. I think artists should profess by accepting their expertise as well as their wily ways. I call for the professing of professionalism, ironizing and making strange professionalization, turning it upside down, to curdle it, to estrange it from itself.

Instead of being forced to answer yes or no to this totally false binary, let's reframe the question. "Should artists and critics profess what they believe in, be more transparent about the stakes that they're making and how they support themselves?" Yes. "Should artists and critics be self-aware of their own circulation within frameworks of power of their own implication and larger systems of financialization and self-management?" Yes. "Should artists advocate for themselves and for social justice more broadly, with an understanding that their fights might have some surprising resonance with other questions of inequity?" Yes. "Should artists also organize with an awareness that they have certain class privileges due to cultural capital, even if that cultural capital does not always easily translate into actual political power or long-term financial security?" Yes. "Should artists fictionalize rather than financialize, make shit up, falsify, infiltrate?" Yes. "Should artists with art school educations be aware that just because they are underpaid does not mean that they are underclass?" Yes. "Should art historians and critics acknowledge our profound privilege as tastemakers?" Yes. "Should we all take more risks, but all the time acknowledge that the risks we take are not equivalent to many other people's and the risks they live?" Yes.

(Loud applause, cheering)

Gould: Can Julia and I start our own "middle team"?

(Laughter)

O'Brian: That is the end of round one, to which you gave great applause. Thank you. We now move on to round two which will last about a similar period of time and in which the exchanges can come in any order, from any quarter that the speakers like. Because Julia has just spoken, I will invite the other side to speak first.

Bruguera: Julia, can you read the last sentence?

Bryan-Wilson: "Should we all take more risks but all the time acknowledge that the risks we take are not necessarily equivalent to many other people's and the risks they live?"

Bruguera: Yes, that's the problem.

Bryan-Wilson: You know, I wrote this before I saw your talk in the Q&A this morning, FYI. I wrote that last night before I saw you talk, and I know, because your talk was a lot about risk.

Bruguera: Don't get defensive. You were very good at saying yes at everything in your position to influence people's minds. I saw that, good technique! Very [Baruch] Spinoza-like.
  So basically, I really like your presentation, but the problem is: How do we see the positioning of

the artist in society? This is part of the discussion about professionalization. When you professionalize practice, you are making a niche, an isolation, a space in society where you are belonging to it, instead of it giving you the flexibility to move across disciplines and across practices. This is a problem. I think artists should not be in the protected zone when they are talking about what happened, but they should be *in* what happened, and helping to develop what happens. I already think that model (motions to Bryan-Wilson) is problematic; it is precisely a consequence of professionalization.

Gould: To further your argument— it creates an "otherness" of the artist, this "special role" that we play— which is not true. [As if, as] an artist, you have this special knowledge that other people don't have. That "otherness" is something that art workers need to consider if they care about creating the types of spaces of "equity" that Julia discussed. We have to divest ourselves from this notion of otherness. We need to start with our desires [and find] commonalities with others on a flattened, nonhierarchical landscape.

O'Brian: So, Sam, are you addressing that to Tania, or to this side?

Gould: I'm addressing that to the entire world…

Bruguera: I'm very interested in the capacity an artist could have when inside the system, as part of the system. To criticize the system, [an artist has to be] willing to self-sabotage [themselves] and [their] own practice. It's hard to renounce all of the privilege and the comfort that comes with being part of the system.

One last point: Are we also professionalizing the audience? Are we also professionalizing other aspects of practice? I'm very sad to see that in this era of art practice, it is more important to have the good judgment of institutions, collectors, and curators, than your own peers. That is something that is lost with professionalization. It doesn't matter how successful you were in the system, it's about the work you produce. Personally, I care more about what another artist thinks about my work than any curator or historian, because he or she knows if I am cheating or not. And we can cheat in art very easily.

Gould: What do you say to that?

Derksen: Maybe we should have a brief board meeting before we…

(Laughter)

Bryan-Wilson: I just want to pick up on Candice's idea about professionalization, in response to marginalization. And again, nobody on this team thinks that we are talking about sending people into the commercial art gallery with a clean conscience. We are trying to turn the question against itself and argue something different.

I think it is very interesting to think about building structures for yourself, to advocate for yourself, when you have been given no voice and how to create a space for that voice—which is about, in some ways, also creating and supporting audiences and collaborating with different communities. I just wanted to highlight that point because I thought it was really interesting, and it is something that

I am thinking about in my own work because I have moved into thinking about sometimes quite anonymous amateur craftspeople and it is an extremely interesting realm when you think about how these people have not been given the identity of "artist." But they might, in fact, *organize* themselves into collectives, or as artisans, and in that way, [they might] professionalize themselves as artists. This might actually be a means to some enfranchisement in a system that has otherwise completely overlooked them.

Tancons: We are obviously not against artists organizing to better their own work and the society around them. I think that there is a point that we don't seem to manage to go beyond, which again is the difference between self-organization and the organizations whose rules we feel we need to abide by. Right? I think that is one of the crucibles of this conversation.

Gould: I think that notion of "who you abide by" is incredibly important. The rigidity of these structures break the most important thing within art—the space of reflexivity. When talking about a structure for reflexivity, I mean *whose* structure? Who gets to say what those paradigms are? If it's different for each art worker, is that professionalization? Or is that just mindfulness? I think there is a core difference.

Bryan-Wilson: Can I ask what you mean by "art worker"? Can you just expand on that term and how you use it? Because you used it a number of times.

Gould: Yeah, absolutely. I use "art worker" in a political sense. In that there are people who…how do I put this…

Bruguera: Go baby, you can do it!

Gould: I use "art worker" in a political sense in that there are people who, while they have different jobs, work in concert towards shared goals. I use it succinctly—as opposed to "artist." This is not to devalue those who would consider themselves artists, but I [think of] myself as an art worker and am in solidarity with other art workers. We have certain concerns that are different from say, someone who might call themselves an artist. For me, the notion of art worker contains a certain politics of equitability.

Audience Member: Class war!

Gould: Class war. That could be. Sure.

Bryan-Wilson: I would actually like to hear you say more about how you feel the word "art worker" functions in terms of a class positioning.

Gould: A class positioning? Yeah, I think it levels the playing field. I think…

Bryan-Wilson: Is it an equivalency that you're proposing?

Gould: Well, I think what it does is that this notion of solidarity…. An "art worker" is someone who is in conversation with other workers. We work together. It's the difference from, say, artist-as-entrepreneur or artist-as-CEO—[which feels like] someone who is working in a completely solitary fashion.

Derksen: Wouldn't that art worker actually project a solidarity outside

the profession or outside the act of art to other workers? That to me would seem to be the definition. Not that the art worker works on art but that the art worker stands in solidarity with other workers.

Gould: Yeah, absolutely. My particular "craft," if you will, happens to be cultural production. It's anybody who also believes that the job that they have shares values with other jobs. And therefore you are in conversation along those lines.

But I do think that is very different from this notion of professionalization because we are defining professionalization strictly in regard to structure. I think those types of relationships between workers can be very fluid. And they can be based on our relationship to our day-to-day lives and how we are experiencing our lives with one another. But these structures that we are discussing I think generally have us try to see each day as the continuation of much the same because therefore it creates a sort of cookie-cutter packaging of what is needed to be produced.

Derksen: I think what our panel is rejecting is an equivalency of structures. So maybe I'll turn to poetry because we've talked a little about poetry—you invoked Gertrude Stein who said, "There's no need for a centre." I also remind you that she wrote a poem called "Banking in Boston" as well. She very much needed a centre to keep her money in.

(Laughter)

So there's contradictions even at the beautiful heart of Gertrude Stein. But I think we are rejecting the equivalency of structures, so I'll turn to one of my favourite structuralists: a guy named Yuri Lotman who talks about setting up structures that break other structures. For Lotman, the moment of maximum poetic meaning is when a structure is set up and then broken by another structure. Through an expectation, it is broken. I saw this at the very poetic heart of what Candice was saying—that we need structures that operate differently than hegemonic structures to open up spaces—if we are going to use a spatial metaphor—for those who have been excluded by these vertical structures.

So, we are not operating on an equivalency of structures, but rather seeing these structures as something—yes, that are fluid—[created] between relations, between workers, and not just between isolated CEOs. That there is a power that one is able to utilize [through] self-management and self-organization.

Bruguera: I think that is so beautiful. Without any irony—I love it. That is exactly the type of practice that I do. Create and break institutions—exactly. The only problem is, that in a professionalized situation, what are the measures of success? This is where the problem comes. What you have said is a beautiful thing that can be done in multiple ways, but it is being judged at some point. It has to be judged; it is not only judged poetically, but it is also judged as part of the poetry of our times. And part of the poetry in our times is "success," right? Unfortunately.

Who is measuring success? Who is establishing the concept of what is successful and what is not? Under professionalization, I think this becomes very problematic.

Bryan-Wilson: I want to get back to "art workers."

Gould: You know, you wrote a whole damn book on this, don't quiz me.

(Laughter)

Bryan-Wilson: Well, yeah, I did, and it's a very, very problematic phrase. I wrote a whole dissertation and it turned into a book about how incredibly problematic it is and how this phantasmatic solidarity that it tries to transcribe within itself is so infrequently returned. So the idea that you, by calling yourself an "art worker," have some kind of relationship or equivalency with the working class is…

Gould: That's not what I'm saying though! You're putting words in my mouth.

Bruguera: No, no, no! Don't get in the trap—that's a trap. I'll tell you something.

Bryan-Wilson: Nobody calls themselves an "Artist CEO."

Gould: I think Damien Hirst or Jeff Koons would call themselves an Artist CEO.

Bruguera: Can I say two things very quickly here? Sorry, I'm in a fire here. So, two things:

First, they call themselves CEOs sometimes as an ironic gesture that becomes reality later. That's the problem: the transformation from an ironic gesture to an actual [one].

Secondly, I think the word "solidarity" should be changed to "identification." I think the word "solidarity" does not operate in the art worker's context. I think we should use "identification." Why? Because, as you rightly state, it is a false presentation that we are going to be in solidarity with everybody. I live in a socialist country and it is not so easy to be in solidarity. But "identification" is different, because if you're an art worker you can identify yourself with other workers and can establish points of entry. It could be contradictory, against, oppositional. So on our team, if it is OK, we should substitute "solidarity" with "identification."

Tancons: Maybe we should start thinking about concrete examples and concrete models of artistic practices and what we see them to have achieved. For the last ten minutes I've been thinking about two radically different practices coming from two revered Italian artists: Michelangelo Pistoletto and Maurizio Cattelan. I do believe that Pistolletto has achieved more for the field of art at large with the work he started to build in the '70s—with the zoo and other similarly related theatrical practices—than Maurizio Cattelan ever will by constantly promoting himself and following a starkly professionalizing model. [Despite this professionalization,] I do not believe we can argue that Maurizio Cattelan is a better artist than Pistoletto.

Bryan-Wilson: Well, I have a question for the audience—even though you are very dark. How many people here have received either a Canada Council for the Arts grant or a regional grant?

Quite a few of you. Wow, that's a lot.

I just looked up something on the website because I was curious. There are two main requirements.

Does anyone know? Number one, you have to be a Canadian citizen and there's lots of rules about that. Number two, you have to be—and it says this on the website—a "professional artist." And this is how they define that: "A professional artist is someone who has specialized training in the field [not necessarily in academic institutions], is recognized by peers [artists working in the same artistic tradition], and has a history of public presentation or publication."

I just thought it was fascinating that we're arguing about artists and if they should professionalize or not when it's the very ground on which so many livings are made. That, in order to "professionalize," you already have to be "professional." Like, with the Ontario Arts Council, the "emerging artists" category for visual artists is open to artists with at least three years of professional practice and some record of exhibition. So I think, just as Claire was saying, in order to get specific, it's very interesting to me that in this country with a lot of state support for the arts—which not every country has—professionalization is defined in very specific and concrete ways.

Bruguera: We said at the very beginning that there is a difference between being "a professional"—being "part of a profession"—and the "professionalization" of practice. Yes, you have to be dedicated full-time to a practice, but that doesn't [define] what kind of dedication or mechanism you have in that practice.

Gould: I have a question for Julia. What do you see as the difference between "being a professional" and "working"?

Bryan-Wilson: Being a professional and working? Maybe there is not one.

Bruguera: Who determines [this]? Not to you (gestures at Julia), I don't want to attack you, I love you, but…. This is maybe why I should attack you.

(Laughter)

I work at the University of Chicago; I have never seen a more fearful, aggressive, and intense practice in academia. It is the only academic place I've been….

(Laughter)

But you know what I mean—there is a professionalization of practice [from] being in academia. I've lost respect for many, many people… the way they have to bend their asses over the institution because they are professionalized. And they have to respond not to their own needs as professionals, but to the institution's.

Bryan-Wilson: I completely agree with you. It's a horrible, horrible thing, the compromises you have to make. For myself, I refuse to apologize for having prepared in advance and written something up, you know? And two….

Bruguera: No, no, no—we should have been prepared too. But the thing is that….

Tancons: Being professional is being ready to react in any circumstance, whether prepared or unprepared…

Bruguera: So the thing is, that if you are in an institutional format,

like academia, people who are in academia have to respond to the institution. Otherwise they lose their jobs. So if we have that model and we put it into art practice, what will happen?

Gould: "Who are you responsible to at the end of the day?"

Bruguera: Yeah! Who do you have to answer to? Who do you have to bend over to?

Bryan-Wilson: Well, I have tenure, so…

(Laughter)

Bruguera: No, we're not personalizing the debate!

Gould: And who's the one talking about privilege?

Bryan-Wilson: I don't make bones about that.

Bruguera: I'm talking about models. I'm not talking about the specific practices in academia…

Tancons: What I still don't understand is what the alternative structure is to the [Canada Council] rules you read. My understanding of that is that Jeff in particular was advocating for a different structure based on horizontalism. So how does that horizontal structure respond to trying to get an art grant based on these rules? Just to be very clear.

Derksen: I think that this is a distortion of the larger point that we've been aiming at. We spun away from the art worker discussion and now we seem to be worried about how tenured or nontenured professors are treated within academic institutions. Frankly, I thought that Candice made a very powerful argument against exactly that kind of narrowing and professionalization of the *stakes*. [Her] argument [focused on] a politics and ethics to fight against exclusion. No stolen art, no stolen land: that would be one rubric of success. I think we've drifted away from the types of alternative, structured models that our side was arguing for.

Even within an academy. I don't want to be a solo, neoliberal, atomized individual. We have a "faculty association"; I would prefer that it was a union. I would prefer that it was a community council. We don't have those. And I certainly don't want to be "bent over the barrel"—as the image we've been using—within an academy.

(Laughter)

I want to have vectors of solidarities and I want them to extend beyond the academy.

That was a really powerful point that Candice brought up. All of those things that she was moving through were towards ways that structures— that perhaps we could think were "overly structured" or are "hardened" in a sense—are hardened in a way that they pierce the hardness of other structures and open up spaces for those who have been excluded and also illuminate some moments of social justice or moments of spatial justice.

Gould: But, Jeff, aren't those structures inherently vertical? How can you have a structure that doesn't create hierarchies? Maybe you can, I don't know. but I would like you to explain that a little bit more…

Derksen: Yes, I believe we can. On the one hand, I could talk about poetic structures that are non-hierarchical. There was a poetics movement that used devices and structures that tried to take away hierarchies, that tried to make shitty and mess up hierarchical relationships between the reader and the writer. If you look at the implication of *horizontalidad*, you will see that it really is around the notion of producing new social subjects rather than reproducing existing social structures or existing social relations. I'm not so much concerned about how the actual structures will look, I'm more concerned with, let's say, the affective software or the political software that it generates for relations between subjects.

Bruguera: And I have a question then: to whom does it serve that artists are professionalized?

Derksen: Not only artists.

Bruguera: Exactly, that's the thing.

Derksen: And see, that's the thing…. I'm doing this weird gender thing, standing up for Candice here. No stolen opinions either…

(Laughter)

But, for me, it has to go outside. Social justice has to go outside of simply artists. And that's where I get tangled up with this idea of artists/ workers.

Hopkins: I think it's not an either/or situation. It's both. And I think that's what you've been talking about. Sam, you were discussing spaces of equity, and Tania, you were talking about a common understanding, trying to find a sense of ethics. I think ethics work both individually and collectively and I think that when things are out of order, you find it your duty to call attention to it. And that is a characteristic of being professional.

O'Brian: We now come to round three which are closing statements that last one to two minutes. And we'll start off with "No" and end with "Yes." Who is going to go first?

Tancons: Tania's question was left unanswered, and is very important. Whom does it benefit when artists professionalize? This is where cynicism might creep in again, because we all know who it is that it benefits the most: the art system. I think that in many ways we've been speaking about the art system more so than about artistic practice, which is already revealing of a state of professionalization that we should be bucking against—not by trying to insert ourselves within it, but by radically resisting it.

(Applause)

O'Brian: Thank you. First speaker for the "Yes" side.

Bryan-Wilson: I'm coming from the United States, in a context in which—we're in election season—debates really do matter. So it feels a little absurd to have this dog and pony show. But it was a very interesting format to have a conversation and I would like to thank you all.

I agree with a lot of what the other team said, obviously. I would love it—to the audience—my charge to you, if at the end, you would hold up both the blue and the yellow to reject the premise of this false dichotomy. And

to all of you who raised your hand about having a Canada Council for the Arts grant: it's a little disingenuous to hold up that "blue" if you have already acknowledged that you are a professional artist in that context. But, yes, hold up both at once. I think that would be a great sign of the many shades of grey and the murkiness that we all inhabit.

(Applause)

O'Brian: Thank you.

Bruguera: I'll just say to the people who hold the blue because they got a grant: you can always repent.

Gould: I think the best thing that we can do as art workers is to cause disruptions. Disruptions within these structures that we're discussing. We need—as people working within cultural practices—to be able to create spaces for questioning, spaces wherein you don't have to have a particular answer. We need to ask more questions and, specifically, ask ourselves more questions. I don't think "professionalization" calls for that. I think it specifically asks us not to consider some of the more problematic aspects of our day-to-day lives. We need to [find] spaces of reflexivity and equitability for ourselves and for the people who are around us.

(Applause)

Derksen: I can invert that and say that I would call for a form of "professionalization" that doesn't frame the question in a way that says we have to be mindful of the people around us, but to have a structure that breaks down the barriers where we think that there are people around us and that we are not actually also "people around us" and around other folks.

So to the question of who benefits when artists professionalize, I'd say that the least of my concerns in this is that artists benefit from that. And certainly even less than that would be that the art system benefits. But rather—and again, I'll just extend this out to artists professionalizing, and this is ironic in a sense because of the false binaries of it—artists professionalize in a way that aims at creating a hardened point or structure that breaks other structures and opens up to spatial and social justice. Now in the spirit that we actually did set up having written statements, I did have a statement I wanted to share.

In the movie *Gung Ho*, directed by Ron Howard and starring Michael Keaton, a car factory in rust belt America is bought by a Japanese car company, saving the jobs for the autoworkers. But once the new, stern Japanese management style is implemented, the slothful American workers are resentful. The workers must professionalize to the Japanese standard. Skulduggery and the feminization of the Japanese incurs to ease the rupture of masculine American hegemony. In the end, capitalism wins. The factory remains under management's control. Artists, let's not let capitalism win. Let's not embrace the false freedom of verticality, nor the false freedom of structuralessness.

(Applause)

O'Brian: Tania?

Bruguera: I don't think I have anything to add. I only want to say that as artists, you have to remember that you are the one who has to decide what you want to do, what you want to be. Never mistake your art production, your oeuvre, with [your] career.

(Applause)

O'Brian: Thank you.

(Applause)

Candice?

Hopkins: I just have one [last thing to add]: I think we are not amateurs, we are not hobbyists; art is a serious thing and I think that's why we are all here.

(Applause)

O'Brian: What extraordinary speakers and debaters. If it weren't invidious, I would say they're all pros.

I would like, on behalf of you all, to thank them very much before we then take the vote.

(Applause)

So to put the question again and for the last time: Should artists professionalize?

(Scans audience)

Yea?

(Audience holds up votes)

That's more than last time. No?

(Audience holds up votes)

And lots together. It looks like it's a tie.

(Applause)

Dana Claxton and Tania Willard
Imperfect Compliance

A Trajectory of Transformation

If "no one is starving in Cuba"—what lesson can we learn from that system?

A student suggested:
"We need to hold pedagogy responsible."

A panellist remarked:
"We need to unmask the lie."

A convention delegate asked:
"How can you Free Pussy Riot?"[1]

Art conferences can be ceremonies—with people gathering to create new ways of knowing and being in the world. As attendees and participants, we become invested in knowledges shared by our colleagues and sit together pondering questions, looking and feeling deep inside ourselves and inside art. Art brings people together. When we think of conference as ceremony we invite, through intention, the potential of transformation. The beauty of these conferences is their ability to make the invisible visible and to invoke thoughts, discussion, fears, and desires. As in ceremony there is a set of rituals we come to expect in conferences: the alignment of speaker tables, introductions, the reading out loud of biographies, the goblets of water and microphones atop tables adorned with fancy table skirts. At the *Institutions by Artists* conference, AA Bronson started his keynote presentation with what he called an "invocation" of artists and peers from his own past. What he evoked through this act was an intentional space of reflection and possibility within the conference structure. This space, breath, pause, and moment is where the ceremony continues to work within us, even after the conference has closed. Spirit needs room to breathe.

Institutions by Artists was strategic in providing such room, allowing ruptures to occur and encouraging debate and self-critique. This is the space where artist-run culture is still radical, in that it invites the possibility of transformation. Despite funding challenges and bureaucratic pressures in Canada, artists here continue to experiment with ways of organizing themselves. The conference exposed these manifestations: from ideas of timely demise, or the unorganizing of institutions, to ideas of appropriating dominant or corporate forms of organizing in order to subvert them. It is within the shifting ground of questioning, experimentation, and engaging with nonartists that we might come together to create models that further challenge current forms of power, whether in the context of art or otherwise. As an extension of the decolonization of knowledge and an exercise in critical or red pedagogy,[2] we as cultural workers need to start at places of *not knowing* in order to build up knowledge together. Artists are hunters, artists are on welfare, artists are kids, artists are caregivers, artists are janitors, artists are powerful, artists are refugees, artists are blind, artists are working other jobs, artists pay rent, artists sell art to live, artists are born every minute...

Approval of Minutes:

In order to translate minutes from board meetings into music, we mapped out the terminology and operations from Robert's Rules of Order *onto [Walter] Piston's* Harmony, *finding*

possible points of similarity and connection between these two systems, and developed a harmonic rule base for the minutes. The resulting graphical scores are not complete musical compositions, but represent frameworks upon which music might be made—they are musical works in potential.
 —Kathleen Ritter and James B. Maxwell, *Call to Order*

Kathleen Ritter and James B. Maxwell's composition *Call to Order*, commissioned by the Pacific Association of Artist Run Centres, copresenters of the *Institutions by Artists* conference, used minutes from local artist-run centre meetings as the framework for a possible musical score interpreted by musicians, which offered a backdrop to the conference's evening debates. The concept of turning the mundane into this potential for and interpretation of music echoed the sense of transformation that artist-run culture has been invoking and playing with in its forty-year experiment in Canada. Ironically, the sound behind the concept, a concept that really illustrated a sense of potentiality, was used as a cue to warn people when time was up. Thus in some ways the music returned a set of transformed minutes back into something that was again ordered and predictable in nature. *Call to Order* and its subsequent use throughout the conference is symbolic of the journey of artist-run culture—a reciprocal relationship between the possibility of transformation and the organizing and administration of that transformative potential.[3]

Points of Dis-Order:

The beauty of *Institutions by Artists* is that it allowed artists to discuss themselves and locate their greatness, failings, and possibilities for interruption, intervention, and transformation. The word "beauty" in this instance refers to the Navajo philosophy of "walking in beauty," which arises when we surround ourselves with well-being and balance with all beings (in the four directions, above and below), and that "with beauty all around me may I walk" further, the potential for equality and perhaps justice will emerge as a result. The belief is that beauty is made from a balanced life, and we believe the *Institutions by Artists* convention was attempting to walk in beauty by way of questioning, unpacking, critiquing the artist institution's role or potential role and function in society. Although institution is a considerable, intimidating word and conjures up all sorts of structures, rules, hierarchies, and enclosures, the conference offered a measure of institutional critique. But we do wonder how the institutionalization of art, whether driven by artists or large institutions, creates yet another rubric of proper taste—meaning another standard by which someone sanctions what art is and isn't, or determines when it's bad or good, or says when it's art or craft. The specialized languages that form along with the compartmentalization of a skill set or profession—as in "art speak"—are, in fact, exclusionary: "I don't even know enough about feminism to be a woman," remarked performance artist Skeena Reece during the conference. Although she was raised by an original Red Power Woman (her mother is Cleo Reece,[4] who comes from an intertribal, matrilineal society), when confronted with feminist discourse, Reece announced that she was in uncharted territory. Reece, invited by the conference organizers as a performance respondent of sorts, highlighted in her interventions womanhood and motherhood in a language falling outside of mainstream feminist analysis, and yet, despite this difference in context, the issues remained the same—equality and inclusion. Her performance was honest, funny, disruptive, and pointed in the way it addressed issues of accessibility for Native peoples and more implicitly Native women.

The recording of a reinterpreted musical score played as a soundtrack at times during the conference and Reece's performative actions were, in fact, the conference's key moments of possibility, where we were able to move beyond an interrogation of self as artists within artist-run centre culture towards the potential of transformation. But in advance of transformation we do need to understand where we were coming from to see where we are going. Artist-run initiatives started out as voices against institutional power and now some have become too predictable as sites of institutionalization. A transformation is needed in order to get back to the original spirit of artist-run culture in Canada, as opposed to the institutionalization of artist culture everywhere. Further, artists need to ponder the implications of corporate-sponsored sites, such as the Goldcorp Centre for the Arts, where the conference was held. We believe this is a symptom and symbol of the art power that we are attempting to transform.

[Regarding] the vibrancy and real flair of artist-run culture that it had when it began in the '70s, we have lost a lot of that intensity to our own bureaucratic stupidity.

—Deirdre Logue and Allyson Mitchell[5]

The roots of the artist-run centre (ARC) movement in Canada since the 1960s have been defined through the creation of spaces for artist-led projects and conversations, yet in practice have fallen into modes of organization that are anything but self-determined. Would any artists' organization really choose to follow the Society Act[6] if they were really self-determined? The fact is that most artist-run centres are incorporated, not-for-profit organizations with a particular, bureaucratic method of organizing (i.e., defined by writing funding reports, systematizing annual general meetings, reaching quorums, and following grant applications that keep them beholden to funders). In organizing ARCs, artists can become occupied with systems that they originally tried to subvert—namely, bureaucracies with systems of power, which influence control over the production, presentation, distribution, and contextualization of contemporary art. Ideas of egalitarianism among participants in artist-run culture are talked about as seeds that were sown in the 1960s and 1970s in Canada with movements for marginalized peoples, feminism, queer rights, cultural diversity, and workers' rights.

The concern for social justice within the production of art is an area that continues to be relevant within the geopolitics and sociopolitical realities of Indigenous peoples on the continent. During the 1960s there was an outburst of activity associated with liberation movements that operated outside of art, but trickled into the gallery space. More than one presenter at the conference referred to the Art Workers' Coalition's historic 1971 protest outside of the Guggenheim Museum in support of artists' rights and its closer examination of the art world's social and political responsibilities. At the conference, some presenters notably explored the naming of artists as cultural workers, art workers, or art labourers as a way to align artists with the working class within an ideological structure that seeks to place the rights and dignity of workers within the very function and purpose of art in society. Claire Fontaine remarked that art needs "to protect those who create nothing and have nothing to do with art," suggesting that the artist's role is to protect and remind society of something and, by extension, that art indeed has power. We always want to probe what art does with its power, for which reasons, and why. If art's power can reveal injustice and protect people, then we must also look inward at our entanglements within established systems of knowledge production and the circulation of art power, and by doing so, establish our own way again, as artists, historians, curators, and so forth, as concerned and engaged culture-makers with ideals of responsibility, purpose, and ethics and not get subsumed by those systems, instead letting those systems get subsumed by a culture of freedom determined by the artist.

The process of institutionalization or incorporation of ARCs, exemplified in the development of boards of directors, has compromised the initial freedom or experimental nature of the artist-run centre movement. By building institutions, the once radical artist-led movement has almost settled into a normalized and standardized practice or profession. The difference between an art careerist, defined as someone who wants an arts career without social justice, and an engaged arts professional seems to be in the realm of responsibility, purpose, and ethics. Do all participants in artist-run culture have to be engaged citizens? This question circulated as an undercurrent at the conference and suggested artists have a responsibility to something.

Our question is, do careerists as well?

There are many members of smaller collectives and alterNative spaces that are questioning or critiquing bureaucracy while resisting formalized institutional structures and maintaining transparency and accountability to their members. However, generally, artists working outside of the prescribed protocols and networks that the artist-run context has established are excluded from participation in this context. Often marginal voices to this system are brought in under the realm of social justice on a project-to-project basis, or not at all. Institutions by artists need to be cognitive of how they create themselves—occupying an organizational space outside corporate models that engage in capitalistic competition and class/race/gender biases.

Maintenance Report:

Art machinery (by which art power is distributed) and subjective maintenance schedule:

The idea that artists are "forced to be responsible for things that we do not have anything to do with" (i.e., abuses of power) as announced by Claire Fontaine and that "those affected by this are dependent on artists" denies art history's role in the structural dehumanization of the Other through its production of art discourse, which defines what art is. Certainly, the role of artistic production can expand questions about justice, but to claim that art has no relationship to abuses of power over the subjugated is a complete denial of art history's complicity in the dehumanizing of the Other through systems of aesthetic value and judgment. Not only has the *primitive* not been able to make art in the annals of Western art history, but women have only very recently entered the discourse. And, in some cases, women have also supported the devaluing of other cultural modes of production that do not fit in with subscribed systems of contemporary art discourse primarily determined by the West. The privileged site of contemporary art production is fraught with its own abuse of power in its very analysis, or lack thereof.

Maintenance Required:

1. Does your organization have a mix of members from diverse cultures, religions, and sexual orientations? Do identity politics still scare you and your friends? If not, please perform Maintenance Schedule B: Deconstructing Art Power 101.

2. If Schedule B is complete, please review and make changes according to Maintenance Schedule C: Questioning Your Very Existence and Relinquishing the Organization Ego.

Troubleshooting:

Many of the origins behind ideas of social justice, egalitarianism, and democracy are more properly attributed to Indigenous societies in the Americas and colonial interaction with, and understanding of, those societies. We are not suggesting a return to some kind of pre-colonial utopia, but at least a reconsideration of the influence Indigenous-centred knowledges had on the collective community building ideas of the 1960s and 1970s and how Indigenous thought, politics, struggles, and aesthetics have influenced art on this continent and beyond. We are suggesting the implementation of Indigenous knowledges that promote generosity, bravery, wisdom, and fortitude. We need to be aware of the self-reflexivity of artist-run culture and not limit its vision and sense of self. So, to start with, we want a deeper sense of roots, not just a hollow acknowledgment of "being on traditional Coast Salish Territory," which, while an important declaration, cannot actually assist with justice for the Salish community nor can it provide an understanding of why we continue to OCCUPY contested lands.

Housekeeping Report:

Dirty diapers need to be changed. Let's move on …
—Skeena Reece

Regarding the professionalization of the artist: All professions have a level of training and skill so participants can function, deliver, or even organize politically. The broader question is, what happens when that professionalization becomes hierarchical and exclusionary? What was once a "movement" (i.e., artist-run) has now become an institutional model that functions with presidents and vice presidents, and in this transformation the role of the collective has been co-opted to meet bureaucratic structures internal to artist-run centres and funding and public demands that are external to them. The call to disorder and to challenge institutional models of art within the artist-run movement is now pale, predictable, and de-radicalized. The standardization that plagues the cultural industry has seeped into artist culture through the mimicry of larger institutions. These once radical sites of cultural production are now either lying in archival boxes, offering launch pads for artists to get into exhibitions at larger institutions, or providing safe havens for artists to return to. Artist-run centres function both within and outside the corporate art world (defined by commercial art dealers and institutions who have corporate sponsorship), as do artists, curators, art historians, technicians, and installers, among others. The flow between mid-size and large public institutions and artist-run culture is reciprocal in strange and wonderful ways, especially in Vancouver. The circulation of art, thought, and bodies go from space to space with fluidity, but perhaps everyone is wearing the same interpretative uniform dyed in the same prescribed notions of power. All in a single day one can go from a large to mid-size public art gallery over to a commercial gallery, and then on to an artist-run centre and sometimes encounter the same artist, curator, or historian. Note that we are not saying the people or art here are "bad," but rather that the uniform they wear is the same. Although we are all in the same field, the conference questioned if, indeed, our field needs to expand its borders, as well as its fixed boundaries.

In Canada, an artist might exhibit in an international biennial one day and an artist-run centre the next, such that the lines are getting blurrier and blurrier between the practice of international art production and artist-run initiatives, thus creating a relationship between corporate art power and the art establishment. The professionalization of the arts now signifies a network of relationships between the academy, artist-run initiatives, mid-size and large public institutions, and the market. The blur between is almost gone. Is this the kind of blur that artists in artist-run culture really want? Do we allow the blur to disintegrate completely, or do we question how to stay radically separate without continuing the relationship with visible hierarchical models that artist-run culture is playing with? Artists operating within artist-run culture have worked really hard and established themselves as participants in exhibitions and discourse, and parts of the conference suggested that artists need to question where they are located and where they are heading. It became apparent that artists need to have clear lines drawn between the corporate art-power system and a sense of self outside those systems. Perhaps it's too late for some, and perhaps some may not be interested in exiting from the art-power system—but how can artist-run culture maintain autonomy from those systems while working from within it without becoming too similar? And, if one is working inside it, should one take on an infiltrator role? How can artists continue to challenge power without becoming pure or dirty power? If knowledge is power, we believe that wisdom is manna. How can artist culture practice manna within the realm of justice and equality? We use manna as a nurturing spirit.

Safety Report (Part 1: Risks):

Artist-run centres in Canada have taken on different modes of regional and national operation. What seems to be unique about Vancouver is that organizations that were once working outside of established institutions and practicing institutional critique have begun to transition into institutionalized, established spaces that maintain enormous art power and are now in need of self-critique—unpacking the implications of the dominant narrative they have established nationally and further afield. After forty years of artistic production, curation, and exhibition, participants in the artist-run centre movement in Canada have established themselves as leaders and experts in the field of contemporary art. Each centre in the ARC network has a unique mandate to fulfil through artist-led curatorial practice and the acceptance of unsolicited submissions, although some centres have now become curator driven in the sense that professional curators select works, artists, and programs to present at these institutions. Thus, the once relatively democratic practice of posting an open call juried by artists has become less frequent with the professionalization of curators. The shift from artist-driven to curator-driven practice has changed the ecology of some ARCs. Since most of the curators in these organizations have attended graduate-level curatorial or art programs, is the field producing cookie-cutter curators and artists? Since artist-run centres are now filled with BFA, BA, MA, MFA, PhD graduates trained within systems of knowledge that maintain meta-narratives, what can be radical in these spaces? Can any of us get away from the institutionalization and professionalization of the arts? Since artist-run culture in Canada is now firmly established and maintains institutionalized art discourses, and, by extension, art power, the *Institutions by Artists* conference attempted to unpack this power and recognize the artist's responsibility to that power. Artist-run centres have enormous art power, developed through years of dedication. Now, with the globalized professionalization of the artist, artist-led initiatives are now even more important and urgent. Artists need to reclaim their own spaces, outside of any institution, as hegemony lingers in the most liberal of spaces. From Romania to Beijing to Cuba, the conference presenters showed how processes of artist-run initiatives intersect in various ways through the professionalization of process (i.e., curators and art historians are professionally trained and they come from an institutional context or are headed towards one). How does institutionalized training affect the creative process, especially regarding the work and outlook of art historians, curators, and artists? What role has pedagogy occupied in reproducing dominant approaches to art-making and analysis? Neoliberalism may be a Western condition, but certainly in other countries the professionalization of the arts is tightly linked to the market, capital, the elite, individuals, and a formal education system. How does cognitive imperialism function within art history, curation, and artistic production?

Review and expose the gaps. Interrogate the gaps.

Safety Report (Part 2: Incident Report):

The claim that artist-run spaces can exist free from hegemonic influence seems slippery, and the nature of the dissemination of art knowledge within fixed frameworks of thought and hierarchies makes artist-run culture complicit in how the circulation of art power continues in ways that are not always identified and perhaps reside within the realm of denial, refusal, and enclosure. If, by the nature of the conference, artist culture is critiquing its own power, how and who decides which power mechanisms in the field will remain and which mechanisms, whether pure or dirty, will be discarded?

An intervention into areas of power can create various degrees of anxiety, frustration, or pleasure for those witnessing the event. Whether issues of stolen land, freedom of speech, reframing history, or Pussy Power, the call to order changes into a call to bear witness. If the viewer witnessing the intervention fails to receive the gift, how will the transference of a different kind of institution of life be received?

Someone at the convention asked the question, "Can we struggle together?"

And we ask further:
Is art a struggle for pure liberation?
Can gender, race, and class struggles even be fought or won in an arts arena?
What is the artist's role in class struggle?
How can artists fight against oppression for the working woman and man?
What can artists learn from class struggles?
Do artists have an obligation to the poor?
Do artists have an obligation to the oppressed?

Ongoing Maintenance Schedule:

1. Host an event for real, live, working-class people.
2. Ask yourself: Do you struggle against neoliberalism?
3. Talk to Glenn Alteen at the grunt gallery.[7]

Artists have witnessed some gender scuffles with some wins and losses on art's battlefield. Race in the field of contemporary art in Canada has played a role over the last twenty years and Indigenous/First Nations/Indian voices have been heard in many of Canada's large public institutions. What role do American curators, gallery directors, and art historians have in the continued dehumanization of American Indian people by denying visibility of contemporary American Indian art? Concerning this matter, most large, mainstream American institutions have never shown Indigenous contemporary art and the matter can be extended to the global, international art community. Why are there so few Indigenous artists circulating in that arena? The fact that Canadian and American Indian/Native/First Nations/Aboriginal peoples have a mythic presence internationally yet don't exist in contemporary consciousness, especially in contemporary art discourse, is an example of how art power is exercised over an entire people who do not get to participate. The fear and denial of the existence of Indian people is still very real in the United States, so much so that our art is refused a place within contemporary life.

Safety Equipment Needed:

The transference of Indigenous knowledges to various larger publics through the dissemination of contemporary Indigenous art.

Auditor's Report:

There is a need to discuss money, as financial concerns came up in a number of panels at the conference. In Canada, artist-run centres are subjected to and organized in response to funding guidelines and systems provided by municipal, provincial, and federal governments. Although as jury members and committee members artists have played a significant role in determining where funding should be allocated in Canada, the government's arts agenda and policies still influence artists and ARCs that apply for public funding. There are set guidelines and requirements that must be met before institutions receive funds. Many panellists at the conference suggested other models to work from rather than state support—from the artist-entrepreneur, to collectivization, or revenue sharing through networks in a "matronage" model proposed by the Feminist Art Gallery. The cultural public purse for funding, especially in Canada, has allowed for artist-run culture to flourish, and because these funds are limited—and in some countries don't exist at all—artists are finding alterNative ways to develop economies in arts production or funding. Artists stepping outside conventional institutional spaces and funding models are essential to challenging and examining how established institutions and funding sources are not serving artists—which is not to say they *shouldn't* serve artists; almost all artists in the conference would agree or stated that there should be more funding for the arts, but the methods of delivering, judging, and organizing that funding should be questioned.

Recommendations:

If you can, make an annual donation to an artist-run gallery or artist collective of your choice.

The Red Paper Report:

The emergence of Aboriginal artist-run culture was a response to the exclusion of Aboriginal art and curatorial practice nationally and materialized in the wake of artist-run culture in Canada. The Professional Native Indian Artists Association/Indian Group of Seven opened up spaces inside the field of contemporary art in Canada, followed by the Society of Canadian Artists of Native Ancestry (SCANA), who advocated for spaces for Aboriginal expression within art institutions. The 1972 exhibition *Treaty Numbers 23, 287 and 1171*, featuring work by Daphne Odjig, Jackson Beardy, and Alex Janvier, was a landmark exhibition in that it brought a new sensibility of Indigenous critical artistic practice to Canadian art audiences. Despite the fact that SCANA and the Professional Native Indian Artists Association were both in operation for only short periods of time, their influence on generations of Aboriginal artists is significant. And, over the last two decades, SCANA activities surface from time to time. This legacy of Indigenous artists who claimed space within contemporary Canadian art discourse has also had a major impact on artist-run culture and funding. For instance, the Canada Council for the Arts and the BC Arts Council both have mandates to specifically support Aboriginal practice, and while we can point to insufficiencies in funding, these strategic priorities are a result of Aboriginal artists and supporters advocating for inclusion.

Ironically, discourse around contemporary American Indian art in the United States, while lagging behind Canada in some senses, has been successful in creating large public institutions like the Smithsonian's National Museum of the American Indian. Although this museum is not governed by Indian people or Indian imperatives, it has dedicated exhibition spaces for American Indian art. The Museum of Contemporary Native Art (MOCNA), within the Institute of American Indian Arts (IAIA, Santa Fe), which is part of an Indian-operated arts educational institution, exhibits and collects art. In addition, the Eiteljorg Museum of American Indians and Western Art offers a fellowship, awarded biannually to American and Canadian Indians, through the purchase of art, and now holds one of the most significant collections of contemporary Native art in the United States. In Canada, we have no nationally significant gallery for Indigenous representation, though the National Gallery now collects Indigenous art and the inclusion of Native curators has been vitally important for securing exhibitions and building such a collection.

Although all these spaces (MOCNA, National Museum of the American Indian, and Eiteljorg Museum of American Indians and Western Art) are outside the artist-centred realm and still governed by a board and donors within prohibitively expensive institutional walls, they are dedicated to exclusively exhibiting Indigenous art. Failing the sudden political will to create Indigenous models of art structures, education, and interaction, we need to look to the artist-run centre movement to identify opportunities to create novel hypothetical/discursive spaces where new ideas can inform and invoke ancient knowledges. The seeds are there: from site-specific, Indigenous performative actions to installations and direct land interventions. The body of knowledges that exists within contemporary Indigenous artistic practices can be nurtured, germinating seeds to form roots. These are practices in which art is felt, heard, and touched, or where birds and animals and plants are a part of the audience, or where board meetings transpire in ceremonies, or openings take place with feasts. Indigenous knowledges and aesthetics can be integrated into a new institution of life, not just art. The moment we connect our hands and our hearts to the land around us: this is what our ancestors would call art. We respond to the land, from basketry to making clothing, and we enter into holistic engagements with animals and food. These acts are interconnected relationships to the land where we live. Our languages are here in the earth, the rocks, the trees, and our art is here too.

In practice, a more complete sense of equality and accessibility for Aboriginal artists has been more elusive. Despite Aboriginal artists represented in art institutions and some forms of Aboriginal-run spaces, like the Urban Shaman Gallery in Winnipeg, the proliferation of alterNative methods of organizing, interpreting, and appreciating non-Western art traditions is not yet apparent. The bifurcated presentation of Indigenous arts within museum and gallery contexts still exists as work is compartmentalized into pre-contact artifacts relegated to museums. Contemporary Aboriginal artists need to be informed about contemporary art systems in order to be permitted entrance on their own terms. If these knowledge bases around "art speak," theory, and established networks are missing, admission to the art world is tainted by paternalism and primitivism. Artists created the Professional Native Indian Artists Association and SCANA to have a voice and claim space, but are we now just fitting ourselves in between the cracks (as the cracks get wider) instead of creating our own circles? Is an Indian art gallery really just a copy of a Western-style art gallery? Is there potential for it to be something else?

Should it be not exclusively Indigenous but rather guided by Indigenous principles in some way? We have been successful in intervening and claiming space inside external institutions but we have not yet truly created our own.

There are no contemporary art galleries or artist-run centres on First Nation reserves/reservations because people have been too busy surviving. We want to ask the spirits: Is it a good idea to have Indigenous art galleries on a reserve or on the land? What do Indigenous artist-run centres look like on Indian land? Do they just look like artist-run centres in cities?

We want a natural gallery, which has no space and no money but rather spirit and thought. There is no particular way of organizing it and we haven't had any exhibitions there yet. Think no money and no building and no institution. It is a space to make art, but the openings are attended by bears harvesting the last of the berries before hibernation and maybe the neighbours' horses or cows are grazing, and there are crows, reservation dogs, and the spirit of the land, lots of spirits. This gallery is a gallery of the land, of Indigenous culture(s) and language(s); this gallery can show new media with basketry, beading with installation art, performance art, and storytelling. This natural gallery can exist anywhere, but it has to start at the root—the root is radical, literally: *radicalis* "of or having roots."

Other Business:

The West likes slaughtering things—people, animal nations, and the natural world. The Western art world likes slaughtering things as well, with the death of painting, originality, authenticity, the subject, and the author. Now it seems the Western art world is trying to kill itself in order to liberate itself from its own overestimated, inflated value. If there should be no more art after capitalism, presumably this means no more Western art. The Western art world has been plagued by its own idleness and neoliberalism. The long overdue collapse of agency (read: domination) in the crisis of its own value (read: domination)[8] in Western art is a result of centuries of interpretive art power over the entire field of art discourses. The killing of self through self-sacrifice and beginning anew will allow for "desert creatures"[9] to show themselves and to begin anew. This is a courageous, generous, fortuitously wise gestural action that will make a new institution of life for artist-run culture, especially in Canada. And, through this act, the gift for other countries from Canada's forty-year history of artist-run culture is the gift to question how dominance circulates even in the most liberated of art spaces.

Operators' Manual:
Institution + Intuition = Transformation

Now that we have discussed maintenance, safety, troubleshooting, risks, and incidents, we are left to consider the realm of operations. Where do we go from here? The conference presented debates, ideas, interpretations, critiques, and examples, so where do we take them? How does the ceremony of the conference continue to work inside of us? These operational guidelines are a series of actions, symbolic and spiritual actions used to invoke an altered state of organizational consciousness. Instead of better or more institutions by artists, let's have more intuition. Intuition stands in opposition to institution, to logical, hierarchical organization. Institutions need intuition. Intuition keeps us honest, wild, and allows the realm of spirit entry into this domain. The possibility of transformation requires the collapse of hierarchies and rules to allow the nuanced, the unspoken, the spirit to be heard. Institution is the body, intuition is the spirit, we need both but they have to be in relationship and responsive to each other, and when they are, we have inspiration, a sudden intuition as part of solving a problem or getting to the "root" of the problem.

Mitakuye Oyasin—pronounced mee-tah-koo-yay o-yah-seen[10]—is a Lakota (Sioux) belief that means "everything is related," and sometimes is spoken as "all my relations." The core meaning is everything is related—plants, sky, water, animal and bird nations, and people. This phrase is an offering acknowledging that everything is related. When stated as "all my relations" we are acknowledging our ancestors as well. Further, *mitakuye oyasin* means we are all related—all bodies, all spirits, all rivers, all mountains, all beings—and by being related, we entrust in each other the care for each other.

Mitakuye Oyasin is a prayer, a manifesto, to ask how we use the experience of the conference to transcend and transform ourselves or our organizations into all possibilities, where we can make our dreams and visions real. We need to open the doors, allow the ruptures, unorganize—that is to say, organize as assembly as opposed to organize as an exclusionary act of professionalization or institutionalization. We have a gift before us, this ceremony has given us a gift, and now we carry it and what we do with the gift is up to us. We don't have to have faith in anything, but just a belief that: ART IS...

Note on the use of *Indian*, *Native*, *First Nations*, *Indigenous*, and *Aboriginal*: These are terms we use to define ourselves and that others use to define us. We use them interchangeably throughout as they of course all have different political connotations and relationships; we invoke all of them, all of we who have been defined as and how we define ourselves. We also say NdN or skin or sister or brother. We are fluid in our definitions.

1. The excerpts from the *Institutions by Artists* conference belong to, in order, Tania Bruguera, an unidentified student, Jaleh Mansoor, and Damien Petryshyn.

2. Indigenous authors and artists have written extensively around ideas of decolonization, criticizing colonial thought, and incorporating Indigenous customs and knowledge into academic writing and research as a way of decolonizing dominant forms of knowledge formed out of the European Renaissance and processes of capitalist/patriarchal/imperialist dominance in the Americas. Critical pedagogy is a method of education that holds criticality as important in deconstructing authoritarian approaches to education and advocates connecting knowledge to power and the ability to take constructive action. Red pedagogy is a method of education and advocacy that is Indigenous centred. The common agenda in critical and red pedagogy is a process of knowledge-making that could lead to liberation.

3. Kathleen Ritter and James B. Maxwell, *Call to Order*, 2011–12, https://fillip.ca/8uqd.

4. Cleo Reece is Cree from Fort McMurray. She is one of the organizers of the Keepers of the Athabasca Healing Walk, an annual sacred walk for Mother Earth in northern Alberta.

For two decades she was an active and influential figure in Vancouver's Aboriginal grassroots movement. She started the Indigenous Media Arts Group in Vancouver, which organized the ImagiNATION Film Festival for eight years, and was active with Co-op Radio for ten years. She is now a Band Council Member of her reserve.

5. Deirdre Logue and Allyson Mitchell (Feminist Art Gallery), "Institutional Time: Facts & Fictions" panel, moderated by Magnolia Pauker, *Institutions by Artists* conference, Goldcorp Centre for the Arts, Vancouver, October 12, 2012.

6. Incorporation as a not-for-profit organization requires the adoption of the standard Society Act within a given Canadian province or the Companies Act if federally incorporated. These acts set out the legal contract for how an incorporated society should act—for example, necessitating a board of directors, annual general meetings, voting, etc.

7. Glenn Alteen and grunt gallery in Vancouver have demonstrated an important commitment and mandate to exhibit Aboriginal artists and community-engaged practice, as well as innovative, collaborative, and provocative Canadian and international contemporary art for the last twenty years.

8. At the conference, Jaleh Mansoor proposed art's collapse of agency and a crisis of value. Our emphasis is domination all around.

9. A conference delegate suggested that we should have no fear of the unknown or new, and that desert creatures will survive. We didn't see his face, but the voice sounded like Vancouver artist Damien Petryshyn's.

10. (Lakota language) Takuya: to be related, to have kinship with. Oya's'in: all as individuals or units, everything, everyone.

Ken Becker is an artist and curator living in Berkeley, California. Becker runs the ceramics cooperative International Cup Makers Union and facilitates artists' projects in the Bay Area. On the side, he pieces together winter-weight quilts and has been trying to understand the rudiments of dance music. Becker received his MA in Curatorial Practice from California College of the Arts, Oakland, CA, in 2014.

Matei Bejenaru is an artist based in Iași, Romania. He is cofounder of the Vector Association and the Centre of Contemporary Photography, the founder of the Periferic Biennial for Contemporary Art, and a co-organizer of the Camera Plus Biennial of Contemporary Photography and Moving Image (all in Iași). Bejenaru's artwork examines the post-communist condition, politics of representation in documentary photography and film, and methods of generation of hybrid art projects at the confluence between visual arts, poetry, experimental music, and scientific research. His work has been exhibited at venues worldwide, including the Taipei Biennial (2008); Western Front, Vancouver (2011); Kettle's Yard, Cambridge, UK (2012); and BOZAR, Brussels (2018), among others. Bejenaru's conversation with Livia Pancu and Kristina Lee Podesva was published in *Institutions by Artists: Volume 1* (2012).

Tania Bruguera is an artist and activist who lives and works between New York and Havana. Her performances and installations examine political power structures and their effect on society's most vulnerable people. Her long-term projects are intensive interventions in the institutional structure of collective memory, education, and politics. Bruguera has received honours such as the Robert Rauschenberg Award (2019) and Guggenheim Fellowship (1998). She was a Prince Claus Award laureate in 2008. Her work has been extensively exhibited around the world, including a commission for the Turbine Hall at Tate Modern, London (2018–19) and documenta11, Kassel, Germany (2002). Bruguera's work is in the collections of the Solomon R. Guggenheim Museum, New York; Museum of Modern Art, New York; Van Abbemuseum, Eindhoven; Tate Modern, London; and Museo Nacional de Bellas Artes de La Habana.

Julia Bryan-Wilson is the Doris and Clarence Malo Professor of Modern and Contemporary Art at the University of California, Berkeley, and Director of the UC Berkeley Arts Research Center. She is also Adjunct Curator at the Museu de Arte de São Paulo. She is the author of *Art Workers: Radical Practice in the Vietnam War Era* (University of California Press, 2011) and *Fray: Art and Textile Politics* (University of Chicago Press, 2017), which won the ASAP Book Prize, Frank Jewett Mather Award, and Robert Motherwell Book Award.

Dana Claxton is a Vancouver-based artist. Her family reserve is Lakota First Nations – Wood Mountain. Claxton works in film, video, photography, and performance art, and her practice investigates beauty, the body, the sociopolitical, and the spiritual. She is Head of the Department of Art History, Visual Art & Theory at the University of British Columbia, Vancouver. Her work has been shown at venues including the Museum of Modern Art, New York (1994); Walker Art Center,

Minneapolis (2000); Sundance Film Festival, Park City, UT; Eiteljorg Museum, Indianapolis (2007); 17th Biennale of Sydney (2010); and Biennale de Montréal (2007). In 2018, Claxton was selected for a career survey at the Vancouver Art Gallery. Claxton was awarded the Hnatyshyn Foundation Award for Outstanding Achievement as an Artist in 2019, and in 2020, she received a Governor General's Award in Visual and Media Arts and the Scotiabank Photography Award.

Christopher Cozier is a Trinidad-based artist. He is Codirector of Alice Yard, a contemporary art space and network in Port of Spain. His work investigates how Caribbean historical and current experiences can inform understanding in the wider contemporary world. Cozier's exhibitions include the 5th and 7th Havana Biennials (1994, 2000–01); *Infinite Island*, Brooklyn Museum, New York (2007); *Afro Modern: Journeys through the Black Atlantic*, Tate Liverpool (2010); *Entanglements*, Broad Museum, East Lansing, MI (2015); *Relational Undercurrents*, Museum of Latin American Art, Los Angeles (2017); and *The Sea Is History*, Historisk museum, Oslo (2019). Cozier participated in the public program of the 10th Berlin Biennale (2018), exhibited at Sharjah Biennial 14 (2019), and will show in the 11th Liverpool Biennial in 2021. He was awarded a Pollock-Krasner Foundation Grant in 2004 and was a Prince Claus Award laureate in 2013.

Jeff Derksen is a Vancouver- and Vienna-based poet. He is a founding member of the Kootenay School of Writing and Artspeak Gallery, Vancouver. Formerly a research fellow at the Center for Place, Culture and Politics at the City University of New York, he is currently Dean of Graduate and Postdoctoral Studies at Simon Fraser University, Vancouver. With Sabine Bitter and Helmut Weber, he is a member of the research collective Urban Subjects. His books include *The Vestiges* (Talonbooks, 2013), *Annihilated Time: Poetry and Other Politics* (Talonbooks, 2009), and *After Euphoria* (JRP|Ringier, 2014). Derksen's writing on art has been included in publications from *Fillip*; Secession, Vienna; Museum of Contemporary Art of Rome; Vancouver Art Gallery; Artspeak Gallery, Vancouver; documenta 12, Kassel, Germany; Camera Austria, Graz; Landesgalerie Linz, Austria; Malta Contemporary Art, Valletta; and Berlage Institute, Rotterdam.

Sean Dockray is a Canberra-based artist and writer. His work explores the politics of technology, with a particular emphasis on artificial intelligences and the algorithmic Web. He is a Founding Director of the Los Angeles nonprofit Telic Arts Exchange and an initiator of the knowledge-sharing platforms the Public School and AAAARG.ORG. Dockray is Lecturer in Sculpture and Spatial Practice at the Australian National University, Canberra, and is currently researching the rise of listening machines.

Chris Fitzpatrick is a San Fransisco-based curator. He was Director of Kunstverein München from 2015 to 2019 and Director of Objectif Exhibitions, Antwerp, from 2012 to 2015. Prior to these positions, he did the peripatetic curator thing in Canada, China, Estonia, Italy, Lithuania, Mexico, the Netherlands, the United States, and so on.

Dirk Fleischmann is an artist based in Berlin and Seoul. He has been creating a business conglomerate since 1997 through which his art inhabits economic forms and capitalist structures. His projects create financial profits that are re-invested into future projects. Fleischmann's work has been presented at Seoul Mediacity Biennale (2018); Moderna Museet, Stockholm (2016); Centre Pompidou-Metz, France (2016); Sharjah Art Foundation (2012); steirischer herbst, Graz, Austria (2012); 4th Gwangju Design Biennale (2011); Kunstverein Hannover (2011); HAU1, Berlin (2006); Musée d'art contemporain de Lyon (2004); and Manifesta 4, Frankfurt (2002).

Sam Gould is a Minneapolis-based artist, writer, and activist. He cofounded the cultural collective Red76, facilitates the neighbourhood-based initiative Beyond Repair, and is a cofounder and Director of Confluence: An Eastlake Studio for Community Design in Minneapolis. Devoted to ideas of publication as an act of public making, his work often focuses on sociality, education, and encountering the political within daily life. Gould has taught and lectured internationally and is a recipient of a McKnight Mid-career Grant and McKnight Visual Arts Fellowship, among other acknowledgments.

Candice Hopkins is a curator and writer and a citizen of Carcross/Tagish First Nation. She lives between Albuquerque, New Mexico, and Toronto. She is Senior Curator of the 2019 and 2021 editions of the Toronto Biennial of Art. Hopkins was co-curator of major exhibitions including the Canadian Pavilion for the 58th Venice Biennale (2019);

2018 SITE Santa Fe Biennial: *Casa tomada*; documenta 14, Athens and Kassel, Germany (2017); *Sakahàn: International Indigenous Art*, National Gallery of Canada, Ottawa (2013); and the exhibition *Close Encounters: The Next 500 Years*, held across multiple venues in Winnipeg (2011). Her writing is published widely and her recent essays and presentations include "The Appropriation Debates (or The Gallows of History)," for MIT Press; "Outlawed Social Life," for *South as a State of Mind*; and "The Gilded Gaze: Wealth and Economies on the Colonial Frontier," for *The documenta 14 Reader*.

Jesi Khadivi is an independent curator and writer based in Berlin. Together with the artist David Horvitz she runs PORCINO, one of the city's smallest exhibition spaces. Khadivi has curated exhibitions at the Fondation d'enterprise Ricard, Paris (2018); PS120, Berlin (2019); and Wattis Institute for Contemporary Arts, San Francisco (2013), among other venues. Her essays have appeared in numerous artist monographs and edited volumes, as well as periodicals such as *Texte zur Kunst*, *Frieze*, *Fillip*, *Flash Art*, *Kaleidoscope*, and the *Brooklyn Rail*.

Deirdre Logue is a Toronto-based artist, prolific and steadfast in her engagement with the moving image. Her work explores anxiety, the queer body, and the limits of ability through video installation and projection. She is Development Director at Vtape, Toronto, and also directs the FAG Feminist Art Gallery, Toronto, with her partner, Allyson Mitchell. Recently, Logue and Mitchell presented *Killjoy's Kastle: A Lesbian Feminist Haunted House* (Toronto, 2013; London, 2014; Los

Angeles, 2015; Philadelphia, 2019), a large-scale installation and performance that presents a nightmarish vision of feminist terror in which visitors are encouraged to engage in dialogue about contemporary queer politics. Logue and Mitchell also collaborate on video installations that put radical feminist texts in productive conversation with contemporary queer theory using puppets, cats, and papier mâché.

Sarah Lowndes is a writer, curator, and lecturer based in Norwich, and is Research Fellow at Norwich University of the Arts. Between 2002 and 2015, she was a lecturer at Glasgow School of Art. Her publications include *Contemporary Artists Working Outside the City: Creative Retreat* (Routledge, 2018), *The DIY Movement in Art, Music and Publishing* (Routledge, 2016), *All Art Is Political: Writings on Performative Art* (Luath Press, 2014), and *Social Sculpture: The Rise of the Glasgow Art Scene* (Luath Press, 2010). Under the auspices of Kunsthalle Cromer in North Norfolk, she curated and produced *Panoramic Sea Happening* (2017), *Esplanade: A Procession for Women* (2018), and the writing and publication projects *Like the Sea I Think* (2019) and *Field Work* (2020).

Jaleh Mansoor is Associate Professor of Art History at the University of British Columbia (UBC), Vancouver. Her areas of teaching and research include modernism and the avant-gardes, European art since 1945, Marxism and the Frankfurt School, formalism, Marxist feminism, and social reproduction theory. Mansoor has also acted as Director of UBC's Critical and Curatorial Studies program. Her current project is entitled *Universal Prostitution: A Counter*

History of Abstraction, 1888–2008, forthcoming from Duke University Press in 2022. Her other publications include *Communities of Sense: Rethinking Aesthetics and Politics* (Duke University Press, 2010) and *Marshall Plan Modernism: Italian Postwar Abstraction and the Beginnings of Autonomia* (Duke University Press, 2016).

Philip Monk is a writer who lives in Toronto. He was Director of the Art Gallery of York University (2003–17) and previously was Senior Curator at the Power Plant (1994–2003) and the Art Gallery of Ontario (1985–94) (all in Toronto). A writer since 1977, his most recent publications are *Migrating the Margins: Circumlocating the Future of Toronto Art* with Emelie Chhangur (Art Gallery of York University, 2019), *Is Toronto Burning?: Three Years in the Making (and Unmaking) of the Toronto Art Scene* (Black Dog Publishing, 2016), and *Glamour Is Theft: A User's Guide to General Idea* (Art Gallery of York University, 2012).

John O'Brian is an art historian, writer, and curator. Until 2017, he taught at the University of British Columbia, Vancouver. He has written or edited twenty books, including *Clement Greenberg: The Collected Essays and Criticism* (University of Chicago Press, 1988)—one of the New York Times' "Notable Books of the Year"—and *Camera Atomica* (Black Dog Publishing, 2015), the catalogue for the first comprehensive exhibition on post-war nuclear photography. He is a recipient of the Thakore Award in Human Rights and Peace Studies from Simon Fraser University, Vancouver.

<u>Post Brothers</u> is a critical enterprise that includes Matthew Post, an enthusiast, word processor, and curator living in Kolonia Koplany, a small village near Białystok, Poland. From 2016 through 2019, Post Brothers was Curator at Kunstverein München, and he has curated exhibitions and presented projects in Poland, Mexico, Canada, Spain, the United States, Portugal, Denmark, Greece, Estonia, Germany, Austria, Lithuania, Italy, Sweden, Finland, Belgium, Latvia, the Netherlands, and China. His essays and articles have been published in *Annual Magazine*, *The Baltic Notebooks of Anthony Blunt*, *CURA*, *Fillip*, *Kaleidoscope*, *Mousse*, *Nero*, *Art Papers*, *Pazmaker*, *Spike Art Quarterly*, and *TANK*, as well as in a litany of artist publications and exhibition catalogues. Post Brothers also regularly participates in exhibitions with text-based and performative contributions, and lectures and teaches workshops throughout Europe.

<u>Christopher Régimbal</u> is Senior Exhibition Manager at the National Gallery of Canada, Ottawa. He has coordinated more than thirty exhibitions of modern and contemporary art in museums and galleries across Canada and Europe and is the author of *Agnes Martin: Life and Work* (Art Canada Institute, 2019).

<u>Slavs and Tatars</u>, cofounded by Kasia Korczak and Payam Sharifi, is an internationally renowned art collective devoted to an area east of the former Berlin Wall and west of the Great Wall of China, known as Eurasia. The collective's practice is based on three activities: exhibitions, publications, and lecture-performances. Their work has been the subject of solo exhibitions at the Museum of Modern Art, New York (2012); SALT Galata, Istanbul (2014, 2014–15, 2017); Secession, Vienna (2012); Kunsthalle Zürich (2014); Albertinum, Dresden (2018); and Ujazdowski Castle Centre for Contemporary Art, Warsaw (2016–17), among others. In addition to their translation of the legendary Azerbaijani satirical periodical *Molla Nasreddin* (currently in its second edition with I.B. Tauris), Slavs and Tatars has published more than ten books to date, most recently *Wripped Scripped* (Hatje Cantz, 2018), on the politics of alphabets and transliteration.

<u>Gregory Sholette</u> is an artist, activist, and writer, and he is curator of the project *Imaginary Archive* (a peripatetic collection of documents speculating on a past whose future never arrived). His art and research theorize and document issues of collective cultural labour, activist art, and decolonial historical representation after 1968. With Chloë Bass, Sholette codirects Social Practice CUNY (SPCUNY), an art and social justice initiative at the Graduate Center, City University of New York. He is a founding member of the collectives Political Art Documentation/ Distribution (1980–88), REPOhistory (1989–2000), and Gulf Labor Coalition (2010–). He is author of *The Art of Activism and the Activism of Art* (Lund Humphries, 2021); *Art as Social Action*, with Chloë Bass (Allworth Press, 2018); and *Delirium and Resistance: Activist Art and the Crisis of Capitalism* (Pluto Press, 2017), among other publications.

<u>Claire Tancons</u> is a curator, writer, and researcher invested in the postcolonial politics of art production and exhibition. She publishes

for and speaks at artistic and academic venues, as well as teaches. She is the inaugural Mellon Global Curatorial Fellow at the Graduate Center, City University of New York. Notable curatorial projects include *EN MAS': Carnival and Performance Art of the Caribbean* (2015–18); *Up Hill Down Hall*, Tate Modern, London (2014); *Tide by Side*, Faena Forum, Miami Beach (2016); and *etcetera: a civic ritual*, Printemps de Septembre, Toulouse (2017). Tancons has curated for biennials including those in New Orleans (2008–09), Gwangju (2008), Cape Town (2009), Bénin (2012), Gothenburg (2013), and Sharjah (2017–19). She is the recipient of fellowships, grants, and awards from the Andy Warhol Foundation, Prince Claus Fund, Foundation for Arts Initiatives, Emily Hall Tremaine Foundation, and Creative Capital.

Tania Willard, of Secwépemc Nation and settler heritage, works within a land-based context, wherein Indigenous land rights and pedagogies are entwined with decolonial praxis. Willard's ongoing collaborative project, *BUSH gallery*, is a conceptual land-based gallery on an Indian reserve grounded in Indigenous knowledges and relational art practices. Willard has exhibited nationally and produced multiple public art commissions. Her artistic practice intersects with curatorial work, for which she received an award from the Hnatyshyn Foundation in 2016. Willard is Assistant Professor at the University of British Columbia, Okanagan, in Syilx territories (Kelowna, BC) and her current research intersects with Indigenous resurgence and land-based art practices.

Institutions by Artists
October 12–14, 2012
Goldcorp Centre for the Arts
Simon Fraser University
Vancouver, BC

Organized by the Artist-Run Centres and Collectives
  Conference (ARCA), Fillip, and the Pacific Association
  of Artist Run Centres (PAARC)

Program Chair: Kristina Lee Podesva
Program Committe: Lorna Brown, Jeff Khonsary,
  Jonathan Middleton (Advisor), Pelin Tan (Advisor),
  Anton Vidokle (Advisor)
Project Manager: Lorna Brown
Event Manager: Allison Collins
Research and Communications Assistants:
  Mariane Bourcheix-Laporte, Jesi Khadivi

Funding Partners
The Canada Council for the Arts,
Heritage Canada Languages Support
Program, the British Columbia Arts
Council, the City of Vancouver, Simon
Fraser University School for the Con-
temporary Arts, Simon Fraser Univer-
sity Library

Presenting Partners
The Andy Warhol Foundation for the
Arts, the Goethe Institut, the Consulat
général de France à Vancouver, the
Audain Gallery, SFU Woodward's,
*Yishu Journal of Contemporary Chinese
Art*, the Morris and Helen Belkin Art
Gallery, the Critical and Curatorial
Studies Program of the Department
of Art History, Visual Art and Theory
at the University of British Columbia,
Emily Carr University of Art and
Design, the Contemporary Art Gallery

Fillip gratefully acknowledges the ongoing support of the
Canada Council for the Arts, the City of Vancouver, and
the British Columbia Arts Council. Additional assistance provided by the Andy Warhol Foundation for the
Visual Arts.

Colophon

Fillip Folio Series: E
Institutions by Artists: Volume Two
Published by Fillip and the Pacific Association
  of Artist Run Centres
ISBN: 978-1-927354-27-8

Editors: Jeff Khonsary and Antonia Pinter
Editing: Jaclyn Arndt
Transcription: Robert Dayton and Josh Gabert-Doyon
Copyediting: Bryne McLaughlin
Proofreading: Bryne McLaughlin, Kate Woolf
Printed in Belgium by die Keure

This book was made possible through the support of the
Canada Council for the Arts and the Andy Warhol Foundation for the Visual Arts.

Fillip
305 Cambie Street
Vancouver, BC
Canada V6B 2N4
www.fillip.ca